Angus Buchan is a tough, straightforward South African farmer of Scottish extraction, whose gentle but uncompromising faith has carried him through drought, financial crisis and family tragedy. Called by God to preach the gospel, he found the Holy Spirit working through him in amazing miracles of provision and healing.

His story is told in his autobiography, *Faith like Potatoes*, now a successful film.

A FARMER'S YEAR

ANGUS
BUCHAN

MONARCH
BOOKS

Oxford, UK & Grand Rapids, Michigan, USA

Originally published in South Africa in 2007 under the title 'A Farmer's Journal'.
This edition first published in the UK in 2007 by Monarch Books
(a publishing imprint of Lion Hudson plc),
Wilkinson House, Jordan Hill Road, Oxford OX2 8DR.
Tel: +44 (0)1865 302750 Fax: +44 (0)1865 302757
Email: monarch@lionhudson.com
www.lionhudson.com

Reprinted 2007.

ISBN: 978-1-85424-850-3 (UK)
ISBN: 978-0-8254-6183-5 (USA)

Distributed by:
UK: Marston Book Services Ltd, PO Box 269, Abingdon, Oxon OX14 4YN;
USA: Kregel Publications, PO Box 2607, Grand Rapids, Michigan 49501

Unless otherwise stated, Scripture quotations are taken from the Holy Bible, New King James Version. Copyright © 1982 by Thomas Nelson, Inc. Used by permission. All rights reserved.

The text paper used in this book has been made from wood independently certified as having come from sustainable forests.

British Library Cataloguing Data
A catalogue record for this book is available from the British Library.

Printed and bound in Hong Kong.

Acknowledgments

Without these special friends this book would never have been completed. First of all, my co-author, Val Waldeck, who has become more than a co-worker for Jesus, but a dear sister to me and Jill. We thank God for her, and the example that she has been to us as a woman of God, who lives by faith in God and walks in integrity.

Special thanks to Clive Thompson for the photography and assisting with the cover and layout of the journal, and to our proofreaders – Malcolm Gage, Joanne Buchan, Morag Collier, Lorna Jackson and Ann Melvill.

All photographs featured were taken at Shalom Farm.

All scripture quotations are from the New King James Version (NKJV) of the Bible.

Dedication

Dedicated to Jill, my wife (and best friend),
and my family. Without your faith in Jesus, and
releasing me to preach the gospel,
I would never have been able to do it.

Preface

As a farmer, I look upon my Bible as an agricultural handbook. There is one most important principle in the Bible that God has impressed upon me and it is found in Hebrews 11:6, which says: "But without faith it is impossible to please God."

In fact, without faith we cannot live this life or finish the race which Jesus has set before us. We cannot be effective farmers, housewives, businessmen, students, or preachers. But more important than that, we cannot please GOD without faith.

At the farm, we have adopted a saying which goes like this: "Good people don't go to heaven. Believers go to heaven." We please God when we trust Him, call on His Name, and ask for His help. We say, "The farmer makes a plan" – "I'll do it my way" – but that does not impress our Creator one little bit. In fact, it reeks of selfish pride – and pride always comes before a fall.

We plant our seed by faith, and trust Jesus to make it grow. We get out of the boat by faith, and trust Jesus to enable us to walk on the water [by the way, the boat is full of dry rot, and sinking anyway].

So we trust that this book will enable you to see that Jesus is indeed the rewarder of those who diligently seek Him.

Angus Buchan
Greytown, South Africa

JANUARY

A new beginning

"Therefore we also, since we are surrounded by so great a cloud of witnesses, let us lay aside every weight, and the sin which so easily ensnares us, and let us run with endurance the race that is set before us."
– Hebrews 12:1

This is a new beginning – a new year – a brand new start. Whatever happened yesterday has been forgotten. It is history.

I heard a dear friend of mine preaching recently. He said, "God is not interested in your history. He is interested in your destiny."

Good farmers know that the worst thing a man can do is look behind him when he is ploughing, because he will not plough a straight furrow. Whatever has happened in your life during the past year, do not look back. There may be things that you have not been able to rectify because the other party is not interested in reconciliation. Leave those things under the blood of the Lamb. Jesus Christ died on the cross of Calvary so that your sins may be forgiven. Make sure you do whatever you can from your side to rectify any undone situation, and then press on.

We are surrounded by a cloud of witnesses. There are loved ones in heaven who have gone ahead of us. If they could speak to you, they would say, "Keep running!" Think of the famous Comrades Marathon run in South Africa every year. The finish line, my dear friend, is closer than you think, so don't stop. Don't get tired. Press on. Run the race to completion. This is a brand new year, with brand new opportunities for you to take hold of. God goes before you.

Have a wonderful year as you go into the future with Jesus Christ, the Managing Director of your farm, business, family or career – indeed, your very life.

Spending our time wisely

"To everything there is a season, a time for every purpose under heaven."
— Ecclesiastes 3:1

You may be the best farmer or businessman in your community. You may grow the best crops and produce the finest animals. Your farms and businesses may run like clockwork. But if your wife is not your best friend and your children have no relationship with you, then you have not spent your time wisely.

Billy Graham, in his book "Just As I Am," said he was grateful for the way God had used him during 50 years of campaigning. But, he said, if he had his life to live over again, he would spend more time with his family. He would speak less and study more. He would spend more time in prayer, seeking to grow closer to God and to become more like the Lord Jesus Christ.

I visited a man one day on a neighbouring farm. He had spent most of his life building the house of his dreams. He had lived in it a mere three months and was sitting on the front verandah, totally wasted away from a terminal disease. "What a beautiful house," I said. Tears filled his eyes. "Yes, Angus," he responded, "but what for?" Three weeks later he died.

We must spend our time wisely. The Bible records the parable of the rich man in Luke 12:16. Jesus said this man had an abundant crop and decided to pull down his barns and build bigger ones to store his crops. "Take your ease, eat, drink and be merry," he said to himself. But Jesus said, "You fool, don't you realise that this night your soul will be required of you."

As we go into this new year, ask the Lord: "What would You have me do with my time?" And then do it, with all your heart.

Rejoicing in tribulation

"And not only that, but we also glory in tribulations, knowing that
tribulation produces perseverance; and perseverance, character; and
character, hope." – Romans 5:3,4

Paul says that we rejoice in our tribulation because it produces perseverance. Perseverance produces character and character produces hope.

I once had a most incredible crop of seed maize. It stood at least seven to eight feet tall and was at a most critical stage in its development. One unforgettable afternoon a wind blew over our farm in the KwaZulu–Natal midlands. Dark greenish-black clouds filled the sky and huge hailstones fell as the wind blew and the rain pelted down. My home is made of wattle and daub with a tin roof and no ceiling. The noise was unbelievable.

All kinds of things were going through my mind. How was I going to face my bank manager? How was I going to get through the next year? This disaster would leave us totally bankrupt. "This will be the end of your farm," the devil gloated. "You will have to sell and move out."

As I was crying out to God, the hail suddenly stopped, the clouds parted, and the sun came out. I felt devastated when I saw 250 acres of beautiful seed maize lying flat on the ground.

But God is faithful. The next morning that maize crop was literally standing up and we had a bumper crop that year. The maize had a permanent curve – a reminder from God of what had happened – but I appreciated that crop of maize more than any other I've ever grown in thirty years of farming. If my faith had not been tested, I doubt that I would have appreciated it as much.

So we rejoice in our tribulation, because it causes us to trust in a God who never fails. We know that "ALL things work together for good to those who love God, to those who are the called according to His purpose." (Romans 8:28).

Trusting God

"He who observes the wind will not sow, and he who regards the clouds will not reap." – Ecclesiastes 11:4

As children of God, we are not to be dictated to by our circumstances, but rather to be guided by the Word of God.

Many years ago my son Andy came home from university and saw that Jill and I were very tired. "Go away somewhere and have a week's break," he said, "I will look after the farm."

The maize crop was at a crucial stage. Unfortunately, we were having a dry spell and the lack of rain caused the maize to wilt. Andy became very perturbed. He kept looking at the clouds and observing the wind. One day he parked his pickup truck in the middle of the maize fields and began praying earnestly. As he pleaded with God, a wonderful thing happened. A big black cloud came up from the northwest and it started to rain. Clouds of dust shot up as the raindrops hit the parched ground and Andy began to rejoice.

To his dismay, a strong east wind then began blowing. It split the storm in two. One half went left and the other right and our farm got no rain at all. Andy went back to our farm office. He picked up his Bible and read Ecclesiastes 11:4, "He who observes the wind will not sow and he who regards the clouds will not reap."

My young son repented before God and the Lord heard his prayer. That night the south wind blew gentle rain onto our farm and drenched the entire maize crop. Needless to say, we had a bumper crop that year.

Do not look at your circumstances, but keep your eyes on the Lord Jesus Christ.

Sowing good seed

"But this I say: he who sows sparingly will also reap sparingly, and he who sows bountifully will also reap bountifully." – 2 Corinthians 9:6

The Father says to us at the start of this new day that, just like the wise farmer who ploughs his ground, prepares his land, sows his crop with a heart of faith and expects a bountiful yield, so too, we must go forward with the same heart attitude.

I have met farmers who always seem to be negative. They sow negatively. "If there's going to be a drought," they say, "we would rather space out our seed wide and use less. That way it won't cost so much, and we won't have to pay back as much if it fails." They cut back on the fertilizer and on cultivation in order to save costs.

But the farmer, or businessman, who is walking according to God's statutes, will do exactly the opposite. He will use more seed and more fertilizer, plough deeper and prepare the land more carefully, expecting a bountiful crop by faith. That man is the man who reaps a bountiful crop. The negative one reaps a marginal crop and often ends up going bankrupt.

As we go out and face this new day, let us do everything with a heart full of faith, believing in the promises of God. He is for us and not against us, and He wants us to prosper and not fail. Let us not only sow bountifully in our fields, but also in everything we do. Let us sow good seed into the lives of our staff, our families and all those we come into contact with. We especially need to spend quality time with our loved ones.

Sow good seed today bountifully, expecting a wonderful and abundant return.

Resting

"Then God blessed the seventh day and sanctified it, because in it He rested from all His work which God had created and made." – Genesis 2:3

Are you adhering to the principle of sabbath rest? A lot of people feel that they simply cannot afford to set aside time to stop and worship God. My dear friend, you cannot afford not to rest regularly. We were created to rest one day out of seven.

The sabbath is a "type" of salvation according to Hebrews chapter 4. But that does not release us from the principle of sabbath rest. Don't think for one moment that you are more powerful and self-sufficient than the Creator. If Jehovah chose to rest on the sabbath, surely you and I must take seriously the principle of sabbath rest. The early Christians chose the first day of the week, ie Sunday, for their day of rest and they left us a good example to follow.

An interesting thing took place in France just after the French Revolution. The nation adopted the metric system and decided to change their horses' rest cycle from every seventh to every tenth day. Soon they had to revert back to a seven-day cycle because the animals were dying from over-exertion.

Purely from a business point of view, it is not profitable for a man to work seven straight days, without a rest day. If we neglect the principle of sabbath rest, the return on the work we do during the following week is much less. Our attitude always determines our altitude. There is nothing worse than working straight through the week without a break and starting the new week tired, without incentive, imagination and drive.

Spend time on the Lord's Day meditating on what the Lord Jesus Christ has done for us and Monday morning will find you refreshed – mentally, physically and spiritually.

Never look back

"But Jesus said to him, no one, having put his hand to the plough, and looking back, is fit for the kingdom of God." – Luke 9:62

I did my agricultural training in Scotland and was taught the importance of doing things properly. Sadly, craftsmanship seems to be a thing of the past, when people took pride in their work.

That is especially true when setting a plough. The first line must be cut very straight. Any curves in your ploughing will work against you. When setting the plough, you look at the horizon and select a church steeple, tree, or a house, and line it up with the arrow on the bonnet of your tractor. Then you plough, keeping your eyes on the horizon and never looking back.

If you follow your natural inclination to glance behind you to check if the plough is out of the ground, or if it is ploughing deeply enough, you will pull the steering wheel and the plough will make a little kink in the first furrow. When you turn your tractor around, the wheel that is running in the furrow to cut the next line will follow the kink. That kink will eventually get bigger and bigger, and by the time you get to the end of the field, there will be a big sweep in your line and it will be anything but straight.

The same applies in your life. If you keep looking behind at what happened yesterday, and you don't leave it at the foot of the cross, you are in trouble. You must trust the Lord Jesus Christ to forgive you for all that is past.

This day, put behind you those things you did yesterday. Ask forgiveness for losing your temper or speaking roughly to your staff or family. Set your eyes on Jesus Christ and don't look behind you. Keep on keeping on.

Have faith in God

"Now faith is the substance of things hoped for, the evidence of things not seen." – Hebrews 11:1

It is very difficult, if not impossible, to farm without having faith in God. Farmers who lack faith are often depressed, bad-tempered, fearful, and uncertain. Many have committed suicide, ended up as alcoholics, or had nervous breakdowns because of the pressure. To be able to farm effectively, one must have faith in God.

How arrogant we farmers sometimes become when we see a beautiful crop of wheat or corn, and have the audacity to take the credit for it. We know very well that if it does not rain, our crops will not grow. We have to trust God. You cannot put a seed in the ground and then dig it up every day to make sure it is germinating. It will never grow. We plant the crop and do our best to cultivate it, but we must leave the rest to God.

That is exactly how we must conduct ourselves when we go about our daily lives. Remember always do your best and let God do the rest. The Bible says in Hebrews 11:6 that "without faith it is impossible to please Him, for he who comes to God must believe that He is, and that He is a rewarder of those who diligently seek Him."

Earnestly seek out the will of God for your life. Find out whether He wants you to plant a crop of wheat or corn, buy or sell a house, start or close a business. When you know the will of God, do it by faith with all of your heart and leave the rest to Him. You will be very well pleased with the result.

Seeking the Lord first

"But seek first the kingdom of God and His righteousness, and all these things shall be added to you." – Matthew 6:33

Seek first the kingdom of God and His righteousness and everything else will fall into place. That's His promise. We need to make sure every day that we are in touch with our Lord Jesus Christ. It is vital for us to spend time with Him before we do anything else. Our early morning time of devotions with Him is essential.

I make it a point to meet with God every day. There is nothing about agriculture, business or family life that He does not know. How vital it is to meet first with Him and get my daily instructions directly from Him.

When I meet with my staff, we spend time every morning in daily devotions. In my time – not theirs – we sing praises to the Lord's name, read the Bible and meditate on the Word. It is absolutely incredible how this changes the mood and spirit on the farm. I have seen our labourers come to work, looking depressed and tired, but, after singing praises to the Lord Jesus Christ and being encouraged by the Word of God, I see an immediate change. The atmosphere lightens. There are smiles on their faces and an excitement about getting to work.

My wife and I used to spend time with our children every morning before they went to school. We made sure they were ready for their day and properly dressed, not only in their school clothes, but in the armour of God. What soldier would go out to battle without his armour?

We must be equipped when we go into the world and face the challenges of day-to-day living, so be sure to seek the Lord Jesus Christ this morning before you leave your home.

Our manual for living

"Your word is a lamp to my feet and a light to my path." – Psalm 119:105

I call the Bible my agricultural manual. It is the very compass of life. I take the Word of God wherever I go, whether it is into the fields or to visit my bank manager. Everything we need to know about living our daily lives is found in God's Holy Word.

The Word of God gives me good counsel. I was challenged once on the fact that my land needs to lie fallow one year in seven. Just like everything else it needs to rest. "Lord," I said, " If I leave my whole farm fallow for one year, I am sure to go bankrupt." I sensed the Holy Spirit gently speaking to me, "Well then, leave a seventh of your farm fallow every year." And that is what I do. Every year I leave one-seventh of the farm fallow and I can assure you it works! In agriculture, we say, "One year's seeds equals seven years' weeds."

In modern agriculture you are often taught to "hammer" the land. As weeds grow up, you are told to disc them into the ground. But the Lord says, leave it fallow. Since doing that, I have found my yields increasing. The humus, the compost and the soil profile are so much richer.

I was once driving around the farm with an economist. He asked me why a field was lying vacant, with the weeds standing six feet high. I said, "Do you really want to know?" "Yes," he said. I drove the pickup truck into the field, turned off the motor and shared the gospel of Jesus Christ with him. He made a commitment to Christ and accepted Jesus as his personal Lord and Saviour.

God will do amazing things for us when we obey His Word.

Taking care of your workers

"You shall not muzzle an ox while it treads out the grain." – Deuteronomy 25:4; 1 Corinthians 9:9

Sometimes we concentrate on every aspect of our business, but neglect the welfare of our workers. The Lord says we must feed the ox that is treading out the corn. If you look after your workforce, they will look after you. It doesn't matter who they are. Look after their needs and God will look after yours. I'm not only talking about financial well-being, but every aspect of their employment.

We work with many Zulu labourers on our farm. Unfortunately, because of the history of our nation the Zulu people are often very distrustful of white farmers. Since giving my life to the Lord Jesus Christ I've been trying to work my farm according to godly principles and I believe that I have, slowly but surely, earned the trust of my people. I am becoming more concerned, not only about making sure that they are rewarded financially for their work, but also that other needs which lead to a better quality of life, are catered for. It is a great honour for me when my farm workers start sharing about things that matter to them. They talk to me about all sorts of things and it brings me great joy to be able to counsel and help them.

They also give me good counsel. Often I'll confide in my foreman and ask him what type of season he feels it's going to be. He loves to encourage me and we discuss together whether we should increase or decrease our plant population. He has years of experience and usually gives me good counsel.

Do not muzzle the ox that treads out the corn. Firstly, because God said so; secondly, because it is beneficial to our fellow man and, thirdly, because it is a good economic principle.

Doing the will of God

"Jesus said to them, My food is to do the will of Him who sent Me, and to finish His work." – John 4:34

I know a man who longed to be an accountant. He is a very intelligent person and I have a high regard for him. However, he is the son of a farmer and his dad told him from an early age: "This farm must continue with the family name. You are my son and you have an obligation to make sure of that." The result was that he became a poor farmer, eventually went bankrupt and had to sell the farm. He did not enjoy what he was doing.

I love farming, but my first love is to preach the gospel of Jesus Christ, to see souls coming into the kingdom of God, the sick healed, the broken-hearted restored and the captives set free.

My second love is to get out onto the land and see the glory of God demonstrated through His creation. I love smelling a newly ploughed field, or watching a newly born calf stand up on its shaky legs while the mother cleans it, making it all nice and fluffy. I love watching the combine-harvester harvesting a field, smelling the beautiful fragrance of a pine plantation just after a shower of rain, or putting my hand into the soil and turning it over. I enjoy the work God has given me to do.

If you are not enjoying what you are doing today, stop and seek the face of God. Find out what God wants you to do. Jesus said, "My meat, (my food) is to do the will of Him who sent me and to finish His work."

A new you

"Therefore, if anyone is in Christ, he is a new creation; old things have passed away; behold, all things have become new." – 2 Corinthians 5:17

I believe the Lord is saying to you today that you are a new creation and old things have passed away.

Imagine planting a crop of vegetables and, for one reason or another, the crop grows up diseased. A farmer will plough in the crop, take a light disc and disc it over, preparing his land to start again. He will plant with new seed, making a completely new beginning. One thing that farming has taught me is perseverance – never to take no for an answer.

This scripture is very special to me because the Lord is saying that, if you are in Christ, you are a new person. You are a new creation. All those old filthy habits – that diseased crop – have been ploughed under and have now become fertilizer for the new you. God says you can start again this morning, a brand new crop that is going to yield not thirty-fold, not sixty-fold, but one hundredfold.

Go this day with the knowledge that, because you are in Christ Jesus, all things have become new.

Perseverance

"Many are the afflictions of the righteous, but the LORD delivers him out of them all." – Psalm 34:19

So often we are condemned by the evil one when things don't go the way we think they should. We feel that it must be because we are out of God's will, that there is sin in our lives, or a curse on our business or farm. This is not always the case. As the psalmist said, "Many are the afflictions of the righteous, but the Lord delivers him from them all."

If there's one thing a farmer has to develop, it is persistence. He has to carry on, no matter what is happening. Many times we have had to nurse a crop of corn right through to harvest because of severe drought. Farmers and businessmen who are half-hearted and half-committed – not believing firmly in what they are doing – end up going bankrupt. The Lord says that He knows how to deliver us in times of affliction if we will but trust and obey Him.

That is how it is in the life of a Christian too. In times of affliction, we must keep on persevering. These are times of tremendous sifting and we have to stand firm. My dear friend, if you are not totally committed to Jesus Christ – born-again, baptised in water and the Holy Spirit – if He is not Lord of your life, then I can tell you now that you will not finish the race.

I exhort you to press on, no matter what mountain lies before you this day, assured that "If God is for us, who can be against us?" (Romans 8:31).

Judging

"And why do you look at the speck in your brother's eye, but do not consider the plank in your own eye?" – Matthew 7:3

We are so quick to judge. The Lord tells us that we will be judged with the same measure we use to judge others and He has taught me, through my agricultural experiences over the years, how important it is to understand the other man's position before we judge him.

I remember driving around a neighbour's farm one day. Suddenly, he stopped the pickup truck and shouted at his tractor driver, criticising him severely for not driving the tractor in the right gear and not ploughing evenly. It was most embarrassing for the farmer when the driver got off the tractor and asked the farmer to show him how to do it. That farmer's face became very red because he did not know how to do the job properly himself. He just mumbled, "Well, just try your best to do it better."

My dear late dad, who was a blacksmith and a self-made man, sent me to Scotland where I was taught to farm. I started off using a pick and shovel, eventually graduating to driving a tractor and learning to use the implements correctly. If we want to gain respect from the world, we need to lead by example. How much better it would have been for that farmer if he had been able to show the tractor driver which gear to drive in and how to set the plough properly.

Unfortunately, in the Christian walk, there are many Christians who love telling people how to live, but they themselves are no example whatsoever. There's no love, no compassion, no understanding and no forgiveness.

When we go out today, let us lead by example. Let us concentrate first on getting the plank out of our own eye before we try to take the speck – the splinter – out of our brother's eye.

Open doors

"I know your works. See, I have set before you an open door, and no one can shut it; for you have a little strength, have kept My word, and have not denied My name." – Revelation 3:8

Some of the most terrible situations we find ourselves in occur because we do not allow the Lord to open the door for us. We get an idea in our heads and are determined – at all costs – to do what we think is best.

A farmer came to our area from a part of South Africa that is very dry and where they do a lot of mechanical cultivation of their crops. The farmers tried to give him good counsel. "In this area we spray our crops with herbicides to keep the weeds down," they told him. "It is very hard do this with mechanical cultivation due to the high rainfall area in which we are living." He completely disregarded their counsel and stubbornly insisted that he would do what he had always done. Within two years that man was declared insolvent and had to sell that beautiful farm for a mere pittance.

The Lord says He delights to open doors that no man can close if we will but heed His counsel. When I have been at my weakest, the Lord has opened doors for me. He has given me creative ideas, and enabled me to make use of opportunities to grow different types of crops on our farm. He has inspired us to try different business methods to improve the day-to-day living of our farming community. He opened the doors. All I had to do was just walk straight through.

Be sure to allow God to open doors for you. If a door is closed, leave it alone. Do not try to force it open. You will only bring much pain, grief, and devastation upon yourself, your loved ones and your business. Spend time with God and always wait for Him to open the right doors.

A new day

"If we confess our sins, He is faithful and just to forgive us our sins and to cleanse us from all unrighteousness." – 1 John 1:9

After working all day out in the fields one tends to get sticky and hot, and also a bit aggravated when things don't go the way they should. Perhaps the tractor has broken down, or the fences have collapsed and the cattle have got into the crops. You try to get them out, while doing a makeshift job on the fence, when you get a telephone message to say your wife's car has broken down and you should come immediately and help her. You are on a very short fuse and perhaps even say a couple of things you don't really mean. That night you go to bed feeling very frustrated.

You awaken early the next morning to find that a lovely shower of rain has fallen on the farm during the night. The dust has settled and there is a beautiful fragrance in the air. You feel new energy coursing through your veins. The motor car has been repaired, the cattle are safely where they should be and the crops are standing up again, looking none the worse for their encounter with the cattle. The tractor is repaired and you can face a new day. All the anger and frustration have gone.

That is what it is like when we repent of our sin and experience God's forgiveness and cleansing. He says if we confess our sins he is faithful and just to forgive and cleanse us. We can start afresh this morning. We don't have to carry anything over from yesterday. We can leave everything behind us and start anew because "there is no condemnation for those who are in Christ Jesus" (Romans 8:1).

Spiritual pearls

"Do not give what is holy to the dogs; nor cast your pearls before swine, lest they trample them under their feet, and turn and tear you in pieces." – Matthew 7:6

Do not cast your pearls before swine. In other words, do not share things which are precious to you with those who will not understand. It's like a dairy farmer trying to explain the finer points of milk production to a forester who does not understand or appreciate the fine lines in a good quality, pedigree, dairy cow. He will not understand the butterfat content required in top quality milk. Nor will he understand the importance of lactation of a cow, the length of time that a cow must be milked before she is dried off, or the fact that she has to be steamed up and got into good condition before she calves down again.

The Lord Jesus Christ is encouraging you today to guard carefully your spiritual pearls, or that beautiful vision God has given you of the work you are going to do in service to Him. Pray with another believer who has the same heart as you and let them counsel you. Do not go to somebody who does not know Jesus Christ as Saviour and expect them to be sympathetic to your spiritual needs or requirements. Seek out men and women who have the same level of spiritual maturity as you before you share your vision.

Most important of all, share your innermost aspirations and dreams with Jesus Himself. Talk to Him about your future and the decisions you feel the Holy Spirit is calling you to make. He will give you the answer through scripture and you will experience the inner peace that comes from spending time with Him.

The return of Jesus

"He who testifies to these things says, 'Surely I am coming quickly.' Amen. Even so, come, Lord Jesus!" – Revelation 22:20

The Lord Jesus says, "Surely I am coming quickly." This is the second last verse in the whole Bible and I really believe the Lord is saying to us that it is a time of tremendous urgency on the earth. We must be sure that we are ready to stand before the Lord Jesus Christ on the great Day of Judgment. I have written in red ink in my Bible: "Keep short accounts with God and with man."

We have a beautiful picture in our family room. It was given to me after a gospel campaign in the Johannesburg area two years ago. There are two words written across the picture in gold lettering: "Perhaps today". Whatever we put our hand to today, let us be sure that we are ready, if necessary, to face the King of Kings, the Lord of Lords, the Saviour of the world.

Be sure that everything is in order, especially in your own personal life, before you leave home. Make certain you have nothing against anyone, that you have settled all accounts and done everything the Lord Jesus Christ has called you to do. Then go out and enjoy the day.

Martin Luther, the great theologian, was once asked what he would do if he knew the Lord was coming tomorrow. His answer was, "I would plant an apple tree today." What he meant was, he would just carry on with his day-to-day living – working, producing food and farming for Jesus until the Lord came.

My friend, be sure this day that you are ready for His coming.

God's faithfulness

"I have been young, and now am old; yet I have not seen the righteous forsaken, nor his descendants begging bread." – Psalm 37:25

Our God is ever merciful and faithful. When I look back over thirty years of farming experience, I can say that the Lord has never forsaken me.

Has the Lord ever forsaken you? If you have a big decision to make, meditate on this question. The answer must be – has to be – "No, never!" So why should He choose to forsake you now? Or why should He leave your children hungry? There is no reason.

Just before I gave my life to Christ, I remember walking through the fields to check my crops with my second eldest daughter. She was about two or three years old at the time. Her little hand clutched the small finger on my left hand and she sang happily as we walked along together. I remember thinking, "How am I going to take care of this little one? What will happen if the crops fail? What will I do if the farm doesn't make it?" That daughter of mine is now an adult, fully qualified as a High School English teacher, and serving the Lord Jesus Christ as her personal Saviour. The Lord has never, ever, let her down. She has never gone hungry or been without a meal because He is a faithful God.

The evil one will try to discourage you, but the only thing the devil can do (and he can do it very well!) is tell lies. He is called the father of all lies, the deceiver of the brethren.

The Lord has given you a promise this morning. He has promised that He will never forsake you. He has said that your descendants will have bread to eat. He will take care of all their needs. All you need to do is make sure that you are walking in righteousness before Him.

Freedom

"Stand fast therefore in the liberty by which Christ has made us free, and do not be entangled again with a yoke of bondage." – Galatians 5:1

We have a couple of donkeys on our farm that we use to transport fertilizer, vegetables or seed from one side of the farm to the other. These two little donkeys pull a small half-ton trailer quite easily. Every morning a yoke has to be put around their necks so that they can pull the load together. As you know, donkeys are stubborn animals. If one donkey decides he's going to pull to the left-hand side, and the other donkey decides he's going to pull to the right-hand side, the cart will not move.

I believe that the Lord is telling us today not to get entangled again with a yoke of bondage. We must not be pulling in two different directions. He says we need to stand fast in the liberty He has given us.

When we met the Lord Jesus Christ as our personal Lord and Saviour, we were set at liberty. The law no longer governs us. We do not have to try to earn our salvation. We are justified through grace by faith, which is unmerited favour and undeserved loving kindness. We are not to go back under that yoke of bondage we were set free from. Having started so well in the spirit, why do we so often try to finish the race in the flesh?

Whatever our business may be today, the Lord is commanding us not to put on the yoke of bondage again, lest we lose the freedom of walking in liberty and forfeit the grace of our Lord Jesus Christ.

So let us go to work today, knowing that the Lord Jesus Christ goes before us, assured that the yoke He has given us is one of Christian liberty. He will make a way for us where there seems to be no way. No matter what challenges today may hold, we may be confident that "He who has begun a good work in us will complete it until the day of Jesus Christ" (Philippians 1:6).

My shepherd

"The LORD is my shepherd; I shall not want." – Psalm 23:1

In the days when our Master walked in Israel, shepherds led their sheep. Unlike modern shepherds today, who chase their sheep from behind with sheep dogs, Middle Eastern shepherds used to lead their sheep from the front. Many of them still do. There are no paddocks or fencing to contain the sheep. The sheep walk with the shepherd and he leads them to grazing.

Our scripture today says, "The Lord is my shepherd and I shall not want (lack)." He will show you where to go today. He will show you where to find food, where to find business and how to direct your operation. Trust Him.

In the olden days, the shepherds brought their sheep down to a particular watering hole (a well). Bear in mind that water has always been in short supply in the Middle East. I've heard it said that the shepherds would sit together underneath a tree and talk about the day's affairs while all the sheep mixed together. There might be five or six different flocks mingling. When they had finished watering, the shepherds simply stood up, said goodbye to their fellows, and whistled for their sheep. When they heard their shepherd's call, all his sheep would leave the crowd and follow him, because they knew him.

The Lord says to you today, be sure that you know the voice of the Shepherd. How do you get to know anyone? By spending quality time with them. Spend time with the Shepherd this morning and He will direct your paths throughout the day.

Commitment

"So then, because you are lukewarm, and neither cold nor hot, I will vomit you out of My mouth." – Revelation 3:16

These are extremely strong words from the Master Himself, the Lord Jesus Christ. What He is saying is that He has no time whatsoever for compromisers, or for those who do things half-heartedly. Whatever you do today, my dear friend, do it with all your heart. The Lord says that He would rather we were ice cold than lukewarm. He would prefer us be unbelievers rather than lukewarm believers.

In my farming experience I have found that when you are planting a field of corn, you need to work with all your heart. It is not the time to worry about whether this will be an El Nino year, without much rain. A farmer who does that will hold back on fertilizer, or cut back on seed distribution, "just in case," and he will suffer loss. A man with this kind of attitude will never succeed. He will never make it.

The Lord is saying very clearly that whatever you do today, do it with all of your heart. Give one hundred per cent to the task at hand. Whether it be a business deal, a decision that has to be made concerning the farm, or even your family, pray, seek the face of God, and then do it with all of your heart. You'll find that you will succeed.

I believe that this is a word for us today. The Lord is saying very clearly that, if we're going to succeed, we must not look behind us. We must not leave the back door half open, but commit ourselves one hundred per cent to whatever we put our hands and hearts to do. The Lord Jesus Christ will honour that and we will succeed. And when it happens, we must be quick to give Him all the praise, the honour and the glory.

The ministry of the Holy Spirit

"Not by might nor by power, but by My Spirit, Says the LORD of hosts." –
Zechariah 4:6

This day the Lord says that He wants us to work, achieve and accomplish whatever we are going to do, by the Spirit.

We have a favourite saying at Shalom: "If your vision does not scare you, it's not big enough." What this really means is, if your vision is not bigger than you, it is not from God. It's probably a man-made, or man-given, vision. Whatever you are attempting to do today, if you feel absolutely capable of accomplishing it in your own strength, I can assure you it is not from God.

We also say that our vision must be to attempt something so big, that if it is not of God it is doomed to failure. The reason for this is that the Lord will not share His glory with any man. "Not by might, nor by power, but by My Spirit, says the Lord." Whatever we do in life, let it bring glory to Almighty God.

We have a little farm school with approximately two hundred students. One day I drove into the grounds and my heart leapt when I saw what the school principal had painted on the side of the school in bold letters, "Set a goal and go for it." I want to encourage you today, as you go about what God has called you to do. Do it with all your heart, with all your mind, and with all your strength. But above all, trust that the Holy Spirit is going before you and He will make it happen by His power.

St Francis of Assisi said, "Preach the gospel at all times, if necessary, use words." When we eventually achieve our goal and people see how limited our natural resources are, they will give glory to God and say, "surely they could not have achieved that project or that goal by themselves. It must have been God."

So, Holy Spirit, as we go out today, we ask that you go with each one of us and give us guidance and strength to achieve great things for our Lord Jesus Christ.

Overcomers

"He who has an ear, let him hear what the Spirit says to the churches. He who overcomes shall not be hurt by the second death." – Revelation 2:11

The Lord is interested in overcomers. He does not have a problem with people who fail, but our Master has a major problem with a person who fails and won't get up and start again. We are in a war. The Lord says to us very clearly in 2 Corinthians 10:4 that "the weapons of our warfare are not carnal but mighty in God for the pulling down of strongholds." The Lord says at least five times in two chapters of the Book of Revelation: "To him who overcomes." I would say He is trying to tell us something!

As a farmer, I have found that the crop we put in the ground doesn't always look like a bumper crop to begin with. In fact, it may often suffer insect damage. There may be a lot of weeds growing up with the crop, or the rains may cease for a while and the crop will suffer a lot of stress. But if we continue to cultivate it faithfully, it will flourish. As good husbandmen, we must get rid of the grass, blank in all the gaps, make sure the colour of the crop is right, and nurture the crop continually. The result will be a bumper yield.

The Lord says to you today, it does not matter what happened yesterday or how well your business is doing at the moment. It does not really matter what your job situation is, or if you are facing a financial crisis in your life, or any other problem. What is important is that He has never changed. He's "the same yesterday, today and forever" (Hebrews 13:8). What we have to do is to overcome, and the best form of defence is attack. We must use the Word of God. We must continue to "cultivate" the situation, so that the Lord can bless and prosper it, and we will become the overcomers He's asking us to be.

Walking our talk

"They profess to know God, but in works they deny Him." – Titus 1:16

As we go about our work today, let us pray that the Lord will enable us to have the grace to operate by faith and most of all, by the love of God. It's so easy to be a Christian on Sunday morning in church and then lose our witness in the workplace.

The Lord says, "why do you call me Lord, Lord, and you do not do the things I tell you?" Make a decision today to do what the Holy Spirit tells you, even though it may not make sense in the world of business and economics.

Consider the story of Lot and Abraham. Abraham gave Lot the opportunity to choose the best land – and he did. He took the bottom lands, the fertile plains, and Abraham was left with the mountains. But we know the story of Sodom and Gomorrah and at the end of the day, Abraham had to come and bail out his nephew when Sodom and Gomorrah were obliterated from the face of the earth.

What may seem to be a good business deal, may not have the sanction and blessing of God. You may even be tempted to bend the rules. Don't do it. Let people know you are a child of God, not by what you say or profess, but rather by what you do.

Family time

"Husbands, love your wives, just as Christ also loved the church and gave Himself for her." – Ephesians 5:25

John 15:13 says "Greater love has no one than this, than to lay down his life for his friends." That is what God expects us to do for our wives. If there are any young men reading this book, you may be husbands one day, so please take note.

The biggest mistake we make as breadwinners is to spend so much time at work that we neglect our homes and families. When our wives want to spend more time with us, the reason (or excuse) we give for not doing so is that we are working hard to feed our families and to take care of them. Is that really true?

I remember early on in my farming career, spending long hours in the fields. I made sure that the crop looked absolutely magnificent, that my livestock – my cattle and my sheep – were fat and clean, that the fences were all pulled up tight, that the gates were nicely painted and the road was properly graded. When my dear wife, Jill, would ask me, "When are you coming in? When are you going to knock off?" I would gently protest and say, "I'm doing all this for you and the children." I wanted to be known as a good husband who was providing properly for his family.

Of course, when the family wanted to see more of me, I continued to insist that I was doing it for them. It took the Holy Spirit to reveal the truth to me. The reason I was working such long hours was for self-glorification and I had to repent of it. "For what will it profit a man if he gains the whole world, and loses his own soul?" (Mark 8:36).

The most important thing is, God first; then the family, and then the business.

So today, work hard and as my young son always tells me, "Work smart." But remember at the end of the day, to spend time with your wife and love her.

Practical Christian living

"Masters, give your bondservants what is just and fair, knowing that you also have a Master in heaven." – Colossians 4:1

This morning as we go to work, whether we are in charge of one man or a thousand, the Lord is saying that we must deal in a just and fair manner with those under our care and management. Remember that we also have a Master in heaven. I think if we realise that we are going to be judged and receive exactly the same amount of grace, forgiveness and mercy that we give to those who are working under us, we would change our attitude very quickly.

The truth of the matter is that is exactly what is going to happen in heaven. Whatever we do today, whatever decisions we have to make, whatever justice needs to be meted out, let it be done with the love of God.

My late dad always told me never to ask a man to do a job that I cannot do myself. That makes things very fair. Before giving someone a task – whether it is digging a ditch, fixing a broken-down vehicle, ploughing a field, putting up a fence or driving a lorry – make sure that you can do it yourself. Ask yourself how long it would take you to do the job, add at least a third of the time and that will be a fair task for the person involved.

Remember one thing, my friend, our Lord Jesus is a practical God. He walked on this earth and never asked anyone to do a job that He couldn't do Himself. The day He washed the disciples' feet, He never asked one of them to do it. He did it Himself. What a wonderful mentor and example we have. Let us do the same today.

Balancing the books

"And Jesus said to him, 'Today salvation has come to this house, because he also is a son of Abraham.' – Luke 19:9

The word "restitution" means to make right. The dictionary says restitution is the act of giving back something that was stolen. Jesus said salvation had come to the house of Zacchaeus and I believe that it was because Zacchaeus was a changed man. He saw the love and the power of God come into his home and it changed his life completely. Has Jesus changed your life, my friend? Or are you just going through the motions? We're not talking about good works; we are talking about the power of God making a practical change in your life.

If anything in your life is not right today then, before you go to work this morning, make sure that you've made things right, first of all between you and God and secondly, between you and your fellow man. It might be your wife; it might be your children. Make restitution. Go to them and say, "Sorry for the way I spoke to you yesterday. Please forgive me." Even if it is not your fault, sort it out. You are the Christian.

The Word of God says that if you've done something wrong, you need to put it right. Zacchaeus was so touched by God he gave half his riches to the poor. He also paid back four hundred per cent more to anyone he had taken anything from. In those days tax collectors were considered to be evil. They had no respect for anyone. Zacchaeus took money that wasn't his. He abused and misused the old pensioners and the poor folk, and yet Jesus came into his life and made a difference.

As you go to work today, be sure to deal with any unsettled accounts. If God has laid something on your heart this morning, make restitution where necessary, say you're sorry, pay that income tax, or that VAT. Do it now so that God can bless your life. Often, all it takes is just one telephone call or a visit to say, "I'm sorry."

Keep on keeping on

"And let us not grow weary while doing good, for in due season we shall reap if we do not lose heart." – Galatians 6:9

Some of us may not particularly feel like going to work this morning. We may be tired of the daily grind and of doing good works, even for the Lord Jesus Christ. Some may be disappointed because they don't immediately see the results of their labours. The Lord says that we must press on. We must walk by faith and not by sight (2 Corinthians 5:7), and we must keep on being obedient to the call of God in our lives.

I always refer to the cornfield as my green cathedral. It's a place where I often pray and talk with the Lord. It reminds me that the Lord said we must not grow weary in doing good, because in due season we will reap if we do not lose heart. Sometimes just one more effort will bring the breakthrough.

Hudson Taylor was responsible for taking over a thousand families to China to preach the gospel. It was very, very tough going. Europeans were treated with great suspicion and it was extremely hard to win converts. Yet they continued by faith, to sow seed. Then an awful thing happened. The Boxer Rebellion broke out in China and the Chinese people revolted against the European residents and literally slaughtered them. Eventually, every European family was expelled from China under the Communist regime.

Never forget that our reward is not here on earth, but in heaven. Continue to do what God has called you to do, because He has promised us that in due season we shall reap if we do not lose heart.

The Caleb spirit

"But My servant Caleb, because he has a different spirit in him and has followed Me fully, I will bring into the land where he went, and his descendants shall inherit it." – Numbers 14:24

This is one of my favourite scriptures. Time and again the Bible tells us that without faith we cannot please God (Hebrews 11:6). This morning I believe the Lord would have us meditate on a "Caleb spirit."

Caleb was different from the rest of his generation. Moses sent twelve spies into the Promised Land. Ten spies – the majority – came back with a bad report. "Do not go in there," they said, "The giants are too big. They will kill you. We will never make it. Let's just stay where we are."

Caleb and Joshua went in with a spirit of faith and they came back with a good report. "The biggest grapes and pomegranates – the biggest fruit we have ever seen – are in that land," they said. "It flows with milk and honey." Later Caleb asked Joshua to send him to one of the most difficult areas so he could conquer it.

I want to encourage you today. You will be as strong as you see yourself to be. If you feel that you cannot cope, you will not cope. If you feel today that you will not be an overcomer, you will not overcome. If you feel that the job is too big for you, it will be too big for you. But if you go out with an attitude like Caleb today and say, "Lord, I can't do it in my own strength, but I know that I can do all things through Christ who strengthens me" (Philipians 4:13), then there is nothing that will hold you back. There is nothing that will keep you from victory. There is nothing that will keep you from success.

Get refocused today. Don't focus on the giants but rather focus on the possibilities that are available to you in the land of milk and honey the Lord is leading you to. Focus on the fact that you are going to achieve, not through your own strength, but through the power of the Lord Jesus Christ.

FEBRUARY

God is with us

"So he answered, 'Do not fear, for those who are with us are more than those who are with them.'" – 2 Kings 6:16

Remember we are in the majority if we are walking with the Lord Jesus Christ. It doesn't matter how big the task or how many messengers of the devil are working against us. Elisha's servant could see only the enemy and Elisha prayed that the Lord would open his eyes to see the chariots and the army of God standing on the hills.

Some years ago a farmer in Zimbabwe left his farm early in the morning to take his cattle to market. He had to leave his wife and young children alone on the farm, in spite of the danger that prevailed in those days.

Unbeknown to the family, terrorists arrived at the farm, planning to blow the farmhouse to pieces with mortar fire. The mother was hanging out washing when she felt the Holy Spirit urging her to go inside with the children. She obeyed immediately, locked the door and then prayed, calling on the Lord for protection. About ten minutes later the security forces came screeching up in their jeeps. "Who called you?" she asked.

"We have an amazing story to tell you," they said. "The terrorists who were planning to blow your house up came to us and surrendered. They said you were out in the garden hanging up the washing and they watched you as they set their mortars in position. Suddenly, they saw four shining soldiers about nine feet tall, standing at each corner of the house, holding glowing shields and swords. They were so frightened that they left all their weapons and ran straight into the arms of the security forces and surrendered."

No matter what you're doing today, be assured that God is with you. And if He's with you, then His angels will be with you too.

Honouring God

"And He said to them, 'Go into all the world and preach the gospel to every creature.' And they went out and preached everywhere, the Lord working with them and confirming the word through the accompanying signs. Amen." – Mark 16:15, 20

Whatever our profession may be, the Lord requires us to preach the gospel by example and by our lifestyle, not only by our words.

In all the years I've walked with the Lord Jesus Christ, He has never let me down. He has always honoured my decisions when I have done business in a godly manner. At an Eastern Cape Farmers' Association meeting, I was once asked whether there was anything wrong with water divining. The community was experiencing tremendous drought at the time and stock was dying. "We have drilling machines," they said," but we don't know where to look for water."

The Bible says clearly that divination is an abomination. "It is a form of witchcraft and totally unacceptable to God," I replied. "What can we do?" they asked. I advised them to visit their local geological office and find out where the different rock types met and where there were rock faults. "Drill there," I told them. "You will find water." "But," they protested, "a fault can run for a hundred metres." "That's where faith comes in," I responded. "You need to pray and God will show you where to drill."

I know this is true because I did exactly that on my own farm. The first peg I put in the ground by faith was right behind my house. Being a good Scotsman, I thought there was no point in putting the peg miles away – it would need more piping! When we started drilling, we got eight thousand litres of water per hour. We put another peg on top of a hill next to our chapel. There we got something like sixty thousand litres per hour and were able to use it for irrigation.

God will honour us if we honour and obey Him and He will confirm His word with signs and wonders.

Obeying God

"Pursue peace with all people, and holiness, without which no one will see the Lord." – Hebrews 12:14

Holiness is the end product of obedience. When we obey the Word of God, we become holy people and the Lord Jesus Christ will honour everything we do.

Living together without being married, for example, is not walking in holiness. I've just returned from a campaign in Cape Town where we saw two couples respond to the challenge of holiness. They were determined to do things God's way and they got married right away. God will honour their stand.

The Lord says clearly in Matthew 5:8 that "the pure in heart shall see God." Many of us have no victory in our lives because we are compromising our stand and not walking in holiness. I believe the Holy Spirit wants us to get our lives in order. Then we will see the power of God demonstrated. He is a holy God. He can see everything we do, the things we have failed to do and what we intend to do in the future.

When God told us to leave part of our land fallow one year in seven, I determined to obey Him. The word "fallow" means "leave it untouched." We allowed our cattle and other animals to graze the land, but other than that we left it alone. Since then, God has blessed our crops more than ever before. I don't even believe that it is only because the land is resting. I believe it is because we obeyed God, releasing His blessing in our lives.

Whatever you do today, do what is right in the eyes of God. God will grant you His favour.

Making a difference

"If My people who are called by My name will humble themselves, and pray and seek My face, and turn from their wicked ways, then I will hear from heaven, and will forgive their sin and heal their land." – 2 Chronicles 7:14

This is a very well-known scripture and it challenges us to stop complaining about the world system; the way it does its business and conducts its affairs. People of the world do not know the Lord Jesus Christ and therefore, they walk in darkness. They have a reason – not an excuse – for living the way they do.

This does not apply to the believer. We have absolutely no excuse or reason for walking in an ungodly manner, or for using ungodly principles in business. The Lord has said that the destiny of our nation, our country, our business, our farm, and our family, lies fairly and squarely in the hands of the believer. "If my people..." – not people of other religions or those who do not know the Lord – will pray, then God promises to act on their behalf.

So today, as we go about our business, let us be challenged by this tremendous promise. Romans 8:19 tells us that "All creation is waiting with expectation for the manifestation of the sons of God." The world has no answer to the dilemma and predicament of our world, but we do. So let's go out and make a difference.

Effective witnesses in the marketplace

"So, because he was of the same trade, he stayed with them and worked; for by occupation they were tentmakers." – Acts 18:3

We often hear the term "tentmaker." It refers to a Christian preacher who provides his own income by the profession or the occupation God has given him. Paul, who in my opinion was probably the greatest evangelist/preacher/apostle of all time, was also a businessman and was often found working as a tentmaker. He wrote many times that he tried not to be a burden to anyone. He worked to meet his own needs.

I would like to encourage you this morning, whatever your profession or business, not to despise the occupation God has given you. You can be as effective a witness in your place of work as a man God has called to a full-time preaching ministry.

God has opened many doors for me simply because I am recognised as a farmer. I've had meetings with kings, prime ministers and other dignitaries and been invited to speak to nations across the world about the Lord Jesus Christ. An added advantage is that I am able to speak from the heart – to shoot from the hip, as they say – and it is received, because I am seen as a fellow tradesman. I think if a theologian were to say some of the things I say, he would be "stoned in the market place"! Do not despise your occupation. Do it with all your heart. Use it to share the gospel, whatever your profession or job may be. Use every opportunity that comes your way to preach the undiluted Word of God.

Standing on the Word of God

"Now the Lord spoke to Paul in the night by a vision, 'Do not be afraid, but speak, and do not keep silent." – Acts 18:9

The words the Lord Jesus Christ used when He called Paul into the ministry were the same words He used when He called me. He said, "Do not be afraid, but speak and do not keep silent."

Has God called you into full-time ministry? Are you longing to do more for God? Do you have a passion to serve Him? Do you have a vision you long to see fulfilled? If the answer is, "Yes," I would ask you, has God confirmed this to you through His Word? Whatever plans you may have, whether they relate to the ministry or business or any other activity in your life, I want to exhort you and encourage you to seek the face of God and seek confirmation through the Holy Word of God.

When God called me to be an evangelist He gave me clear direction. The scripture He gave me was Acts 18:9, the verse we are considering today. I only found out about twenty years later that this was the very scripture God used when He called the great evangelist George Whitfield, a man who spoke to literally hundreds of thousands of people in the British Isles and America about two hundred years ago.

God always confirms His call through His written Word. During difficult times we need to stand firmly on that Word. There will often be times of severe testing when the venture or vision is not going according to plan and you are feeling the pressure. That is when you have to stand on the Word of God and believe God.

Find out what it is that God wants of you and get it confirmed by scripture.

A godly wife

"He who finds a wife finds a good thing, and obtains favour from the LORD." – Proverbs 18:22

I'm often asked to speak at farmers' conventions, men's breakfasts and business meetings. Sometimes, just to get the attention of the men, I start by saying that unless your wife is your best friend, you are a failure. In Proverbs 18:22 the Lord says, "He who finds a wife finds a good thing and obtains favour from the Lord."

My wife is my best friend and confidante. We pray together and talk about everything. Others may tell me what I want to hear but my wife will tell me the undiluted truth, even sometimes if it is painful, because she loves me. If your wife is not like that, maybe you should ask yourself, why not?

When I was younger, before I became an evangelist, there was nothing I enjoyed more than asking my wife to ride with me around the farm. I appreciated her unbiased, honest opinion and advice. She really enjoyed that. Maybe you ought to involve your wife a bit more, in every aspect of your life. Particularly with regard to your family. The best thing you can do for your whole family is to pray together for them.

I appreciate my wife now more than ever, because I'm away from home so much due to my preaching schedule. When I come home, I enjoy her company immensely because the Lord has given me such a wonderful companion. The Bible says one will chase a thousand but two will chase ten thousand. Your wife is your greatest asset. Never forget that. Without Sarah, Abraham would have accomplished nothing!

Your vision

"Then the LORD answered me and said: 'Write the vision and make it plain on tablets, that he may run who reads it." – Habakkuk 2:2

In South Africa we talk about a "slap chip." That is a soft, soggy, French fried potato. When you hold it up, it just folds in two! That's what a person is like who doesn't have a cause to live for, or a vision to aim at. You know the old saying, "If you aim at nothing, you're sure to hit it."

If you do have a vision, cause or ambition, it's very important to share it with others. That is why the Lord said to Habakkuk, "Write it down, make it plain, (keep it simple) so that he who sees it may run with it."

Do you speak to your employees and your fellow workers about any projects that you have for the future? People you work with can often become totally uninterested unless they know what you're aiming at and can share your vision.

On our farm we don't talk about "my farm," we talk about "our farm," and what we are going to do on "our farm" today. As the vision becomes clear, our workers start to run with it. Our people don't work strictly to the clock. They get the job finished because they take pride in what they are doing. They have a share and a say in it. But if we don't tell them what the vision is, things can get very complicated.

Are you telling your people that you appreciate the work they are doing for you and the company? Do you keep them up to date with what's going on? You say they know... but are you sure they know? Continue to remind them and encourage them and you will see the difference.

The Way, the Truth, the Life

"Jesus said to him, 'I am the way, the truth, and the life. No one comes to the Father except through Me." – John 14:6

As Christians we have to understand one thing very clearly. All roads do not lead to heaven. We are not all praying to the same God. A Muslim once said to a Christian: "Your God and my God are the same." "That cannot be so," said the Christian. "Why not?" responded the Muslim. "Does your God have a son?" asked the Christian. "No. Allah does not have a son." "Well, my God does have a son," said the Christian emphatically, "His name is Jesus Christ. We do not serve the same God."

The great and wonderful truth of this scripture can never be compromised. Jesus Christ is the Way, the Truth and the Life and no one comes to the Father except through Him. The moment we start changing the gospel message we are asking for trouble and this trouble will affect not only our own lives, but those of our families as well. Men are the "high priests" of their households and have the responsibility of ensuring that their children both understand and are brought up in the light of the Truth.

If we want a peaceful, godly home, we have to stand for the uncompromising gospel of Jesus and we should ensure that our homes are run accordingly. Many of us have made a rod for our own backs by not disciplining our children, implementing the Word of God and maintaining Christian principles. We have allowed standards to slip and foreign gods – in terms of worldly influences like music, dress code, and language – to come into our homes.

Let us repent of that this morning and run our homes on the right footing. We will soon see the difference it will make, not only in our own lives, but in the lives of our families as well.

Loving our wives

"Husbands, love your wives, just as Christ also loved the church and gave Himself for her." – Ephesians 5:25

Do we love our wives as Christ loved the Church?

I believe half the problems in our homes arise because husbands do not love their wives properly. The Lord says we are to love our wives as we love our own bodies. We are to cherish and look after them. It's our responsibility to see that accounts are paid, not send our wives to make excuses for us. It's our responsibility to discipline the children when they misbehave. It's our work as the high priest of the home to instruct our children in the things of God. I have often heard men complain that their wives won't submit to them. Well, why should they? What kind of example is set for them? It is easy for a wife to submit to a man who loves and respects her, but who can submit to a man who is a coward and does not take his rightful responsibility and position in the home?

Today, show your wife that you love her. Don't only tell her – show her. Love is a doing word. It's an active word. Spend time with her. When was the last time you bought her flowers? When was the last time you prayed with her? When was the last time you shared things together or just sat in the garden and enjoyed fellowship with her over a cup of tea?

Lord, please forgive us for taking our wives for granted. We repent of that this morning and make a pledge today, to make her the most important person in our lives after you. Lord Jesus, give us the strength to do it. Amen.

Humility

"Therefore whoever humbles himself as this little child is the greatest in the kingdom of heaven." – Matthew 18:4

If we want to be great, then we must be prepared to humble ourselves like little children. I have three grandchildren and it gives me great pleasure to have them come to our home. I love watching them just being themselves, totally natural, without putting on any airs and graces.

Martin Luther, the great reformer, was asked what the three greatest virtues were. He replied that the first one is humility, the second is humility and the third is humility.

William Carey, a poor English cobbler, established a great missionary work in India and was mightily used of God. He was responsible for translating the Bible from English into Sanskrit, Chinese and many other Asiatic languages. One day, someone tried to humiliate him. "I believe you are only a shoemaker," he said, "No, Sir," responded William Carey humbly." I am a cobbler. I cannot make shoes. I can only repair them."

William Duma, the great South African Zulu preacher with a tremendous healing ministry, was asked to preach in a church in Zambia many years ago. At nine o'clock the whole congregation was waiting for the great man of God to come through the front door. A few minutes later they heard a little tap at the back door. The minister opened the door and there stood Pastor Duma. The servant of the Lord had come through the servants' entrance. True greatness is not earned. It is recognised.

As we go out today, let us be humble. Remember, He is the one who gave us the supreme example by taking the basin, filling it with water, and washing His disciples' dirty feet, even as they were debating about who would be the greatest in the kingdom of heaven.

God is for us

"Or do you not know that your body is the temple of the Holy Spirit who is in you, whom you have from God, and you are not your own?"
– 1 Corinthians 6:19

Christianity is not about buildings, churches, organisations or denominations. It is about people. John Wesley said, "Give me a hundred men who fear nothing but sin, and desire no-one but God and I care not one straw whether they be laymen or clergymen." He went on to say, "With those one hundred men I will rattle the gates of hell and bring heaven down to earth," and that is exactly what he did.

Jesus lives inside of the heart of the Christian. Wherever we go today, let us be sure that we treat our bodies as the temple of the Holy Spirit. Dale Carnegie, the great American tycoon said, "If you take away my empire, I will rebuild it in ten years if you leave me with my men." The Bible says clearly in Philippians 4:13 "I can do all things through Christ who strengthens me."

It is Christ in you that will make you a success. The church is the body of believers. We are the church. If you want to be successful, invite Christ to come and take residence inside you. If you want to be successful in business, a good husband or wife, or a good leader, it is very simple. It is "Christ in you, the hope of glory" (Colossians 1:27).

The farmer only plants the seed. The Lord makes it grow. May the Lord bless you today as you go out, and remember, that wherever you go today, God is going with you because He lives inside of you. You need fear nothing. "If God is for us, who can be against us?" (Romans 8:31).

Pray without ceasing

"Pray without ceasing." – I Thessalonians 5:17

Prayer is the most important part of a believer's life. It is possible to pray without ceasing and I would encourage you to pray today, especially if things are not going too well with you. The Lord says in Jeremiah 33:3, "Call unto me and I will answer you. I will show you great and mighty things of which you do not know." Matthew 7:7 says, "Ask and you shall receive, seek and you will find, knock and the door shall be opened unto you." Many times we don't have because we don't ask, and we can only ask by praying and speaking to our Father. That is what prayer is. It is communication with God.

I remember very distinctly one of the most testing times of my life. We had established eighty hectares of pine trees on a slope going into a wetland. The reeds were standing about two metres tall. That day a fire had started in the wetland and the wind was driving it straight towards our plantation. Our pine trees were only about three or four years old and the fire would have completely destroyed them. As I saw the smoke, a neighbour telephoned. "Get to that fire," he said, "It is very urgent."

I remember feeling totally helpless. All we had with us were a couple of beaters. I said, "Let us pray." That may sound futile or ridiculous. Our natural tendency was to get to the fire as quickly as possible and try to extinguish it.

But we got on our knees and we prayed. It wasn't half an hour later when the Lord changed the wind and it took the fire back into the wetland. We never lost one tree. There is power in prayer! Today, wherever you go, pray without ceasing. When we do the possible, God will do the impossible.

Effective prayer

"Confess your trespasses to one another, and pray for one another, that you may be healed. The effective, fervent prayer of a righteous man avails much." – James 5:16

The Word of God says that the effective fervent prayer of a righteous man avails much. We are made righteous by the blood of Jesus only as a result of accepting Him as our Lord and Saviour and being "born again" (John 3:7).

When we pray, we must pray effectively, we must pray fervently and we must be in a right relationship with the Lord Jesus Christ. Then when we pray, God will move mountains. If you have never received Christ as your own personal Lord and Saviour, I would encourage you to do that right now. Kneel at your bed before you do anything else this morning and invite Him into your life. If you are already a Christian, recommit your life to Christ today.

Robert LeTourneau was the man who put the earth-moving business on the map. He was so successful he eventually sold out to Caterpillar. Yet, at the age of forty, he was bankrupt. He repented before God, recommitted his life to Jesus and said, "From this day onwards I give you my life and my everything." He became the first businessman in the United States of America in the 1930s to fly his own aeroplane. He tithed 90% of his income and only kept 10% for himself. He was a multi-billionaire. Why? Because God answered his prayer. He prayed effective, fervent prayers and he was a righteous man.

Bring everything before Christ this morning before you go to work. Then set out with faith and confidence, knowing that God has heard your prayer and He goes before you.

Praying the Word

"In this manner, therefore, pray: Our Father in heaven, hallowed be Your name." – Matthew 6:9

Do you have difficulty praying? If that is the case, I would encourage you to start off with the most complete prayer that has ever been prayed and written – the Lord's Prayer.

George Muller was a great man of God who built the orphanages in Bristol, England, two hundred years ago. Ten thousand children and £6,000 went through his hands without him asking anyone for one penny. He was a man who lived by faith. He said that he struggled quite a bit with his prayer life until he realised that if he focused his mind on the Word of God, he could then pray effectively. That is what I do. I read a portion of scripture systematically from the Old Testament and the New Testament every day and then I pray around what I have just read. You might say that you don't have time to pray. I want to say to you very sincerely, my dear friend, that you cannot afford not to pray.

Martin Luther was a very busy man. He said that the busier he got, the earlier he rose in the morning to pray. You can accurately gauge a man's spirituality by the amount of time he spends praying. Our mentor and example is the Master Himself. We read time and again that when people went looking for the Lord – the busiest man who ever lived – they would find Him in the mountains, praying to His Father.

Let us pray before we go out today and then go forth, knowing that God has gone before us.

Exercising our faith

"Then Jesus answered and said to her, 'O woman, great is your faith! Let it be to you as you desire.' And her daughter was healed from that very hour." – Matthew 15:28

When I pray for the sick, I often stress that I am exercising my faith as I trust God to heal the sick person. I am very aware that the faith of the one I am praying for may well be at an all-time low, simply because they are physically or mentally sick. So it was with this woman. Her daughter was severely demon possessed. She came to the Master and asked Him to heal her daughter. The disciples saw that she was not one of them and told the Lord to send her away. She persevered, even when Jesus told her that He was sent to the lost sheep of the house of Israel. She would not be put off. She kept crying, "Lord, help me." Her persistence and her faith in Him to heal her daughter touched His heart and the child was healed in a moment of time.

How is your faith level this morning? How long have you trusted the Lord Jesus Christ for that miracle in your life? Today could be your day, because of your persistence and faithfulness.

Never forget the woman who persevered until she got an answer. When you think about that family affair, sick person at work, or situation that you just cannot see any way out of, remember that faith is all we need.

How do we get faith? Remember "faith comes by hearing, and hearing by the Word of God" (Romans 10: 17). Write your prayer request down. Don't let anyone dissuade you from seeking God for the answer. Trust Almighty God to do a miracle. He's a good God. He will not fail you.

God has no grandchildren

"For whoever does the will of My Father in heaven is My brother and sister and mother." – Matthew 12:50

The Lord Jesus has no grandchildren. Your father or grandfather may have been a minister of the gospel and a great servant of the Lord, but that does not qualify you to enter into the kingdom of God. The Bible says you must be "born again" (John 3:3). You have to make a new start. You have to declare Jesus Christ as your personal Lord and Saviour. Then you have to live the life of a believer. The Bible says that not all who cry, "Lord, Lord," will enter the kingdom of heaven, but only those who do the will of God. That is what Jesus said in Matthew 7:21.

One day Jesus was speaking to the multitudes when His mother and brothers came to look for Him. Someone came to Jesus and told Him that they were waiting outside. "Who is My mother and who are My brothers?" the Lord asked. And then He answered His own question. "Whoever does the will of My Father in heaven is My brother and sister and mother." (Matthew 12:47–50).

I believe the Lord is asking you and me that very question this morning. The answer is very simple: If you are obeying the Word of God and walking in righteousness, then you are a relative of the Son of God. You are behaving as His brother, sister, or mother. However, if you are purposely walking in disobedience to God, you are in a very dangerous situation.

I exhort you, before you start your day, repent. Stop committing that premeditated sin and start afresh this morning, so that you too may be called a child of the living God.

What do you want the Lord to do for you today?

"So Jesus answered and said to him, 'What do you want Me to do for you?' The blind man said to Him, 'Rabboni, that I may receive my sight.'" – Mark 10:51

What is it that you want the Lord to do for you today?

I remember preaching at a place called Hornchurch on the outskirts of London. The Lord Jesus Christ worked mightily that night. He healed a man who had cancer of the intestine and I prophesied that he would preach the gospel. Two weeks later I received a letter from him confirming that he was healed totally and indeed preaching the gospel. Our God is a mighty God.

There was a lady present in a wheelchair that same night. I watched her wheel herself to the front and asked her, "What do you want the Lord to do for you?" It seems such a ridiculous question. She was there because she was sick. But Jesus asked blind Bartimaeus the same thing when he was led to the Master. I believe if the blind man had said to the Lord that he had backache, earache or arthritis, God would have healed him of his spoken condition. Bartimaeus said, "Lord (Rabboni), that I might receive my sight." The Bible says, "immediately he received his sight" and he followed Jesus.

When I asked this lady what she wanted the Lord to do for her, she said, "I have tremendous pain in my back. I want the Lord Jesus Christ to heal my back." I prayed for her and the pain left her instantaneously. She started rejoicing, but she turned the wheelchair round and to my sorrow, wheeled herself out of the service. She did not desire to walk.

This morning, the Lord is asking you a question, "What is it that you want Me to do for you today?" Tell Him very clearly so that He can work in your life.

Overcoming temptation

"But Jesus answered him, saying, 'It is written, Man shall not live by bread alone, but by every Word of God." – Luke 4:4

How did Jesus overcome the temptation of the devil? It was by quoting scripture. There is tremendous power released when we speak the Word of God. It is an incredible weapon in the hands of God's children. Jesus could have told the devil to get lost, but He did not. He quoted scripture: "It is written, man shall not live by bread alone but by every word of God" (Deuteronomy 8:3).

To be tempted by the devil is not a sin. Sin comes when we succumb to the temptation of the evil one. David, when he was supposed to have gone to war, remained behind, and walked out on to his veranda in the cool of the evening. He looked down and saw a beautiful woman bathing. Her name was Bathsheba. He looked a first time – that was temptation. He looked a second time – that was sin.

Remember today that the evil one will try to tempt you as he did Jesus in the desert. The way to contend with the devil is by doing what Jesus did – quoting the Word of God. If necessary, we even have to flee or run away from temptation. Joseph was in a serious situation when Potiphar's wife tried to tempt him to go to bed with her and he refused. Eventually he ran from her and left his garment in her hands. Sometimes we have to flee from evil in order to have the victory.

Whatever it is that you are wrestling with this morning, whatever the temptation may be, the strongest weapon you have is the same weapon the Master used – the power of the spoken Word of God. Speak scripture and God will strengthen you, causing the evil one to flee.

Faith and doubt

"But let him ask in faith, with no doubting, for he who doubts is like a wave of the sea driven and tossed by the wind." – James 1:6

As I write this, I'm on holiday at the coast. I have been watching the waves of the Indian Ocean these last few days and noticing how their direction constantly changes. When I get up in the morning, the waves are blowing from the east towards the seashore. By mid-afternoon they are blowing from the south. I can see how the waves are dependent on the changing winds. The Lord is showing me that we are living in times of tremendous change. Things are changing all the time. Governments, moral standards and previously acceptable practices of dress and language are changing. But the Word of God never changes.

This scripture tells us that whatever we ask of God, we must ask in faith without doubting. We must take our eyes off the waves of the sea and the winds, and keep our eyes fixed on Jesus Christ, the author and the finisher of our faith. Smith Wigglesworth, that great servant of the Lord – a master plumber by trade and a man of very little education but incredible faith – said, (and I quote) "God said it, I believe it and that settles it." He was used incredibly in the area of divine healing. He was known to have been instrumental in raising twelve or thirteen people from the dead through his faith in God. He was a man of great faith. Faith is not dependent upon sight. Faith is dependent upon the promises of God, which never change.

As we go out today, let us ask God by faith for direction in decision making and thank Him in anticipation and expectation.

Holy conversation

"Neither filthiness, nor foolish talking, nor coarse jesting, which are not fitting, but rather giving of thanks." – Ephesians 5:4

Our Lord is a holy God. He cannot and will not tolerate sin of any description or degree. The Lord says that in the last days, the filthy will become filthier and the righteous will become more righteous. As believers we need to keep ourselves pure and to refrain from indulging in dirty jokes and questionable conversations. We need to guard our tongues and set a good example to our sons and daughters. They may not necessarily do what we say, but they will do what we do.

If you are someone who is walking a fine line between righteousness and ungodliness, you are in trouble. The Lord says very clearly, that instead of wasting time with coarse jesting or foolish talking, we are rather to give thanks to our righteous and holy God for His goodness towards us. We are to encourage those with whom we interact, talking about the things of God and speaking positively of encouraging things.

My dear friend, time is short. Let us spend every moment of the day bringing hope, faith, love and strength to others, so that we might be found honourable before God. Let us watch over the words of our mouths and the meditation of our hearts, in Jesus' name.

Strong in the Lord

"Finally, my brethren, be strong in the Lord and in the power of His might."
– Ephesians 6:10

Are you feeling strong this morning as you start your new day? Or are you feeling weak? Paul says, "When I am weak, then I am strong." The Lord is telling us today, that we must be strong in Him and in the power of His might. That is the safest place to be.

Philippians 4:13 says,"I can do all things through Christ who strengthens me." We have to depend on the strength of God every day. I'm reminded of the Fijian rugby team that ran onto the rugby field with Philippians 4:13 printed on their jerseys. They were making the statement that their strength was in God. No wonder they became world champions.

Where is your strength today? I trust it is not in your ability, even if you are the heavyweight power-lifting champion of the world. The power God is speaking about is found in His Son, our Saviour, the Lord Jesus Christ. He said, "Seek Me first and all of these other things will be added unto you" (Matthew 6:33).

Go forth today, knowing that whether you are strong or weak in the flesh is not the issue. If Christ is for you, there is no one who can stand against you. Our strength is found in the Lord and His written Word. We are further strengthened through prayer, in meditation and in fellowship with other believers.

"My soul, wait silently for God alone, for my expectation is from Him." – Psalm 62:5. Let your expectation today, your very essence, be found in the power of His might.

Perfect peace

"You will keep him in perfect peace, whose mind is stayed on You, because he trusts in You." – Isaiah 26:3

What are you trusting in at this time? Are you trusting in your bank balance? Are you trusting in that beautiful crop that is growing in the fields or that magnificent herd of cattle? Are you trusting in your business? Or are you perhaps trusting in your health, or your IQ? If you are, you are skating on thin ice!

The Lord says to you this morning, "Trust in Me and I will keep you in perfect peace." Keep your mind focused on Jesus, trust Him with all your heart and He will bring it to pass. As Moses said, "If God is not going with us, we're not going!" We can do nothing whatsoever without His blessing and strength.

Sometimes we have to accept situations without knowing the answers. For example, God is using me particularly in the area of divine healing. I am almost speechless with gratitude when I see paralysed people walk, deaf ears unstopped and blind eyes opened. Yet often I will pray the prayer of faith (really believing God has told me to do it) and the person will not be healed. In fact, sometimes they are taken home to heaven. People ask me why and I don't have any answers. Katherine Kuhlman was asked the same thing and she always said, "I don't know, but one day when I get to heaven I'll ask Jesus and He will tell me. Until then I shall carry on praying for the sick, because I've seen so many healed."

Don't ask questions today, my friend. Find out exactly what it is that God wants you to do, and then do it with all of your heart, and you will have perfect peace.

Doing business until He comes

"So he called ten of his servants, delivered to them ten minas, and said to them, 'Do business till I come.'" – Luke 19:13

Are you doing business until He comes? Or are you playing it safe? That's the question the Lord wants to ask you this morning.

Peter stepped out of the boat and was walking on the water towards Jesus. He took his eyes off the Lord, focused them on the water for just a split second and immediately started to sink. He cried out to God for mercy and the Lord Jesus lifted him out of the water. For Peter, the safest place was to be with Jesus.

The Lord says to you and me this morning, "Do business until I come." Trust the Lord. This is no time to play it safe. The safest place to be is out on the water with Jesus. The best form of defence, they say, is attack!

It doesn't matter how hard the going is for you in your occupation. It doesn't matter what the crop of potatoes is looking like, or what the cattle prices are doing. The Lord says, "Do business until I come."

Go out today and continue to do business. He is coming back very soon and He is going to ask us one question: "What did you do with what I gave you?"

Minding our own business

"Let both grow together until the harvest, and at the time of harvest I will say to the reapers, 'First gather together the tares and bind them in bundles to burn them, but gather the wheat into my barn.'" – Matthew 13:30

The Lord would ask you a question this morning. Why are you so concerned about evildoers? Why are you so concerned about the supposed victory that evil people are having? That underhanded person seems to be making so much money and succeeding in so many ways and it frustrates you. The Lord says to you today, "Leave him alone. I will deal with him on the Day of Judgment (or possibly even before). Concentrate on growing the crop that I've called you to grow." Put your effort into the wheat crop and leave the tares (the weeds) for the husbandman, the harvester, Jesus Christ. He will sort out the tares from the wheat in His good time.

Often we get so disillusioned because we are farming according to God's principles, while the man across the road is doing the very opposite. He's not paying his income tax. He's not paying his workers correctly. He is undercutting people and operating in an ungodly and evil manner. The Lord says to you this morning, "I will take care of the tares. You make sure that you grow a good crop of wheat. Don't be concerned about the splinter in someone else's eye. Be concerned about taking the beam out of your own eye."

Today, concentrate on your own field and let the Lord Jesus Christ take care of the tares.

The coming of the Lord

"Now learn this parable from the fig tree: when its branch has already become tender, and puts forth leaves, you know that summer is near." –
Mark 13:28

The Lord says to us, as good farmers (husbandmen), that we know when summer is upon us because we see the trees start to put forth new blossoms.

I believe God is saying to us today that the return of the Lord Jesus Christ is very near. He says that when we see signs of wars and rumours of wars, floods, droughts, disease and pestilence, we know that His coming is at hand. Jesus said, "Now when these things begin to happen, look up and lift up your heads, because your redemption draws near." – Luke 21:28.

Never before in the history of our world have we seen such devastation, disease, hunger or disregard for humanity. AIDS is sweeping across our nation. Immorality is at an all-time high. Churches are openly marrying people of the same sex. According to the Word of God, this is an abomination to Him. We are seeing unprecedented droughts north of our borders, in central and sub-Saharan Africa. Cloning is becoming the order of the day. Scientists are playing with DNA and GM (genetically modified) foods, interfering with God's creation.

Let us rejoice that the fig tree is blooming and Jesus Christ is on His way. At the same time, let us be sure that we have nothing to do with anything that is ungodly. The Lord said, "Watch therefore, for you do not know what hour your Lord is coming." – Matthew 24:42.

I am a cloud watcher because the Word of God tells me that Jesus is coming back on the clouds. I have a plaque in my home with two words beautifully inscribed on it. They read, "Perhaps today." Every day when I go about my work on the farm, I look up and I say, "Lord, is it today?"

Are you ready for His return?

God hears sincere prayer

"Behold, the Lord's hand is not shortened, that it cannot save; nor His ear heavy, that it cannot hear." – Isaiah 59:1

The Lord will save anyone who has a desire to repent and start again. However, if you look at verse two of that same scripture, you will see the Lord says, "but your iniquities have separated you from your God."

He has assured us that His hand is not shortened and His ear is not heavy. You do not need to shout. God can hear you. You can pray in the quietness of your heart. You do not have to be an eloquent prayer. God hears the prayers from a man's heart. In fact, He despises the Pharisee's flamboyant prayers. He prefers the prayers of a genuine sinner saying, "Lord, have mercy on me."

You say, "His hand cannot save me." My dear friend, I'm a living testimony to a miracle-working God. I have seen my God turn the wind so that a fire that was set to burn out my whole farm was stopped. I've seen a herd of cattle that were condemned to be slaughtered because of a TB diagnosis pronounced by a vet, turned around miraculously, so that the farmer still has his herd intact.

The Lord is asking you to call on Him this morning, and He promises to answer you but He is looking for a broken and contrite heart that He can work with. If there is anything in your life this day that you need to repent of, do it. Pray, in His name, earnestly, fervently, and He will hear your prayers. John 14:14 says, "If you ask anything in my name I will do it."

No weapon formed against us shall prosper

"No weapon formed against you shall prosper, and every tongue which rises against you in judgment you shall condemn. This is the heritage of the servants of the LORD, and their righteousness is from Me, says the LORD."
– Isaiah 54:17

This is a beautiful promise to start off the day. The Lord says you do not have to justify yourself because He will deal with the situation for you.

I will never forget getting fully involved in the preparation of a large campaign that was to be held overseas. At the same time I was busy preparing some oxen for a cattle show. To be honest, I spent all my effort and time in preparation for the campaign, spending time in prayer, listening to the voice of God, getting all my contacts ready and making travel arrangements.

For the cattle show all I had to offer were three oxen. Most of my neighbours and fellow competitors were entering strings of up to fourteen head of cattle. The Lord says that the heritage of the servants of the Lord comes from Him. We need fear nothing. He says that every weapon that's formed against us shall fail and every tongue that rises up in judgment against you, you shall condemn. I went to that show and came home with no less than seven trophies. Amongst them was the Grand Champion, the Reserve Champion, the Stockman of the Show and the Most Points in the Show – all out of three animals!

I would say to you today, concentrate on what God has called you to do and He will take care of every single accuser and problem that you have, because this is the heritage of the servants of the Lord.

Humble yourselves

"Humble yourselves in the sight of the Lord, and He will lift you up." –
James 4:10

One of the attributes all great men of God display is humility.

I rode horses in Australia for a while when I was a young man and the Australian cattlemen used to tell me that the bigger the hat the farmer wore, the smaller the farm he had. The smaller the brim of the hat, the bigger the farm. Jesus says if you humble yourself, He will lift you up.

I really feel today that God would have us remember we are nothing except for His grace, and yet at the same time, we can do all things through Christ who strengthens us. The reason we are to remain very humble is simply because any good thing in us came from the Lord in the first place.

The most humble person ever to walk on the face of the earth was the Lord Jesus Christ Himself. When He came down from heaven, God became man. A defenceless baby born in a feed trough (manger), in a little cave in Bethlehem, surrounded by farm animals. He asks you to humble yourself so that He can raise you up into the mighty man or woman of God that He has called you to be.

MARCH

Protection

"When the enemy comes in like a flood, the Spirit of the LORD will lift up a standard against him." – Isaiah 59:19

We live in a particular area where many farm murders have taken place over the last few years. Over two hundred farmers and farm personnel, both black and white, have been murdered but the Lord Jesus Christ has protected us and we thank Him for that. Sometimes it feels as if the enemy is coming in like a flood. We do not have an electric fence around our farmhouse, nor are we able to install an adequate security system or purchase firearms with which to protect ourselves. We are literally relying on the angels of the Lord Jesus Christ to protect us. Our experience every time has been that the Spirit of the Lord has lifted up a standard against the devil.

I remember taking care of a young drug addict who had come to our farm for rehabilitation. She was on mainline drugs and involved with a terrible drug syndicate somewhere in Durban. Unbeknown to us, these men had tried to smuggle drugs to her, but the drugs never arrived. Much later she told us why. They had come all the way from Durban, some 145 km away – a two-hour drive. When they reached the gates of the farm, these hardened gangsters said they saw an incredibly bright light over the farmhouse and they were afraid to come in. They turned around and drove all the way back to Durban with their drugs.

The Spirit of the Lord will raise up a standard against the devil and his agents. Go out today and work hard, knowing that the Lord has got His hand upon your life.

Unconditional faith

"Though He slay me, yet will I trust Him" – Job 13:15

God has a question for you this morning. Are you serving Him unconditionally, or are you serving Him conditionally? In other words, does your prayer life consist of, 'Lord, I will serve You if You do this or that – Lord, I'll make a deal with You – Lord, I promise to give my life to You, if You will take care of all my wants (not my needs).'

Stop right there! No one makes deals with God. God is God, and we are His creation. Job said, "Even though He slay me, yet will I trust Him". Job had a close relationship with the Lord. Do you have one with Jesus Christ? Can you say, "Lord, irrespective of what happens, I will serve You because I love You"?

Abraham, the great father of faith, had such a wonderful relationship with God that he was prepared to offer up his only son, for whom he had waited so long. He knew his God so well that he believed God would be able to restore Isaac out of the very ashes of the sacrifice and give him back to his father.

What about you today? Can you honestly say that whatever the circumstances, you will still serve God? I firmly believe that the decision you make hinges on your relationship with the Lord.

You see, if you know God, you'll know His heart. Our God is not a taker. He is a giver. Our God is not against us – He is for us. Our God wants us to have abundant life and therefore, irrespective of what happens, make a choice today to serve God unconditionally.

"Even though He slay me, yet will I trust Him."

What would Jesus do?

"Blessed is the man who walks not in the counsel of the ungodly, nor stands in the path of sinners, nor sits in the seat of the scornful; but his delight is in the law of the LORD, and on His law he meditates day and night. He shall be like a tree planted by the rivers of water, that brings forth its fruit in its season, whose leaf also shall not wither; and whatever he does shall prosper." – Psalm 1:1–3

Some people wear little wristbands with the letters WWJD emblazoned on them. That stands for "What Would Jesus Do?" I believe our reading today is about that very thing. The saying came, I believe, from a book called "In His Steps" by Charles Sheldon. The story is about a pastor who challenged the congregation one morning to make a decision that they would ask themselves the question "What would Jesus do?" in every situation that confronted them.

A man who was in the service that morning – a publisher and newspaper tycoon – was offered sole rights to cover a bare knuckle prize fight. Immediately, he asked himself the question, "What would Jesus do?" Would Jesus be happy for him to cover that story? The answer was no, because it was absolute savagery. They fought without gloves and pummelled each other almost to death. He told his editor that they would not be covering the story. The editor was shattered and said it would destroy the newspaper; that they were doomed and sure to go under. However, the newspaper publisher stuck to his guns.

An opera singer was about to go on a tour to Europe. She also asked herself the question, "What would Jesus do?" Her friends, to their horror, found her downtown standing on a street corner in the red light district, dressed in a beautiful evening gown, singing to the poor and the needy, to prostitutes and drug addicts. There are many similar stories which always come back to the same question: "What would Jesus do?"

Ask yourself that question today.

Unashamed of the gospel

"For I am not ashamed of the gospel of Christ, for it is the power of God to salvation for everyone who believes, for the Jew first and also for the Greek." – Romans 1:16

We have a thirty-foot cross on our farm. It stands at the highest point, right next to our chapel and at night, the cross lights up. We are making a very simple statement. We are not ashamed to be called Christians.

Paul said, "I'm not ashamed of the gospel of Christ, for it is the power of God to salvation for everyone who believes." All my life I was afraid to stand up and be counted, until I realised that as soon as one becomes apathetic, there is no power. The best thing to do is to be forthright and outspoken. People may not agree with what you stand for but they will at least respect you. Do your neighbours know what you stand for? Do they know that you are a Christian? Do your fellow workers know that you love the Lord Jesus Christ? Why not? How can you keep the good news to yourself?

J Hudson Taylor, during a later visit to China, asked one of his first converts how his Christian walk was going. The Chinaman said, "It's going well. My life is transformed, I've never been so happy." And then he asked Hudson Taylor a question. He said, "There's one thing that is concerning me. You people in the West have had the gospel for two thousand years. How could you keep it to yourselves without telling my people? My father was a dear man and he spent his whole life looking for the truth. He studied Confucius and Buddhism, and he died as an unbeliever. How could you keep the good news to yourself for so long?"

Tell the first three people you meet today that you are not ashamed to be called a believer, a Christian, a child of God.

Firstfruits

"The first of the firstfruits of your land you shall bring into the house of the LORD your God." – Exodus 23:19a

I believe the Lord expects the "firstfruits" of the day and that our "quiet time" should be first thing in the morning so He can give direction for the day.

There have been times when I have been called to speak at a very important men's breakfast, and I have come out of my closet with a changed message. Later I would find that it was the exact word the people needed to hear. If I had gone out with my own thoughts it would have failed dismally to reach the hearts of those who needed to hear from God.

Without a quiet time, there is no power. It is in my quiet time that God gives me specific direction. It was while spending time with Him in the closet that He gave me the size, specifications, colour and type for the Seed Sower vehicle. It was there that the Lord gave me the vision of journeying from the Cape to Jerusalem with the gospel. I have found that I come out of that quiet time with God with calmness in my spirit and clarity of thought, enabling me to unashamedly speak the unadulterated Word of God.

It is vital for Christians to spend time hearing what God is saying in order to be obedient and to do the Will of Him who sent us out to finish His work.

Did you give Him the "firstfruits" this morning?

Good fruit

*"Even so, every good tree bears good fruit, but a bad tree bears bad fruit.
"A good tree cannot bear bad fruit, nor can a bad tree bear good fruit." –
Matthew 7:17,18*

One of my heroes is Dr. David Livingstone. Some have accused him of being a "glory hunter," saying that he detracted from the preaching of the gospel because he was also an explorer and a botanist. If you read his journals, however, you will find he had only one mission – to open up Africa to the gospel in order to stop slavery. He believed that by opening up Africa to commerce and industry, the terrible dealing in human flesh could be stopped.

When Stanley found Livingstone in the middle of darkest Africa, his sole objective was to meet the man and return to America to tell the world that he had found the great missionary. After he had met Livingstone, however, he remained there and lived with him for four months. The day he left he wept bitterly. He gave Livingstone most of his clothes, his food and supplies. He testified on his return to the civilised world that he never heard a negative word proceed from that man of God. Do you have a testimony like that today?

The names of towns and institutions throughout central Africa have been changed to indigenous names, with the exception of those directly connected with David Livingstone. These include the towns of Livingstone, Blantyre (named after the Scottish town where Livingstone was born), the mission station of Livingstonia and the famous Victoria Falls. I don't believe for a minute that the Victoria Falls has been left with its name unchanged because of the love that the local people have for the memory of Queen Victoria. It was because this man of God named it the Victoria Falls that it has been left intact. He did indeed produce good fruit.

Are you producing good fruit today? Let your words be few today and let your actions speak loudly. In fact, let your fruit speak for you.

One who is closer than a brother

"A man who has friends must himself be friendly, but there is a friend who sticks closer than a brother." – Proverbs 18:24

A songwriter was walking through the streets of the East End of London late one night when he saw a little street urchin carrying his brother on his back. The boy was only about ten years old himself, and his brother was the same size and obviously physically handicapped. "Is he not heavy?" asked the songwriter. The boy replied in a strong Cockney accent, "He ain't heavy, he's my brother." That inspired the song immortalising those words.

What the boy meant was, even if his brother weighed a ton, he was not too heavy because he was his brother. That's love. When someone will go the extra mile for his brother.

The Bible says there is a friend who sticks closer than a brother. I have one brother and we are very close. We are not only brothers but also best friends. We used to fight like cat and dog but woe betide anyone who tried to get between us. They soon found out what brothers are all about! We stuck together. Jesus is a friend who sticks even closer than a brother.

I'm reminded of that scripture in John 15:13, which says, "Greater love hath no man than this, that a man lay down his life for his friend." Jesus died for you and for me. He couldn't give any more than His own life. That's how much He loves you. No matter what you're going through, what ordeal, trial or tribulation you are struggling with, remember this: there is a friend who sticks closer than a brother. You need never feel alone with Jesus as your Lord and Saviour.

Respecting your children

"And you, fathers, do not provoke your children to wrath, but bring them up in the training and admonition of the Lord." – Ephesians 6:4

Do you have any children who are in business with you? If so, do you treat them as grown up and responsible or do you provoke them by endless criticism?

Many years ago I preached at a gospel campaign in Bredasdorp, the southernmost town on the continent of Africa. At the end of a week of preaching, some young farmers invited me to visit a local farm. They gave me a splendid breakfast before showing me around. Halfway through the tour, they stopped their vehicle to ask me a question. "Do you have a son?"

"Oh yes," I replied, "In fact, I have two sons." "What age is your eldest?", they asked. I replied that he was twenty-nine years old and happily married, with two children. Those men looked me right in the eye and said, "When are you going to allow him to take over the farm?" I had to swallow hard, because I'd never thought of that. I realised that my son was older than I had been when I started my first farm. He has a university degree in agriculture and is far better qualified than me. He'd been brought up on the farm and was well able to run it. I had not – my father was a blacksmith. That day I repented. I telephoned my son. "When you are ready, come home," I told him.

What about you? Perhaps today you need to sit down with your offspring and say, "It's time we spoke about promotion," and stopped your continual criticism and negative words.

Repent this morning before you go about your business, and ask God to forgive you for the negative words you have spoken over your children. Make a covenant with God that you will speak only life and positive things over your sons and daughters. You will see the change in your family.

The sovereignty of God

"Where were you when I laid the foundations of the earth? Tell Me, if you have understanding." – Job 38:4

This is a direct challenge from the Lord God Almighty to those of us who think we know everything. Human beings are so proud. For example, the farmer plants the seed and then claims to have grown a mighty crop! All he's done, however, is put the seed in the ground. The Lord brings the rain, the sun, and the heat units. He grows the crop. The surgeon performs the operation, but God does the healing. I believe that this was a turning point in Job's life, which sobered him up and turned him around.

God's ways and thoughts are far beyond the comprehension of man. That is why He has written them down in our agricultural handbook – the Bible. We need to be people of "The Book," reading and meditating on its message daily.

Don't ask questions today, my friend. Find out exactly what it is that God wants you to do, and then do it with all of your heart and you will have perfect peace.

Slow to anger

"The discretion of a man makes him slow to anger, and his glory is to overlook a transgression." – Proverbs 19:11

By nature, I have always been a man with a very short fuse. In the days before I met the Lord Jesus Christ, I was very impatient and intolerant of people who didn't do things well. I got angry quickly and could become very aggressive.

For a Christian that is not acceptable and I believe that the love of Christ, when it comes into your heart, changes it. The Lord expect us to be slow to anger and quick to overlook a transgression.

Some years ago I went into the spares department of a tractor company and asked for a spare part. They promised to order it. I impressed on them that it was extremely urgent and went back two days later to collect it. Unbeknown to me, the staff decided to test the genuineness of my Christian witness! They hid the spare part under the counter, claiming that it would arrive after the weekend. These two men, one a Christian and the other an unbeliever, had taken a side bet about how I would react. The unbeliever said I would lose my temper. The believer said I would not. I came out in a cold sweat when I was reminded of the incident the other day. How I thank the Lord Jesus Christ for His grace. Apparently I said, "Oh well, that's unfortunate. I'll come back on Monday." As I walked out of the door they called me back and presented me with the part. An incident like that can speak louder than a thousand sermons.

Today, let your temperament be a testimony to your faith. Let your patience, understanding and forgiving heart be a beacon of light to those who are lost in this world. Be slow to anger and quick to forgive, thereby glorifying the name of Jesus.

Living by faith

"But the just shall live by His faith." – Habakkuk 2:4

How are you running your affairs at this moment? Are you running them by faith, or by sight? Are you planting that crop by faith because God has told you to plant it? Or are you planting because you are watching market trends and your neighbours are planting it?

I realised over twenty–three years ago that our farm at Shalom must be run by faith. I plant the crops by faith and I sometimes do things which seem totally irrational to the economist, and especially the agronomist. Yet every single time the Lord has come through for us.

The Bible says the just shall live by faith. That is repeated in Romans 1:17 and Galatians 3:11, so the Lord has said it three times in His Word. I think He's telling us this morning that we bring joy and pleasure to His heart when we live by faith. That allows the Lord Jesus Christ to be part of our project, our plan, and our enterprise.

Go out in faith today. Walk on the water like Peter did. Do things that seem totally irrational to the world when the Lord directs you to, and it will bring glory to the name of our heavenly Father, the Miracle-worker. Put that crop in. Buy those extra cattle. Clinch that deal. Buy the farm next door. Do whatever you have to do by faith.

Get a Word from God and then do it. God will always honour His Word.

An eye for an eye

"You have heard that it was said, 'An eye for an eye and a tooth for a tooth.'" – Matthew 5:38

Just before the general elections in South Africa, when the violence was at its height, farmers were being targeted in Zululand where I live. Something like two hundred farmers had been murdered and not surprisingly, the farming community was very angry.

The Lord Jesus Christ laid upon my heart to book the massive Absa Rugby Stadium to hold a huge prayer meeting. 2 Chronicles 7:14 was our theme. "If My people who are called by My name will humble themselves, and pray and seek My face, and turn from their wicked ways, then I will hear from heaven, and will forgive their sin and heal their land."

Meetings were held all over the province in order to create interest in the event. At one meeting I'd emphasized that we had to go the extra mile. One big farmer, obviously very angry, stood up and said, "Doesn't the Bible say, 'an eye for an eye and a tooth for a tooth?'" Everybody laughed uneasily and I was completely caught unawares. I prayed to the Holy Spirit for an answer and He faithfully prompted me. "Do you have a wife and children?" I asked the farmer. "Yes," he responded aggressively. "You are a very selfish man," I told him. "Are you prepared to sacrifice your wife and your children for a little bit of revenge?" He became totally silent and I had the attention of all the farmers present. "We need to draw the line. We have to stop somewhere," I exhorted them. "The Bible says revenge is the Lord's. We have to forgive and go the extra mile."

Obey what Jesus said and do it. It takes more courage to turn the other cheek than to take revenge.

The light of His Word

"Your word is a lamp to my feet and a light to my path." – Psalm 119:105

The Lord says to you this morning, "My Word is a lamp to your feet and a light to your path." Before you go out this morning, or make any important decision, seek the face of the Lord.

I get very concerned when people telephone a "prophet", or a man of God, and ask them to pray that God will give them a word so they will know whether they should sell or buy, invest or withdraw their investment, leave the country or stay where they are. They go from pillar to post, looking for confirmation through men of God, instead of going to God himself. He says to you and to me this morning, "My Word is a lamp, my Word is a light."

I can promise you from first-hand experience that He will never forsake you nor leave you. He will not let you down. He will speak to you through His Word and give you the answer you seek.

We do not allow anyone to work with us at Shalom unless they have a clear and distinct scripture from God to say that they are to come here. The scripture might not make any sense to us, but to the person concerned it is the light and the lamp showing them the way ahead. You don't have to take a chance over your decisions today. The Lord will light up your path and He will give you clear direction.

Jesus, our best friend

"The name of the LORD is a strong tower; the righteous run to it and are safe." – Proverbs 18:10

The first change I noticed in my life when I accepted Jesus Christ as my Lord and Saviour, was that I stopped swearing. I used to have a filthy mouth. Every second word was a swear word. The day that I met the Lord Jesus Christ, He cleansed my mouth with Holy Ghost soap.

I know a dear brother in Christ who is a very outspoken man. Whenever anyone uses the Lord's Name in vain, he has no hesitation in saying firmly, "I just heard you speak about my Friend. Please don't talk about Him in that way." The scripture this morning tells us that the name of the Lord is a strong tower. It's a Name that you can call upon at any time. The righteous run to it and are saved.

When I am in a tight spot, I always call on His Name. There are times when I'm busy assisting a cow to calve and we have to use all possible means to get the calf out in order to save the mother. Sometimes it takes a lot of manipulation and hard work. Before we even start, we call on the name of the Lord, our strong tower. Even when I am working with men who are not Christians, I insist they bow their heads and close their eyes as I call upon the Name of the Lord. As soon as the calf is born, we are quick to thank the Lord Jesus Christ for His provision and His help.

In everything you do today, call on the Name of the Lord Jesus Christ and you will find that His name is a strong tower.

Belonging to Christ

"Examine yourselves as to whether you are in the faith. Test yourselves. Do you not know yourselves, that Jesus Christ is in you – unless indeed you are disqualified?" – 2 Corinthians 13:5

My friend, there is no time left to doubt whether or not you are in the faith. The Christian faith is very simple and exceedingly powerful. We are living in perilous times and we need to be sure we belong to the Lord Jesus Christ. It is very simple. Romans 10:9 says "that if you confess with your mouth the Lord Jesus and believe in your heart that God has raised Him from the dead, you will be saved." There is nothing you can do to make the Lord Jesus Christ love you any more than He does, and there is nothing you can do to make Him love you any less. All you have to do is believe, and then to go out by faith and live the life He has called you to. "Faith comes by hearing, and hearing by the word of God." (Romans 10:17).

We have all heard the saying that "he who hesitates is lost." This is definitely not the time to hesitate. The devil is going round like a roaring lion, seeking whom he may devour, and we need to know who we are in Christ. It is so wonderful to sit under the ministry of men and women who make no apologies for preaching the unadulterated Word of God, secure in the knowledge that they belong to the Lord Jesus Christ.

Do not allow yourself to be disqualified this morning by doubting whether you are in the faith. Go out today, "being confident of this very thing, that He who has begun a good work in you will complete it until the day of Jesus Christ." (Philippians 1:6).

A "gratitude attitude"

"A merry heart does good, like medicine, but a broken spirit dries the bones." – Proverbs 17:22

No matter what your burden is today, rejoice in the fact that your name is written in the Lamb's "Book of Life." You have an incredible future ahead of you, if you know Jesus Christ as your Lord and Saviour. A merry heart does good like medicine so develop a "gratitude attitude." Thank the Lord for this day and for the beauty that is all around you. It is His gift.

As countrymen, we have a great advantage over those in the city. We can walk out of the front door and hear the birds singing. What a privilege. Today, whether it is raining or the sun is shining, thank God and rejoice because the Bible says "A merry heart does good like medicine."

We've all heard the joke about the farmer who looked up and saw clouds in the sky. "Here come the floods," he said. A moment later the sun began to peak through the clouds and he remarked, "And here comes the drought!" Indeed, a man like that reminds me of the second part of the scripture, which says "a broken spirit dries the bones." No one wants to be around a negative person. You can see them coming a mile away! Many of us need to repent of that kind of attitude. We are often so negative, always complaining about our lot in life, instead of thanking God for His goodness.

Thank God that you are alive! Thank the Lord for all the things that He's given you – your family, loved ones, and your health. Thank Him most of all for saving your life and bringing you into fellowship with Him. Go about your business today with a merry heart.

Profit or loss?

"For what will it profit a man if he gains the whole world, and loses his own soul?" – Mark 8:36

Where is your heart and where are your thoughts this morning? Even if you are the richest farmer in your whole district, or the most effective businessman or businesswoman in your area, that is not going to save your soul. If we gain the whole world, and lose our soul, how will money help us? How much time are you spending waiting on God compared to building up your business?

The story is told of an old Scottish preacher who went to visit a man who owned a water-wheel. It used it to drive a grindstone in order to grind corn. This man's sole interest was in making money. The preacher took note that the old man was very sick and elderly, and on the threshold of meeting his Maker. The man had organised his bed right next to the grindstone so he could hear the grindstone working, grinding up the corn and bringing in the money. When the preacher tried to talk to him about his soul, he said, "I can't hear you! The grindstone is making too much noise. Come back another day." Eventually the man died and went to hell, because he had made no provision whatsoever for eternal things. He left the grindstone and water-wheel behind, just like you and I will leave our farms and businesses behind, on the day of reckoning.

The Lord is asking us a question today: what will it profit us if we gain the whole world, and become the most efficient farmers in the whole world, and yet lose our souls?

Humility

"Pride goes before destruction, and a haughty spirit before a fall."
– Proverbs 16:18

A godly man once said to me that when you are on your knees you cannot fall any further. The more God uses you, the more humble you must be. The danger is not when things are going badly. It is seldom that a man of God falls when he is under pressure – it is usually when he succeeds, when things were going well and he is prospering.

I remember being invited to meet the king of the Zulus. I had attended a banquet at one of his palaces and later we walked out into the garden. As we were looking at his cattle, I heard him instructing his Induna (Head Man) to slaughter one of his oxen in order that he might give it to me as a gift. It was only later that I realised what a great privilege and honour it was to receive a gift from the king.

One of the stately ladies in the party walked up to me and said, "Mr Buchan, I believe you are a farmer." "Yes," I replied, "I am." "I would like you to explain to me how to start a nursery," she said. "I want to grow seedlings." While we were talking, I asked her who she was. Very humbly she replied, "I am the Queen." I was so embarrassed but she never batted an eyelid and continued talking in a very sweet and gentle way. She was a believer and loved the Lord with all her heart. I will never forget that experience as long as I live.

Humility is the opposite of pride and when we walk in humility God exalts us.

The sufficiency of His grace

"And He said to me, 'My grace is sufficient for you, for My strength is made perfect in weakness ... For when I am weak, then I am strong.'"
– 2 Corinthians 12:9,10

This scripture is one of my favourite Bible verses. It is an unfailing source of encouragement, because it is not about me – it is about Jesus in me.

It reminds me of the famous hymn "Amazing Grace." It is a wonderful hymn. I've heard it played on the bagpipes, which especially appeals to my Scottish heritage. I've heard it sung in pop concerts, and performed by classical orchestras. It has been on the radio and television and is rated as one of the greatest and most popular hymns of all time. Did you know that a man who was in a terrible predicament wrote it? He was the captain of a slave ship. I don't think there can be a more hellish type of employment on earth. When he met the man from Galilee – the Lord Jesus Christ – and experienced his sins washed away, he wrote about the amazing grace of God that saved a wretch like him. A weak man became strong in the Lord.

Today I believe the Lord wants you to take your burden, your reputation and responsibilities and cast them upon Him, because He cares for you (I Peter 5:7). Walk in His strength and His grace and you will experience true freedom. You will soar like an eagle and be free to accomplish things that you never thought possible "through Christ who strengthens you" (Philippians. 4:13).

Today, rejoice in your weaknesses and shortcomings because – as you give them to the Lord – He will turn them into strengths and victories. At the end of the day, remember one thing – it's all about Jesus. To Him belong the praise, honour and glory for your success. If you can grasp that truth, then nothing will hold you back from accomplishing great things and great exploits for Him.

The enemy within

"I have been crucified with Christ; it is no longer I who live, but Christ lives in me; and the life which I now live in the flesh I live by faith in the Son of God, who loved me and gave Himself for me." – Galatians 2:20

My biggest enemy is not the devil. It is self, or the flesh. Paul, the greatest apostle who ever lived, in my opinion, recognised he was his own greatest enemy. That's why he said, "I have been crucified with Christ. It is no longer I who live but Christ who lives in me." If we can put the flesh down – if Angus Buchan can die – then the Lord Jesus Christ has full liberty to work and do something constructive through him. Every time I rear my ugly head, everything comes to nought and I have to start all over again.

At the start of this day, ask the Holy Spirit to enable you to put down the flesh so that the Lord Jesus Christ may have full reign in your life. Do whatever He tells you to do with gusto and enthusiasm, knowing that it is not really important what people think of you or of me. It is not even important whether we succeed or not. What is important is that we have been obedient to the Lord. When we have an attitude like that, then we will succeed, far beyond our wildest dreams, because it will be Christ in us who will accomplish it.

Remember, the symbol of the cross is the symbol of death. It speaks of death to self, so that Christ can live in us.

Tribulation

"And not only that, but we also glory in tribulations, knowing that tribulation produces perseverance; and perseverance, character; and character, hope." – Romans 5:3,4

You may be wondering why you seem to have more tribulations than you had before you became a Christian. You have given your life to Christ, you have cast all your cares upon the Lord, believing that your life would be changed for the better – and it has – but there still seems to be trouble all around.

My dear friend, be encouraged. Trouble builds character. All the great men of God in the Bible went through tribulation. And so have all the great men of God since. William Carey went to India as a missionary and lost his wife and children there. She was mentally ill and he nursed her for fifteen years before she died. And yet God raised that man up to incredible heights and his legacy lives on today.

David Livingstone buried his wife underneath a Baobab tree on the banks of the mighty Zambezi River in Mozambique. Hudson Taylor buried his wife, Maria, in China. She worked herself to a standstill for the gospel of Jesus Christ. Yet these men never thought about turning back. They lost everything they had – everything that was dear to them – for the sake of the gospel of Jesus Christ. That did not mean in any way that they failed. In fact, they grew enormously in stature and character.

I want to encourage you today to take heart whatever problems you are facing. Christ said that He will never leave us nor forsake us (Hebrews 13:5). Go out knowing that God goes with you and you have nothing to fear. The tribulation is just like a storm. It will soon pass, the sun will come out again and there will be a glorious new day. The good news is that you will be twice the man or woman you were before the storm.

Going the extra mile

"And whoever compels you to go one mile, go with him two." – Matthew 5:41

I have just had the privilege of having a Christian farmer come to Shalom to teach us how to grow maize, using the "no tillage pattern." This method is designed particularly for peasant and rural farmers who are unable to use tractor power.

This man says he preaches the upside-down gospel. He preaches turning the other cheek, going the extra mile, loving those who hate you, and praying for those who persecute you. He has lost four farms in Zimbabwe and when we flew him down to us he was in the process of being stripped of his last farm. His wife had been held hostage in the farm office and threatened with death and all they are doing is teaching the peasant farmers how to grow food.

These people are driven by the love of God. There's nothing else in this world that could give a man and his wife the grace and love to pray for those who are persecuting them. They have gone the extra mile, even teaching the invaders how to use their farm equipment. This man humbled me tremendously and I realised afresh that it is only by the grace of God that we can do these things.

As Christians, we have to be different. We have to be the fragrance of Christ in these last days. We have to be the light on a hill. No matter what anyone may say to you today, treat them with the love of Christ. Let me remind you that we are sojourners and travellers in a foreign land and this is not our home. Our home is in heaven.

Peacemakers

"Blessed are the peacemakers, for they shall be called sons of God." –
Matthew 5:9

Let us be known as peacemakers. The Lord does not say, "Blessed are the peace lovers." He says, "Blessed are the peacemakers." There is a clear distinction, and sometimes we have to be controversial in order to make peace. A peacemaker is someone who has a heart after God. Jesus is known as the Prince of Peace (Shalom), yet He went into the temple with a whip and chased out those who were using it as a money-changing house instead of a house of prayer. Jesus always spoke the truth and He was known as a peacemaker. If we are to be known as peacemakers, we also need to speak out the truth. If things are wrong they need to be addressed in truth and love.

At Shalom we start every day with prayer, scripture reading and singing. Some people don't like that, and we have people on our farm from time to time who are not Christians. Our farm is a Christian farm and, because we want to be peacemakers, we are determined to make a stand for Christ and we will not compromise that for anybody or anything. Our Lord and our Saviour, Jesus Christ, is the Prince of Peace indeed but sometimes when we preach about Him, all hell breaks loose because the devil hates that Name.

Our farm is called Shalom. It is a place of peace and many people visit us from all over the world. They come for different reasons – to be healed by God, to be set free, encouraged, or just to rest, but they all say the same thing, "We sense peace here. We feel the presence of God in this place." I can assure you that it is not because we are peace lovers, but because we are standing on the principles of the Word of God.

Bearing fruit

"Therefore bear fruits worthy of repentance," – Matthew 3:8

The Lord is asking you and me this morning to bear fruits worthy of repentance, and He goes on to say that "every tree that does not bear good fruit is cut down and put in the fire" (v10). I've seen many people who have started off serving the Lord but they are no longer bearing fruits worthy of repentance. They have fallen by the wayside and are no longer following Jesus.

What fruits are we talking about this morning? These are fruits that identify us as believers. They are the fruits of a change of heart, the fruit of peace rather than anger, the fruit of love rather than hatred, the fruit of a servant's heart, the fruit of going the extra mile, the fruits of joy, peace, patience, long-suffering and loving-kindness, the "fruit of the spirit" (Galations 5:22 – 23). Are you bearing these fruit, my friend?

People should see that we are believers, not just hear it. They should see the fruit that we are bearing which comes from within. Be different today. You cannot continue living as you lived before you came to know Christ and call yourself a Christian. You need to bear fruits worthy of repentance. If this is not true of your life, then repent today. Ask God to forgive you and start again. Watch and see the difference God will make in your life.

A double portion

"And so it was, when they had crossed over, that Elijah said to Elisha, 'Ask! What may I do for you, before I am taken away from you?' Elisha said, 'Please let a double portion of your spirit be upon me.'" – 2 Kings 2:9

Elisha, the young prophet and understudy of Elijah, was not only determined to have an impartation of the power and anointing of God that rested on Elijah's life, but also asked for a double portion. Are you prepared to ask God for a double portion?

It always saddens me to hear servants of God saying, "Oh well, I don't mind, whatever God wants to give me, I'll take." God wants us to be bold and ask Him for a double portion of His anointing and power so that we may be even more effective in the work or ministry God has called us to. I believe God is looking for men and women who want to receive a double portion of the anointing of His Spirit.

When we began preparing to plant our maize crop this year, we heard negative reports coming from near and far about another El Nino. We had to make a choice either to trust God for a double portion of His blessing, or to play it safe by cutting our fertilizer rates back to half and opening up our seed spacing. We decided that we would be like Elisha and ask for a double portion of God's Spirit to be upon us, the farm and this particular crop. So we doubled up with fertilizer and seed, holding back on nothing. As I am writing this, we are looking at the result – a bumper crop of over eight tons of maize per hectare. Is that a coincidence? No! You see, Elisha would neither take no for an answer, nor give up. He persevered and persisted until God gave him not only the mantle of Elijah, but a double portion of Elijah's anointing.

God bless you today as you become expectant for a double portion from the Lord Jesus Christ.

Friendship with God

"And the Scripture was fulfilled which says, 'Abraham believed God, and it was accounted to him for righteousness.' And he was called the friend of God." – James 2:23

The Bible says that God considered Abraham His friend. How did that come about? Quite simply, because Abraham was a man who took the Word of God at face value and believed it. What about you? Would you like to be known as the friend of God? Do you believe what the Word of God says about you? Do you believe the promises of God, regardless of what you see with your eyes or feel in your body? The Lord Jesus Christ has told us in His Holy Word that "without faith it is impossible to please Him, for he who comes to God must believe that He is, and that He is a rewarder of those who diligently seek Him" (Hebrews 11:6) The Lord wants you to walk on the water. He wants you to go out one more time. My dear friend, Abraham was prepared to sacrifice his only son that he had waited for patiently for one hundred years. As a result, God honoured him.

Do not be like the proverbial farmer who is always making a plan. Make a choice to believe God's plan for your life. "Have faith in God" (Mark 11:22) and let everything you do and say today be done by faith, in the Name of Jesus Christ of Nazareth.

Freedom

"Therefore submit to God. Resist the devil and he will flee from you." –
James 4:7

From the time I gave my life to Jesus I have had no fear of the devil, nor anyone nor anything else. The only person I fear is God Himself. I fear Him with a holy reverence.

The Lord has given us clear instruction in His Word to resist the devil. Do that and he will flee from you. We are not to give the devil any foothold in our lives. We are not to allow ourselves to be contaminated by the world or its system. I know of men who have paid large quantities of money for a witch doctor to throw his bones and stolen cattle have subsequently been recovered. That does not impress me in the slightest. I firmly believe the man who does that opens his door to the power of darkness.

When the Lord Jesus Christ was tempted in the desert, His response was, "It is written." He used the Word of God and the devil had to leave Him alone. You and I need to do exactly the same thing. Superstitions are not of God. Resist the devil and he will flee from you.

I have been wonderfully free from the day I gave my life to the Lord. He convicted me of all the things that opened the door for the evil one and I had a glorious bonfire, and burnt anything, (ie tapes, CD's, pictures, ornaments) that would be displeasing to God, and also cause me to stumble. Maybe you need to do that as well. From that day onwards I felt as though chains had been cut off me with large, heavy-duty bolt cutters. I feel as free as my favourite bird – the African fish eagle – free to soar into the heavenlies.

Is there anything at all in your life that is holding you back?

Giving your burdens to Jesus

"Casting all your care upon Him, for He cares for you." – I Peter 5:7

Whenever our large "Seed Sower" gospel truck goes into Central Africa, I always think about the little chorus which goes, "Higher, higher, lift Jesus higher" and then goes on to say, "Cast your burdens onto Jesus, for He cares for you".

I'll never forget the road that travels from Central Africa right up to where the Great Lakes meet. It is an absolute paradise and a place where farmers could do so much. These lakes look like inland oceans of fresh water. Lake Tanganyika is one of the deepest in the world. We saw multitudes of African people walking on the road and as the big, yellow, twenty-ton Seed Sower passed through on our way home, the young children and the women broke into singing, "Higher, higher, lift Jesus higher. Cast your burdens onto Jesus, for He cares for you." It brought a lump to my throat.

I believe the Lord wants us today to cast our burdens and our cares upon Him, because He cares for us. Whatever is facing you, remember if God goes before you, you have nothing to fear. Cast your cares upon Him and then by faith tackle the workload, knowing that if He goes before you, you are totally indestructible. Spend a few moments in prayer after this reading, name your burdens, give them to Jesus and then go out and face a beautiful carefree day.

Doubt

"The effective, fervent prayer of a righteous man avails much." – James 5:16b

The story is told about an old lady who opened up her curtains early one morning. She had just read the scripture that says if you have the faith the size of a mustard seed, you can tell a mountain to be removed. There was a big mountain outside her window and she said, "Mountain be removed and deposited into the sea." The next morning she got up, opened the curtains, and looked out of the window. The mountain was still there. "Well," she said, "I didn't think it would move anyway."

Do you believe God is going to answer the prayer that you are praying? If the answer is that you're doubting, or you're not sure, your prayer will not be answered. The secret of faith is to find out what God's will is, pray in accordance with His will, and then believe the Lord for the answer. The Lord promises such prayer will avail much.

Start to pray for something that you believe God wants to do and will do for you. Increase your faith. Pray for a good day today for all your loved ones. Pray that there will be no accidents on your farm, that your family will be protected wherever they go, that the wayward child will return home. Then do everything in your power to make it happen. When we do the possible, God delights to do the impossible. Believe and thank Him for what is going to happen.

God's way

"But if not, let it be known to you, O king, that we do not serve your gods, nor will we worship the gold image which you have set up." – Daniel 3:18

This was the response of Shadrach, Meshach, and Abednego to King Nebuchadnezzar in the time of Daniel many years ago.

These three men of God were threatened and told that they would be put in a fiery furnace unless they bowed their knees and served Nebuchadnezzar's god. Are you bowing the knee and doing something that is not strictly of God in order to stay in the race, to keep going, to have a successful operation? If so, you are in severe trouble. The Lord says, "Repent and return to Me and I will see you through."

You may be in a fiery trial at the moment. That is exactly what these three men of God went through, but they were determined to honour God regardless of personal cost. The Bible says that not even one hair on their heads was singed, nor did their clothes even smell of smoke.

The most beautiful part of this whole story is that, when Nebuchadnezzar looked into the fiery furnace, he saw the three men walking about unscathed, but what really opened his eyes was to see the figure of a fourth man "like unto the Son of God."

The Lord has not promised that He would take us out of the fire when we give our hearts to Him but He will walk through the fire with us and we will not be burned.

Today, do it God's way and expect God to honour His Word.

Going with the flow

"Therefore, brethren, stand fast and hold the traditions which you were taught, whether by word or our epistle." – 2 Thessalonians 2:15

We are living in an age when lawlessness is rampant. A few months ago I travelled to Zimbabwe and saw first-hand what happens when lawlessness prevails. The devil is at work everywhere. In these last days we are to stand firm, as the scripture says, holding fast to our traditions (which is the Word of God) and not capitulating in any way for anyone. Gypsy Smith, the great old evangelist, said that it takes a dead fish to flow with the current, but it takes a live one to swim against it.

The Bible says very clearly in Daniel 11:32 that those who know their God shall be strong and carry out great exploits. Let us continue with our traditions (the Word of God), doing exactly what the Lord says – nothing less and nothing more – and we shall prevail and be overcomers because God is with us.

Let us not be like Esau, who traded his inheritance for a bowl of lentil soup. We must never compromise the Word of God, nor the standards of the Lord Jesus Christ, in order to gain what may appear to be an advantage. Rather let us be godly men and women in all that we do, knowing that at the end of the day, the law of God will prevail.

In other words, Christians do not accept bribery, Christians are not intimidated and Christians will not compromise.

APRIL

Dwelling in the shadow of the Most High

"He who dwells in the secret place of the Most High shall abide under the shadow of the Almighty." – Psalm 91:1

Are you dwelling in the secret place of the most High? Perhaps you are feeling severely pressurised financially, physically, or spiritually. If you felt that it was hard to get up this morning to face a new day, I want to ask you a question: are you abiding under the shadow of the Almighty?

I'd like you to picture a massive rock in your mind. In Zimbabwe, Africa, one sees the most incredible rock formations. Massive boulders balance on top of one other. It is a very hot place in the dry season, just before the rains, but if you take shelter underneath the shade of one those rocks, it is wonderfully cool and refreshing. The rocks are so large, they never heat up or grow cold and the temperature remains comfortable.

I believe the Holy Spirit wants us to abide under the shadow of Almighty God. Come out of the heat before you do anything else today. Come aside and He will give you rest and refresh you. He will give you strength to see this day through.

Make it a habit first thing every day – before the cares, heat and pressure of the day get to you – to spend time under the shadow of the Almighty in the cleft of the Rock. Your day will go far more smoothly. No problem will be too big for you because you will have your eyes fixed on Jesus, the Author and the Finisher of your faith.

Receiving from the Lord

"If you ask anything in My name, I will do it. If you love Me, keep My commandments." – John 14:14,15

This is a very encouraging and powerful scripture. When the Lord says "anything," He means anything. But notice what He says next: "If you love Me, keep My commandments." These two scriptures are closely linked.

I believe the Lord is saying that if we walk in righteousness and in holiness, and ask Him anything in faith that will bring glory to His heavenly Father, He will give it to us. What is your prayer request today? Are you asking the Lord to heal your child? Are you asking Him to help you get out of the jaws of debt? Are you praying that God would bring abundant rain on your farm or give you a good market for your crop? The Lord says that He will do it in order that the name of His Father may be glorified. All He requires from you and me is that we walk in righteousness, obedience and faith.

Let us get down on our knees and ask forgiveness for any area in our lives that is holding us back from the blessing of God. Let us repent (in other words, stop doing it) and start again. Ask in faith, believing God for a mighty answer.

Flourishing in the House of God

"Those who are planted in the house of the LORD shall flourish in the courts of our God." – Psalm 92:13

Every farmer knows that if he plants good seed on stony ground it will germinate but, as soon as the heat of the day rises, the seed will frizzle up and blow away. He also knows if he plants his seed amongst thorns and weeds it will germinate but it will be strangled. If he plants his seed in good land, however, it will produce a mighty crop.

Psalm 92:13 says that if we are planted in the house of the Lord, we shall flourish. Is that where you are planted today? The psalmist is talking about being focused on the Lord Jesus Christ. He is talking about putting Christ first, and giving Him precedence over everything in your life.

How do we do that? The only way is through prayer and reading the Word (the Bible). It is also helpful to read good Christian literature. As we spend time with the Lord – waiting upon him – He promises that we shall flourish in the courts of our God. We shall be like a sweet fragrance wherever we go, because we will be concentrating on the things of God. The more time we spend with God, the more the likeness of Christ will be seen in us.

I love taking my mountain bicycle and going for a short ride early in the morning. As I go, I praise God for His goodness, His beauty, and the glory of His creation. I make it a habit to spend time with God first because I know that I shall flourish in the house of the Lord.

Our home is in heaven

"In My Father's house are many mansions; if it were not so, I would have told you. I go to prepare a place for you." – John 14:2

If you are a believer and truly love the Lord Jesus Christ, remember one thing – no matter how beautiful your farm or your house might be, this is not your home. You are a sojourner in a foreign land. You are only here for a very short season of seventy years and, if God gives you added grace, perhaps another ten or twenty. The Lord Jesus Christ has promised us that He has gone ahead to prepare a home for us in paradise.

I love the story about the missionary coming home after he had been on the mission field for forty years. Travelling on the same ship was a very successful football team that had just come back from a victorious tour. As they came into the harbour, the sound of a brass band playing music filled the air. Hundreds of people crowded the wharf, throwing streamers into the air, clapping and welcoming their football team home. The missionary stood to one side, all by himself. Not a single soul had come to welcome him after forty years' service in the mission field and he cried out to God. "Lord," he prayed, "why is it that these men who have just played a mere series of football matches are welcomed home as national heroes and yet I, who have given forty years of my life to the mission field, do not have a soul to welcome me?" "But son, you are not home yet!" said the Lord.

Our home is in heaven and what a welcome will await us on the day we get there. Serve the Lord with all your heart, mind and soul and remember to hold lightly the things of this world. We are not home yet.

Bearing fruit

"They shall still bear fruit in old age; They shall be fresh and flourishing," –
Psalm 92:14

If you spend time with God it will begin to show, especially as you grow older. We have a dear, dear lady at Shalom. Her name is Peggy O'Neill. She is close on 80 years of age and she is flourishing. When she was 70 years old, I was invited to her birthday party. She stood up and addressed her whole family, telling them that she was going to serve the Lord Jesus Christ full-time, as a volunteer worker at Shalom Ministries.

Peggy has been with us all these years and she is still flourishing and bearing much fruit. All her friends who went into old age homes have since passed on. I believe the reason in many instances was because they felt of no use to anyone, and so they just quietly died. But this dear sister in Christ is fresh, she is blooming. There are many people who receive strength and encouragement from her.

What about you today? Are you still bearing fruit? Maybe you're saying, "I'm not even forty years old and I'm not bearing any fruit." My dear friend, get back to the vine, the Lord Jesus Christ. Focus first on Him and His goodness and you will begin to bear fruit and flourish. You will heal physically, mentally and spiritually and you will bear good fruit even in your old age.

Loving one another

"By this all will know that you are My disciples, if you have love for one another." – John 13:35

How will people know today that we are the disciples of Jesus Christ? Quite simply, as this scripture says, we shall be known to be His disciples by the love that we demonstrate towards one another. This, by the way, my dear friend, is a commandment. It is not an option for us to love one another but a command from God.

No matter what is happening in our life, we have to love one another. If the tractor driver has broken the tractor, or the cattleman has allowed the cattle to get out of the paddock and into that beautiful crop of cabbages, or your young son has just dented the back of your prized Land Rover, the Bible says we are to have an attitude of love one to another. Rebuke the person concerned gently, of course. If they have to pay for the damage, fine, but keep a good attitude. Love one another.

If you're not sure what love is, read 1 Corinthians chapter 13. Remember: love does not behave rudely, it does not think evil, it does not seek its own, it does not rejoice in iniquity, it does not envy, it does not parade itself and it is not arrogant.

Have a wonderful day as you walk in love and watch how many new friends you'll make today.

Jesus never fails

"To declare that the LORD is upright; He is my rock, and there is no unrighteousness in Him." – Psalm 92:15

What you say is what you get. As farmers, we are so often guilty of complaining about the weather, our crops, our animals, and our land that we forget about the good things.

In fact, some of the biggest complainers I've ever come across are sheep shearers. You can hear them complaining from the moment they arrive on your farm to shear your sheep. Either the wool is too dry or too wet, or there are too many burrs. There's always something wrong.

Whenever I go to the local farmers' cooperative to get supplies for the farm, farmers often come to me and say, "It's getting a bit dry. You've got a 'hot line' to heaven. Why don't you ask the Lord to send the rain?" I always tell them that the rain will come – and plenty of it – because my God will supply all of my needs, "according to His riches in glory." (Philippians 4:19).

Are you someone who is always complaining? The Lord says this morning, "Declare that I am upright".

I have found that the more I talk about Jesus, the more strength I receive and the more positive I become which, in turn, makes my work more successful. The more I declare the uprightness and the righteousness of my God, the more He seems to bless me. I brag that in my Lord there is no unrighteousness, that He is my rock. There are many people looking for a hero in the world today – someone they can look up to – and Jesus is their answer.

People, organisations and good ideas may fail but Jesus never fails. He has never been accused of abusing a child, stealing, intimidation, or immorality. He is righteousness itself. I declare that He is upright and He is my rock.

Continuous revival

"Therefore... work out your own salvation with fear and trembling;" –
Philippians 2:12

To serve the Lord Jesus Christ is not just a "one off" emotional event. We must be "born again," as the Bible clearly says in John 3:7, but thereafter we have to walk in obedience to our Lord and Saviour. Jesus said, "But why do you call me Lord, Lord, and do not do the things which I say?" (Luke 6:46).

John Wesley, a mighty man of God, turned the British Isles upside down for Christ when he had an experience with the Lord at a little Bible study in Aldersgate, London. When he was in his late 80s, someone asked him what the biggest obstacle was in his walk of faith. He responded, "The lust of the flesh." This godly man continued throughout his life to wrestle with areas that were still troubling him, as we all do. He was working out his salvation with fear and trembling.

What about us? I always feel sad when I hear Christians talking about a revival that took place twenty or thirty years ago, or about some supernatural happening in the mid 1950s. Our faith must be relevant to our generation.

When I was a young man and about to preach my first sermon, the elders of my little church laid their hands on me and began to pray. One of them, a man in his 60s, said to me, "Well, son, get in there and preach the gospel. I've done my bit." I couldn't understand what he meant and I still don't. We never stop walking by faith, living by faith, sharing the gospel by faith and being open and ready for testing in our lives.

Work out that which God has worked in you – through prayer, supplication and repentance – and then press on to take the world for Jesus.

Sons of God

"For the earnest expectation of the creation eagerly waits for the revealing of the sons of God." – Romans 8:19

Today, if Jesus Christ is your Lord and Saviour, then this is a very special verse for you. The Lord says that all of creation is waiting (on tiptoes) to see what the sons of God are going to do.

Many times, in over thirty years of farming, the Holy Spirit has laid it on my heart to call a prayer meeting during a drought cycle. I usually telephone the mayor of the town, book the town hall and then contact the president of the Farmers' Association, the local farmers and every minister of the gospel in the area.

Many of those farmers are not Christians, but they attend because they have a desperate need and they come with all their workers. We come before Almighty God in repentance and ask Him to forgive us. Then we start to pray and ask God for rain. You can always hear whether a man knows God – or only knows about God – by the way he prays. When men of God start to pray, God always hears their prayers, and many times – in fact just about every single time we have prayed together like this – the black clouds start to gather and the Lord Jesus Christ sends rain in abundance. Sadly, few people return to give thanks later.

Do you know God this morning? If not, you need to get on your knees and repent today and say, "Lord, I want you to be my Saviour." Men of the world may blaspheme and ridicule you because you are a believer, but when push comes to shove, they know you have the answer!

A harvest of joy

"Those who sow in tears shall reap in joy." – Psalm 126:5

How often the farmer weeps and sweats as he ploughs, coming home at night with blistered hands. It seems as if he has seen nothing for his day's work. But when reaping time comes and the crop is standing high and golden – ready for harvesting – the farmer still comes home at night with blisters on his hands, tired and weary, with chaff in his hair, but he is happy because he has reaped a rich harvest. Indeed it's a true saying that those who sow in tears shall reap in joy.

That great man of God – one of my heroes and mentors – Dr David Livingstone, wrote in his memoirs, "I am sowing in tears, but there will be those who will come after me who will reap a mighty crop."

I thank God for a man like David Livingstone, who sowed in tears so we could come behind him and reap in joy. Not many people came to Christ through his preaching, but he forged a road into the heart of Central Africa and made it possible for others to take the gospel there. I have personally spent many months preaching the gospel of Jesus Christ in Central Africa as a result of his labours, and I especially honour him for that. We must never forget those who have gone before.

Keep sowing. Keep ploughing. Keep preparing the land. Keep on preaching the gospel! "Keep holding the fort," as William Booth loved to say, because you will reap a bountiful crop if you do not grow weary and give up. Your children will turn to Christ if you stand fast. Your farm will turn round. Your business will not go bankrupt. Keep on sowing in tears and you will eventually reap in joy.

No condemnation

"There is therefore now no condemnation to those who are in Christ Jesus, who do not walk according to the flesh, but according to the Spirit." – Romans 8:1

What a beautiful and invigorating scripture to start off the new day. When God forgives, He forgets and "there is now no condemnation" as far as He is concerned.

People often forgive only to forget as long as it suits them and they can be very quick to remind you of your transgression. Or they say, "I forgive you, but I'll never forget." That's not forgiveness. When Jesus forgives, He forgets. When we go back to the Lord a week later and say, "Lord, you remember when…" the Lord says, "I don't remember a thing". When God forgives, He forgets. Praise His name.

There is no more condemnation. It doesn't matter what happened yesterday or last week. If you lost your temper and behaved badly, the Lord says, "Apologise, ask forgiveness and press on." There is no condemnation for those who walk in the Spirit. If you have been sinned against, forgive and forget. For the born-again Christian, "an eye for an eye and a tooth for a tooth" does not apply.

"But, Angus," you may say, "You don't know the terrible things I've done!" My dear friend, think of a heap of accounts on your desk and see the Lord Jesus Christ taking a pen and signing each one in red, "Paid in full." His blood avails for sinners like you and me.

One of the most humbling things I've had to do, was to stand before my entire staff and apologise for my bad behaviour and ask their forgiveness. I did it reluctantly but it changed the mood and the atmosphere on our farm and my people worked harder and more happily than ever before. They also seemed to treat me with ten times more respect. There is no condemnation for those who are in Christ Jesus and who walk according to the Spirit of God.

The God who answers prayer

"In my distress I cried to the LORD, and He heard me." – Psalm 120:1

Are you in distress this morning? Have you cried to the Lord? "No," you say, "I am a farmer, I'll make a plan." Shame on you. Repent immediately and cry out to the Lord as the psalmist did. He said, "In my distress I cried to the Lord and He heard me." He will hear you too.

You may say, "Well, God doesn't understand farming or business in the 21st century." Oh yes, He does. He is time. He is the same yesterday, today and forever according to Hebrews 13:8. The reason He has not heard you is because you have not cried out to Him. He says to you today, "Cry out to Me and I will hear you. I have heard your prayers. I will undertake for you, because I am God."

I come from a small family and I have only one brother and one sister. My dear brother, Fergus, while working as a golf professional in Bavaria, contracted the dreaded disease, cancer. In his distress he cried out to the Lord and the Lord healed him. There is no cancer left in his body.

Cry out to the Lord this morning. Whatever your problem – whatever your need – cry out and say, "Lord, I don't know what to do. I don't know which way to turn." The Lord will hear you and He will deliver you. Then, by faith, go forward today, work hard and do whatever your hand finds to do. The Lord Jesus Christ will do the rest.

When things don't make sense

"For as many as are led by the Spirit of God, these are sons of God." –
Romans 8:14

When the Holy Spirit is leading you, things do not always make sense because in God's economy two plus two sometimes equals seven. When Jesus told Peter to get out of the boat and walk on water that did not make sense. When Jesus told the disciples to feed the five thousand with two sardines and five barley loaves, it did not make sense either.

In these last days, we need to walk in the Spirit as never before. When the Lord instructs you to do something that does not sound practical or reasonable, but is confirmed from the Word, just do it. Servants came to Jesus' mother at the wedding in Cana and she said, "Do what He tells you to do." They filled up those vats with water at His command and Jesus turned the water into wine.

When the Lord Jesus Christ told me to leave a seventh of my farm fallow every year, it didn't make sense to the agronomist. But I do it, because God told me to and I'm reaping greater crops now than ever before. God told me not to use a diviner to find water on my farm, so I used a geologist and trusted God to show us where to put the peg. I have abundant water in both my boreholes, one producing 60,000 litres an hour and the other 8 000 litres an hour and we are irrigating from borehole water that we found through trusting God. "For as many as are led by the Spirit of God, these are the sons of God."

When the Lord tells you to give a tenth of your "firstfruits" to the storehouse, the place where you receive your spiritual food – namely the church or fellowship that you belong to – do not argue. Do it, so that He can bless you.

Be still and know that I am God

"Be still, and know that I am God; I will be exalted among the nations, I will be exalted in the earth!" – Psalm 46:10

I think in this present day and age the hardest thing for men and women is to be still. There just doesn't seem to be enough time.

The Lord, however, says to you and me this morning, "Be still, and know that I am God." When you start to see God in perspective, your problem literally disintegrates before your very eyes. He says, "Know that I am God." How can we know who He is if we are not prepared to sit down and quietly contemplate the greatness of our God?

Job was a great man of God but he needed to be still before the Lord. The Book of Job records God's challenge to him. "Where were you when I laid the foundations of the earth? Where were you when the morning stars sang together? Who shut in the sea with doors when it burst forth and issued from the womb? Have you commanded the morning since your days began? Have the gates of death been revealed to you? Can you comprehend the breadth of the earth? Tell me if you know all these things."

When you realise who God is, then nothing can make you afraid. Fear will be replaced by faith and joy in God and you will experience the truth of Romans 8:31. "If God be for us, then who can stand against us."

Spend time this morning being still and contemplating just who your God is.

Spiritually minded

"For to be carnally minded is death, but to be spiritually minded is life and peace." – Romans 8:6

According to our scripture verse this morning, if you are operating according to the carnal mind, you are heading for death. If you are spiritually minded, on the other hand, you are going to have a day of peace.

What does it mean to be spiritually minded? It means to owe no man anything, to put your fellow man before yourself, to be gentle, fair, kind and honest. To be carnally minded is to try to get everything you can for yourself as quickly as you can and to do as little work as possible for the most return. Those who have this kind of lifestyle and attitude will not succeed but will experience spiritual death.

To be spiritually minded is to put the Lord Jesus Christ first and His people second. When you do that, you may be sure that He will take care of every one of your needs. You will succeed. You will be the head and not the tail. You will overcome. You will have life abundantly and you will walk in peace. Today, make sure that you are walking in the Spirit and you will succeed.

Lot is an example of a man who was carnally minded. Abraham gave Lot a choice. He didn't have to do that but he chose to. Lot, he said, could choose either the lush fertile plains where Sodom and Gomorrah were located, or the high rocky mountains. Lot chose Sodom and Gomorrah and it cost him dearly.

Do not walk in the flesh. Walk in the Spirit and allow the Lord Jesus Christ full liberty to direct your life.

God's telephone number

"Call to Me, and I will answer you, and show you great and mighty (inaccessible) things, which you do not know." – Jeremiah 33:3

Perhaps you don't know which way to turn today. The Lord says, "Call unto me and I will answer you". Many refer to this scripture as the Lord's telephone number – Jeremiah 333. So pick up the heavenly telephone today and call Him. He has promised that He will show you great and mighty things, which are inaccessible to you now.

How many times have you said, "Lord, I just don't know what to do next!" when, all of a sudden, a simple answer came your way – something you never even dreamed of doing and it just opened up whole new possibilities? That's how God works.

Many years ago we were in a terrible drought situation. Our crop of corn did not even yield enough to pay for the fertilizer. Right out of season – and totally foreign to the Natal Midlands of South Africa – a freak snowstorm hit us. We had snow everywhere, especially in the areas where many timber companies grow wattle and gum trees. These trees are not used to this kind of weather, and they were broken, twisted and bent by the weight of the snow on their branches. The timber companies had thousands of hectares of damaged timber and their plantations were in an absolute mess. They cried out for help. It was an opportunity for the farmers and we purchased four chain saws. The huge staff we had hired to reap our crop of corn cut down the timber. The timber company paid us and we were able to pay our outstanding debts. Yes, we called to God and He answered us, and He showed us "inaccessible things" in a way we never dreamed, enabling us to settle our accounts.

So, today, call unto God and expect Him to show you great and mighty things.

Have faith in God

"Have faith in God." – Mark 11:22

Do you have faith? Have you ever wondered what real faith is? Faith is a "doing–word." Faith is putting your expectation into practise. Faith has got feet. Duncan Campbell, who was involved in the great revival that took place in the North West of Scotland in the 1950s said, "Expectations and aspirations are of no use unless they can be turned into reality." That's what faith does best.

My friend, faith is not froth and bubbles. I'm a farmer and I have my feet firmly planted on the ground. I know that faith is a reality. Faith is God in action.

I've heard it said that God feeds the birds, but He doesn't throw food into their nests. When we do the possible by faith, God will do the impossible. We must pray in faith and trust God for whatever enterprise we are involved in. Then we need to roll up our sleeves, get stuck in and see it through – not forgetting, at the end of the day, to thank the Lord.

The psalmist put it in a nutshell. "My soul, wait silently for God alone, for my expectation is from Him." (Psalm 62:5).

True wisdom

"Behold, the fear of the Lord, that is wisdom, and to depart from evil is understanding." – Job 28:28

I was the speaker at a "Farmers for Jesus" conference in Cathcart, South Africa, a number of years ago when a farmer stood up in the meeting. "Do you believe," he asked me, "that it is a godly thing to pay income tax to a government that professes to be communist?" Before I became a Christian, I thought wisdom was to try to see how we could pay as little income tax as possible, but that day I was caught completely off guard and cried out to the Holy Spirit for wisdom. Immediately, I remembered an incident recorded in the Bible when the Pharisees tried to trip up our Lord Jesus Christ with a similar question. Jesus took the coin and said, "Render unto Caesar what is Caesar's (because the face of Caesar was on that coin), and render unto God what is God's." We have to be honest in all our dealings. That is true wisdom.

The Lord says if we depart from evil, we will understand the things which belong to the kingdom of God and we will become wise. It's a fact of life that we reap what we sow. The Bible says that he who lives by the sword will die by the sword. I've seen it so many times.

Let us make it our aim to reverence the Lord and so become wise people. Let us pay unto Caesar what is Caesar's and unto God what is God's. Let us do things that are right and correct in the eyes of God. It doesn't matter what the collector of taxes sees or doesn't see. What is important is what God sees and He is no man's debtor. If you do things according to His ways, He will see that you prosper in every area of your life.

Empowered by the Holy Spirit

"But you shall receive power when the Holy Spirit has come upon you; and you shall be witnesses to Me in Jerusalem, and in all Judea and Samaria, and to the end of the earth." – Acts 1:8

It is impossible to live life as God intends it without the power of the Holy Spirit.

The disciples could do nothing without the Holy Spirit. Peter was too afraid even to acknowledge that he knew the Lord Jesus Christ, when the little servant girl exposed him on that terrible night our Saviour was arrested and taken to Pilate's palace. That same Peter went out into the streets a few weeks later and preached his first sermon, resulting in around three thousand converts (Acts 2:41). What made the difference? Acts 2:4 tells us. Forty days after the resurrection of Jesus, the Holy Spirit came as a mighty rushing wind, filling the house where the 120 believers were meeting together. Tongues of fire came upon them and they were all filled with the Holy Spirit and began to speak with other tongues. From that moment, they were totally transformed men and women.

What about you? Are you saying, "I have no power. I can hardly get out of bed in the morning"? Well, go and kneel in your room and ask the Holy Spirit to come and fill you with His fire, His love and His power. Ask Him to give you a new tongue. If you've never spoken in tongues before, I can assure you that it is for real and it is a wonderfully blessed experience. Open your mouth and He will fill it with a brand new heavenly prayer language that you can freely use to communicate with Him all day long. You will experience a deeper love for Jesus and a new boldness as you share your faith with others.

The Lord is our helper

"So we may boldly say: 'The LORD is my helper; I will not fear. What can man do to me?" – Hebrews 13:6

There have been times when I have felt totally alone, even when in the company of people, and have had to cry out to the Lord for help. I felt like that during the very first campaign I ever held. It was in a little town named Ladysmith, in Northern KwaZulu–Natal, South Africa. I'd had much support from my friends as I prepared for the first night of the campaign. But I clearly remember feeling terribly alone as I looked into the hall. The meeting was due to start at 7:00 pm. At 6:45 pm there was not a soul in sight, except for the music team, faithfully playing. Ten minutes later, the hall was still empty.

I retreated to the little kitchen underneath the stage, where I had been praying. I felt terrible but it was my hour of testing. I cried out to God in desperation. "Lord, I will preach to the chairs if need be, but I am going to share the gospel no matter what happens." And praise His Name, the Lord is my helper. When I walked onto that platform at 7:00 pm, that town hall was already comfortably full. That was the first night. By the end of that week, there were only fifteen empty seats left in the upstairs balcony.

Are you looking to man to be your helper? Or are you looking to God? Man will fail you every time but you may be sure that God will never let you down. Whether you are a winner or a loser in man's sight means nothing to God. God loves us so much that He gave His only begotten Son for you and for me. So this day, as you go about your business, remember it is the Lord who is your Helper, and not man. Trust Him.

Unity

"Behold, how good and how pleasant it is for brethren to dwell together in unity! It is like the precious oil upon the head, running down on the beard, the beard of Aaron, running down on the edge of his garments." – Psalm 133:1, 2

Unity obviously starts, first of all, between you and God and then extends to your immediate family, your fellow believers, and your working environment.

The Lord commands His blessing when believers dwell together in unity. The Bible says unity is so special that it reminds us of the precious anointing oil poured over the head of His priests in Old Testament times, symbolising the presence of the Holy Spirit. We always pray for the sick at our campaigns and anoint them with oil in the Name of the Father, the Son and the Holy Spirit for the same reason. There is no power in the oil, the power is in the prayer of faith and the healing presence of the Holy Spirit.

I believe what God is saying to you and me today is that when we dwell together in unity the Holy Spirit is present. Take time out today and ask God to forgive you for any relationships that are not going as they should. Even if the other party refuses to forgive you or make peace with you, ask God to take all unforgiveness, awkwardness, rebellion and disobedience out of your heart and go in faith and peace. You will find that the precious oil of the Holy Spirit will be upon you, and you will be a sweet fragrance as you seek to restore unity.

Always remember that it takes two to have an argument. A man cannot argue by himself. If you are prepared to make peace, then unity will prevail and the presence of God will be there. God bless you as you go forth as an ambassador of the Lord Jesus Christ today.

The joy of the Lord

"The joy of the LORD is your strength." – Nehemiah 8:10

When was the last time you had such a good laugh that the tears ran down your face? The Bible says in Proverbs 17:22 that "a merry heart does good like medicine."

The Lord says to you today that if you truly know Him and are confident of His plans for you, the ups and downs of this life will not make any difference to the way you feel deep inside. The fact that your name is written in the Lamb's Book of Life and that you have an incredible inheritance awaiting you in heaven, is good reason to be joyful.

I heard the story about a multi-millionaire who had been told that he had cancer and was going to die. Apparently, he went to a local video shop and bought every comedy video he could find. He went home, sat down and watched every one of them, laughing until he cried. He did this for days on end and I was told that he got stronger and healthier every day. The specialists could not believe what had happened. The cancer had completely left his body.

Our God is a joyful God and we are made in his image and likeness. He wants us to be joyful. We are not talking about walking around with a grin on your face like a Cheshire cat – that is not joy! We are talking about inner peace and the joy of knowing, whatever happens, Jesus Christ has promised that He will never leave nor forsake us.

The Lord will help you over the hurdles of life if you continue to trust in Him daily. Before you go anywhere today, sit down for five minutes and count your blessings. Thank the Lord for each one of them and then, with joy in your heart, go out and face the day.

Time with the Lord

"Now in the morning, having risen a long while before daylight, He went out and departed to a solitary place; and there He prayed." – Mark 1:35

To walk the Christian road can sometimes be extremely lonely. Jesus Himself spent much time on His own before His heavenly Father in prayer.

If you are someone who always has to have people around you then, my friend, look at your heart very carefully today. Are you taking time to build a relationship with the King of Kings and the Lord of Lords? The mark of a Christian – a true believer – is one who can sit and be quiet before God for long periods of time. Those who wait upon the Lord shall renew their strength and mount up with wings like eagles according to Isaiah 40:31. An eagle is a solitary bird that spends much time by itself.

I've travelled a lot, especially in the last few years, ministering all over the world for the Lord and have found it necessary to spend long hours in solitary places with the Lord. That is where I receive my strength. People always graciously want to take me sightseeing and visiting but I have little desire for that. In between meetings all I want is to have time with the Lord. I need to hear His voice as I prepare for the next service. I particularly miss my wife and family when I am away from home and I need time to allow Him to strengthen me when I am feeling lonely and weary. That is exactly what my Master did. When He wasn't ministering, He was spending time in solitary places talking to His Father.

If you are feeling weary, tired, listless, and there is no joy or spark in your life, may I suggest that you take time out to spend with God on your own?

Living the life

"Brethren, join in following my example, and note those who so walk, as you have us for a pattern." – Philippians 3:17

You may be the only example of a Christian some people will ever see or hear. It is in the workplace – when the pressure is on – that people want to see whether this Jesus you keep talking about is real or not. They say you never know what an orange tastes like until it's been squeezed, nor will you smell the fragrance of a rosebud unless the petals are crushed. So it is with a Christian. This is when people see who you really are. Paul says that we have his example to follow. Are you an example for others?

A missionary was once sent out to preach the gospel in the South Sea Islands. His boat was shipwrecked on the rocks and he was the sole surviving member of the group. The inhabitants of the island were hostile, but allowed him to live among them on condition that he did not speak about his God. The man lived the life. He lived the pattern. When he died, they buried him on the island. Some years later another group of missionaries arrived. This time the Polynesians welcomed them and listened carefully. The missionaries were amazed at their reaction. "Do you know about Jesus?" they asked. "Oh yes," said the islanders. "Who told you about Him?" the missionaries asked. "He lived on our island," they said. "The man you are talking about is buried here."

They took the missionaries to the spot where the man of God had been buried. "He is the man you are speaking about," they said, pointing to the grave of a man who was not allowed to speak about Jesus, but who lived the pattern of Jesus.

Does that challenge you today?

Responsibility

"Am I my brother's keeper?" – Genesis 4:9b

"Where is your brother?" the Lord asked Cain. "Am I my brother's keeper?" responded the man who had just murdered his brother Abel. The Lord is asking you and me the same question. What is your response this morning?

My dear friends, the answer is, "Yes, yes" and a third time, "yes." We are our brother's keeper. We are responsible for the people God brings into our lives. Like Peter of old (John 21:17), Jesus expects us to feed and take care of His sheep.

Perhaps you have a problem in the home and you are even contemplating divorcing your spouse. You might be trying to justify it because you've heard that other men of God have divorced their wives. My dear friend, there is no such thing in the Bible. When you made your covenant before God, you said, "Until death do us part." God is holding you to your word today. You are your brother's keeper. You are responsible for your marriage partner.

You are also responsible for your children. Whether or not they respect you, or acknowledge you as head of the house is immaterial. God has put you in that place. You are the authority in your home. If you are a farmer, every person on that farm is your dependant. You are your brother's keeper.

Ask God to give you much grace and love today. Set the standards in your home, on your farm or in your workplace by all means but, at the same time, take care of the people God has brought into your life.

Investing in eternal things

"The Spirit of the LORD is upon Me, because He has anointed Me to preach the gospel to the poor; He has sent Me to heal the broken-hearted, to proclaim liberty to the captives and recovery of sight to the blind, to set at liberty those who are oppressed." – Luke 4:18

God called me to be a preacher, an evangelist. What has He called you to be?

I sometimes hear people say they have been called to be evangelists, and some that their vision is to be the next Billy Graham or Reinhardt Bonnke. When I ask them if they have started, I am seldom surprised to hear that they are still waiting for something to happen in their lives. My dear friends, our congregation is the people among whom we live and work. My congregation is my farm. If I cannot preach the gospel to my own immediate family and to the employees on our farm, how am I ever going to preach to the nations?

The Lord says to you this morning that He has anointed you to preach the gospel to the poor – starting with your wife, husband, children, grandparents and relatives. Home is the hardest then Judea, Samaria, and extend your ministry to the outer ends of the world. We have to start at home base and then move out into our local communities, provinces, country and, finally, the nations of the world. God has anointed you to preach the gospel, not only by word, but also by deed and – most of all – by example.

Let us start today. Let's not be so concerned about making money, but rather about investing in eternal things. If we seek first the kingdom of God and His righteousness, all of these other things will be added unto us (Matthew 6:33). There is nothing nicer than working with a group of people who are happy, joyful and fulfilled; people who are prepared to go the extra mile because they love you, not because they fear you.

Renewing our first love

"Nevertheless I have this against you, that you have left your first love." –
Revelation 2:4

This morning, the Lord is saying He wants to have that intimate relationship with you that He had the day you first gave your life to Him.

Hear the challenge of the Lord to the Church at Ephesus, "But I have this against you – You have left your first love" (Rev 2:1–4).

"What will it profit a man if he gains the whole world and loses his own soul?" (Mark 8:36). The Lord is not really interested in what you can do for Him. His main interest is in what He can do for you. He cannot help you if you are not talking to Him. Remember, the door to your heart has one handle, and it is on the inside. How often the Lord Jesus is left standing on the doorstep of our lives, longing to come in and have fellowship with us.

How long has your door been closed? He says, "Come and sit and talk things over. Come, cry on My shoulder. Sit under the tree with Me and look at the beautiful sunset. Let Me show you what I have created for you." Pull the plug on the telephone. Switch the computer and the television off. Hear the Lord say, "Come, and let us reason together. I love you so much that I gave My very life for you."

He is the God of second chances and He invites you to repent and start again. Let us get our priorities in order. "But seek first the kingdom of God and His righteousness, and all these things shall be added to you" (Matthew 6:33).

Where are you?

"Then the LORD God called to Adam and said to him, 'Where are you?" –
Genesis 3:9

The Lord is asking us a question today – "Where are you?"

God used to have a beautiful relationship with Adam and Eve. In the cool of
the day, He walked and talked with them, until they fell into sin and hid
themselves from His Presence. God knew exactly what had happened and
where Adam was because He knows all things, yet He still asked Adam,
"Where are you?" God knows where you are today and where I am. Are
you also hiding yourself from Him like Adam and Eve? Where are you?

Why did God ask Adam this question and why does He ask it of us? The
reason is simply because He wants us to face up to our sin and make
amends. He wants to have fellowship with you because unconfessed sin
causes a barrier. That issue in your life which is driving you away from God
– that bad habit you just don't seem to be able to break – God asks you
this morning to deal with it so that He can have fellowship with you again.
He longs to walk and talk with you so that He may guide, love and cherish
you.

Do not believe that your sin is too great. It is the very reason God sent His
Only Begotten Son – the Lord Jesus Christ – to die on the Cross of
Calvary. His promise is that "If we confess our sins, He is faithful and just to
forgive us our sins and to cleanse us from all unrighteousness." (1 John 1:9).

Come out of hiding this morning. Confess that sin and start afresh, so that
you may, once again, have beautiful fellowship with the Lord.

Rejoice!

"Rejoice in the Lord always. Again I will say, rejoice!" – Philippians 4:4

This is a command from God. He wants us to rejoice! "But." you may say, "I don't have anything to rejoice about." Oh my friend, that's not true. The greatest reason to rejoice is because your name is written in the Lamb's Book of Life, if you are a "born again" Christian. Perhaps you say, "I'm so full of sin." I want to tell you that Jesus is the friend of sinners. Or you may say, "But I am not a good person." Good people don't go to heaven – believers go to heaven.

Trials and tribulations do not necessarily mean that there is sin in your life, or that God is displeased with you. Did our Lord not suffer? Did the disciples not suffer? Do you know that almost every apostle died a violent death? Do you know that there are more martyrs in the world today than there have been in the history of the world? If you add together every martyr from the first nineteen centuries since Christ died, the total is less than the number who have died during this last century. Does that mean that we are to mourn? No! The Bible says "Rejoice in the Lord always. And again I say rejoice."

Early believers in Roman times were marched into the Colosseum as sport for the citizens of Rome. Hungry lions were allowed to tear godly men, women and children apart. History reports that these precious believers did not scream or weep. They rejoiced. They sang hymns and praised God as the lions attacked them, because they were about to meet Jesus Christ in heaven. The Word of God says, "The Lord is at hand." – Jesus is coming soon!

No matter what that mountain is, or how big it might seem, the Lord tells you today, "Rejoice in the Lord always." And, again He says, "Rejoice."

Godliness with contentment

"Now godliness with contentment is great gain." – I Timothy 6:6

Having been born in Africa and grown up here, I always thought I understood the black man, his culture, his hardships, and lifestyle, but I can honestly say that God taught me some valuable lessons on my trip into the Luapula Province of Zambia. Here I learned afresh the meaning of godliness with contentment.

For one thing, I was amazed at the infinite patience of these people. A mother will wake up early in the morning, sometimes at 3 a.m., and start polishing the floor of her house. The lights will go out. She will try to run water to wash dishes or bathe and the water will stop. Without any show of frustration or anger, she will serenely take a 20 litre container and walk down to the river, sometimes three or four kilometres away, fetch water and bring it home. It is heartbreaking to see the curse of poverty with nothing working, everything needing attention and no money to make repairs. The gap between the "haves" and the "have-nots" in Africa has become a giant chasm.

Yet how contented these believers were in the Lord. It challenged me and I pray that it will challenge you too.

MAY

Is your passport in order?

"For our citizenship is in heaven, from which we also eagerly wait for the Saviour, the Lord Jesus Christ." – Philippians 3:20

What country do you belong to? What citizenship do you hold? What passport do you have? Are you a South African, Italian, Argentinian, American, or maybe a Scotsman? My friend, if you are a believer, that is a temporary passport you are holding. Your country is heaven. Your president is Jesus Christ. Your inheritance is life eternal. Your riches cannot be reckoned. All the cattle on a thousand hills – all the riches of this world – belong to you because they all belong to your Heavenly Father.

The kingdom to which you belong cannot be toppled. The King is in power forever and ever. The citizenship that you hold is eternal. In the place of your destiny, there is no sickness, disease, hunger, poverty or evil. There is no darkness or fear. There is only life eternal. Make sure today that you do not lose your eternal passport – that it is not confiscated by the devil because of double standards or an inward desire to change your citizenship.

Ensure at all times that your passport is up to date and intact. You will be glad you did – for all eternity.

How big is God?

"But as it is written: 'Eye has not seen, nor ear heard, nor have entered into the heart of man the things which God has prepared for those who love Him." – I Corinthians 2:9

Are you feeling very low in spirit or tired in body today? Maybe the buffeting you have been enduring has exhausted you. The Lord has good news for you. He says eye has not seen, nor ear heard, nor has it even entered into the heart of man the wonderful things which God has prepared for those who love Him. Do you understand, my dear friend, what God is saying? He says, before you run onto the rugby field the score is already 44/nil in your favour. Before you strike the ball on the first tee of the golf course, you've already won the tournament – 25 below par. Before you've even walked onto the tennis courts you've won already, game, set and match.

The things He has prepared for you are so wonderful that you cannot even contemplate or imagine them. You have a choice when you walk out of the door this morning. You can believe the lies of the devil, who is saying to you that you're a failure, a loser, and that you will never amount to anything. Or you can tell him, "Get behind me, Satan," just as Jesus did and choose to believe the promises of God. When the Lord Jesus Christ died on the cross of Calvary he said, "It is finished" and He meant it. He has done the job and completed the task. Victory is ours.

Think about this question today: how big is God? The answer is very simple. God is as big as you allow Him to be.

The Lord's temple

"Do you not know that you are the temple of God and that the Spirit of God dwells in you?" – 1 Corinthians 3:16

The Lord asks you a question this morning: how is it with your temple – is it clean, or dirty?

He is not asking how many times a week you do aerobics, how much sport you play, what your blood pressure is, or how many pulses per second your heart beats. Nor is He asking whether you play provincial or international sport, how well-groomed you are, how beautiful your hair is, how bright and shiny your eyes are, what your figure looks like or what your waistline is doing. What He is asking is "How is it with your spirit? Is your temple clean? Can I live inside you? Or are you full of filth and dirt, pornography, evil thinking, ugliness, unforgiveness, hatred, selfishness, and self-centredness?"

Why not ask God today to cleanse you out, to do a complete spring–clean in your spirit so that He can dwell comfortably inside you? Repent, receive forgiveness and walk in obedience to the Holy Spirit from this day forward.

Jesus, our mentor and Lord

" But we have the mind of Christ." – 1 Corinthians 2:16b

It is quite amazing to observe throughout history that, whenever there were serious problems in their nation, many of the great leaders of the world called for men of God to stand by them. Some prime examples in the Bible are Daniel, Joseph, Isaiah and Elijah.

Dr Billy Graham has been the mentor to no less than nine U.S. presidents. Robert Moffat was the personal mentor to the king of the Matabele people in Zimbabwe many years ago. The people of this world sense that the children of God have something about them. No matter how clever, powerful or talented they might be, human wisdom will fail. Even Charles Darwin himself, the very man who propagated the theory of evolution, repented on his death bed and acknowledged that there is a God of wisdom and that this world didn't start with a "Big Bang."

Paul said, "We have the mind of Christ." Never underestimate the power of God in the spirit of a man. John Wesley's definition of a Christian is, "The life of God in the soul of man." There are many people you will meet on life's journey who do not have answers. What a privilege to know that the Christian has the mind of Christ and He is the source of all knowledge.

Remember, my friend, people are not interested in your opinion. They want to know what Christ says about the predicament they are involved in. And they need to know His answer to their dilemma.

Unlimited power

"That your faith should not be in the wisdom of men but in the power of God." – I Corinthians 2:5

The wisdom of men is very limited, especially when you compare it to the unlimited power of God.

I have been an evangelist for well over twenty years and I know that the best message I am capable of preaching will not move or change people, nor motivate them to stand up and be counted for God. However, when the power of God is demonstrated through divine healing and signs and wonders, there is always a spontaneous response. When people see someone they know healed, their hearts are instantly touched. When a man who has never been able to walk and has been bound to a wheelchair all his life, rises up and starts walking, having been anointed with oil and prayed for, you have their full attention. When the power of God touches people, unbelievers will accept Jesus Christ as sovereign Lord, unconditionally.

Paul says that our faith should not be in the wisdom of men but in the power of God. His power is incredible. I've seen a hailstorm rushing straight at a lush crop of corn and cried out to God, pleading the blood of Jesus Christ over my farm – and watched as an easterly wind came up and changed the course of that storm, causing it to bypass the farm. That is what makes a man realise that the power of God is a reality. That's what stops vain arguments and man's weak discussions about the things of God. Yes, I've said it before and I want to say it again – one genuine miracle equals a thousand sermons.

Let your faith be demonstrated through the power of God and not through philosophy.

Glorying in the Lord

"He who glories, let him glory in the LORD." – 1 Corinthians 1:31

Are you glorying in the Lord today, or are you glorying in yourself – what you have done and who you are? Do the words, "I, me and mine" dominate your conversation? My friend, let us be real today. You are nothing but by the grace of God. It does not matter how big your empire is, what great feats you have attained for God, how many farms you own or how many trophies you have in your cabinet. It does not matter how successful you have been or how many degrees you have earned; the Bible says, "He who glories, let him glory in the Lord."

When people come to you and say, "What a wonderful effort. What a fantastic show. What a beautiful farm. What lovely fields you have," thank them and acknowledge that it is all due to the Lord Jesus Christ. The most dangerous thing anyone can do is to touch God's glory. Saul, the first king of Israel, tried that and he lost the power and anointing of God on his life.

Do not touch God's glory. Give Him all the glory, praise and honour for what He has done in your life and that of your family and your business and He will continue to bless you.

Bold as a lion

"The wicked flee when no one pursues, but the righteous are bold as a lion." – Proverbs 28:1

If Jesus Christ is your Lord and Saviour – if you have truly acknowledged Him and confessed all your sins – you are righteous through the blood of Jesus. It is an amazing thing, but the righteousness of God gives you tremendous boldness. As the scripture says, you become bold as a lion. There is no bolder creature in the animal kingdom than the lion. It is a fearless animal. Mary, Queen of Scots, said of John Knox that she feared his prayers more than a legion of soldiers because he was a righteous man.

I vividly remember my visit to the king of the Zulu nation, King Goodwill Zwelethini. As I was escorted into his palace, I saw scores of his people, shouting, saluting, singing songs and saying, "Bayete, Inkosi. Wena Ndlovu,"which means: "We salute you king, you are the elephant." I must admit to being rather nervous, but as I walked into his palace the Holy Spirit reminded me that I am the ambassador of the King of Kings and the Lord of Lords. Immediately, a humble boldness rose up within me and I was able to greet His Majesty in the Name of our risen Lord and Saviour. We had a tremendous day together. The ox he slaughtered as a gift for us was totally unexpected. You are supposed to bring gifts to the king, and not vice versa!

You see, the boldness of the righteous is appealing. People notice and respect you for it. Today, go in the righteousness of the Lord Jesus Christ and be as bold as a lion.

Crowd pleasers

"When they found Him, they said to Him, 'Everyone is looking for You." –
Mark 1:37

Are you a crowd pleaser? Are you someone who constantly desires
acknowledgement, believing that unless you are the centre of attraction,
you must be a dull, depressing person to be with? Or are you like Jesus,
who was totally focused, sure of His calling and not in any way impressed
or swayed by man's opinion?

Jesus' response to the disciples when they told Him that everyone was
looking for Him is challenging. He said, "Let us go into the next town, that
I may preach there also, because for this purpose I have come forth" (Mark
1:38). Can you say that, my friend? Would you be prepared to leave
everything that you have built up over the last number of years and go to
an unknown destiny because the Lord Jesus Christ has called you? Or
would that be too much for you?

The Lord is challenging you this morning. If He requires that you hand over
your complete farming concern to your sons and go into the mission field
– or that you retire or go into another type of business – would you be
able to do it? I would say that you could measure your spirituality by the
decision you make. You've heard that old song, "Take the world but give me
Jesus." Is that your song today? If not, you need to sit down and count the
cost. When the trumpet sounds and the Lord calls us home, everything we
have built up here on earth – our farming concern, ministry, business, home
– will be left behind.

Jesus was not impressed by man's applause. He was interested only in being
obedient to his Father's call. May that be the hallmark of our lives too.

The urgency of the times

"The time is fulfilled, and the kingdom of God is at hand. Repent, and believe in the Gospel." – Mark 1:15

I really feel this morning that the Lord is saying there is an urgency involved in following Jesus. There is urgency in the kingdom. If the message was urgent 2000 plus years ago, my dear friend, it must be vitally important today. We need to be sure that we have repented and believe with our whole hearts the gospel of our Lord Jesus Christ. He says, "The time is fulfilled – the time is up – the kingdom of God is at hand."

We are living in the last seconds of the last hour. Jesus is not only coming soon – He is already on His way. Are you ready? The Word says that two people will be working in the field when He comes. One will be taken and the other left. Two will be lying in bed, He will take one and leave the other. If He were to come today, would you be ready to meet Him in the air. This is an urgent message.

The Lord says, "Do not say there are four months and then the harvest, but lift up your eyes and look. The fields are white unto harvest" (John 4:35). Any good farmer knows there are seasons. There is a season to plant and a season to reap. Many of us need to make sure that all our affairs are in order – that we are no man's debtor, that we have made out our Wills correctly, and that we are in a position, if the Master were to call, to leave immediately. Take time out today. Check your household. Be sure that your family is saved and that your staff know about the Lord Jesus Christ. They may choose to accept or reject the Lord – but give them the opportunity. Be ready for the coming of the Lord.

We, at Shalom, are called the "cloud watchers." Every morning we look up at the clouds and say, "Lord, perhaps today..." Why not join us?

Instant obedience

"They immediately left their nets and followed Him." – Mark 1:18

When the Lord Jesus called the fishermen (Peter, Andrew, James, and John) to be His disciples, they left their nets immediately. What a challenge to our faith. The question is, are we instantly obedient to God's Word? Do we do exactly what God tells us?

A year or so ago I felt the Lord Jesus Christ telling me to sell my entire herd of beef cattle. I had just returned from a preaching campaign and we were financially stretched on the farm. It was not an easy decision but, in obedience, I sold the entire breeding herd and received top prices. Our Lord Jesus is God. He knows all things and that is why it is so important that we do what He tells us without delay. Two weeks after having sold that herd of cattle, we had an outbreak of foot and mouth disease in KwaZulu–Natal and you could not give your cattle away! How glad I was that I had obeyed Him immediately.

The disciples obeyed the voice of the Lord. Will you? Make a pact with God before you walk out the door this morning, that you will do whatever He tells you IMMEDIATELY, so that He can bless you.

The unique Christ

"He is not here; for He is risen, as He said." – Matthew 28:6a

We need to understand one thing clearly – Jesus is God! I remember preaching about that some time ago in Pietermaritzburg, South Africa. To my surprise, someone approached me after the service and said that this was the first time they had ever heard it said that Jesus is God.

Yes, He is the Son of God, but He is God. We are not to make the mistake of comparing the Lord Jesus Christ with any other person or thing on earth. Don't even try to compare Him with great leaders, or people like Confucius, Buddha, Mohammed, Hari Krishna or any superstar – whether it be in music, sport or politics. They are not in the same league. Not one of them has been raised from the dead. None of them has an empty tomb. You can go to the grave sites of many of those leaders and see their bones enshrined.

The tomb of Jesus is empty. "He is risen." He is alive. He is the God you and I serve. He is the same God who stilled the storm when the disciples' boat was about to sink and they cried out, saying, "Who is this man that even the waves and the wind obey Him?" So, today, don't look for Him amongst the dead or famous of this world. It is wonderful news that Jesus is with us today. Wherever you go and whatever you do, you have nothing to fear. The same Holy Spirit, who raised Jesus from the dead, is with you today. There is nothing too big that God cannot handle. Go in the peace and joy of knowing that He is with you

No more tears

" ...And the Lord GOD will wipe away tears from all faces ..." – Isaiah 25:8

This is a special word for those who are weeping today and whose hearts are heavy. If you are sad and feeling that you have been treated badly and people have manipulated and taken advantage of you, the Lord promises that He will wipe away every tear from your face.

Make a decision today to forgive the person who has wounded or hurt you, and press on with the peace of God in your heart. "Is that fair?" you may wonder. "Why should that person get away scot free?" It is fair. God will see that justice is done. "Vengeance is Mine, I will repay, says the Lord." (Romans 12:19). Leave your case with the Lord.

The Day of Judgment is in God's hands. Every man, woman or young person, including you and I, will be held accountable for our actions. Believers will appear before the Judgment Seat of Christ (Romans 14:10) to give account. On that day, the Lord says, He will wipe away every tear from every face. Please don't wait until that day to repent. Make sure that your life is in order, and that you do not have anything against anyone, or that any person has a case against you.

Unbelievers will appear before the Great White Throne on Judgment Day. Tyrants like Idi Amin, Mao Tse-tung, Joseph Stalin and Adolph Hitler will stand before the King of kings and God will deal with them according to their deeds. Do not hate those who hurt you, but rather pray for them.

The Lord says to you and me today, go out and wipe away the tears of those who hurt. Visit the widows and orphans. Feed the hungry and the poor. "Assuredly, I say to you, inasmuch as you did it to one of the least of these My brethren, you did it to Me" (Matthew 25:40).

Drinking His cup

"So He said to them, 'You will indeed drink My cup, and be baptized with the baptism that I am baptized with." – Matthew 20:23a

The disciples wanted to know who would sit on the right and left hand side of the Lord Jesus Christ in glory. The Lord answered them with a strange question, "Can you drink of the cup that I will drink of?" The disciples said, "Yes," and the Lord responded, "You will indeed." And they did. Be careful what you ask of the Lord because you can rest assured that He is listening to you.

On the 17th November 1989, I asked the Lord to use me to preach the gospel. I was driving into the little town of Ladysmith, where I had planned my first preaching campaign, when the Lord asked me a question. "Are you prepared to see less of your family for my sake?" I swallowed hard because I'm a family man. My wife is my best friend. My children are very precious to me. I said, "Lord, only by Your grace," and I sensed His response: "You will indeed."

I've had the privilege of seeing thousands of people bow the knee to the Lord Jesus Christ but it has cost me dearly. As I write this book, I still drink of the cup of loneliness. Sometimes I'm misunderstood, misrepresented and disliked, for the sake of the gospel. But I would never change it for anything, because I am totally fulfilled in the work God has given to me to do. As a result my entire family is serving the Lord Jesus Christ. Our farming enterprise is being blessed. The ministry at Shalom is growing. The orphanage is blossoming. Souls are being saved.

Do not be afraid to drink of the cup the Lord offers you. Just be sure, before you drink it, that you are prepared by all means to walk the road of obedience.

The power of the spoken word

"O dry bones, hear the word of the LORD!" – Ezekiel 37:4b

The prophet Ezekiel had a vision of a valley of bones and God told him to speak the Word of the Lord over those dry bones. I believe the Lord wants us to focus, once again, on the power of the spoken Word of God.

What is your situation today? When you got up this morning and looked around, perhaps all you saw were the dry bones of bankruptcy, separation from your family, sickness, poverty, and hopelessness.

The Lord says to you today, speak to the dry bones. Speak the Word of the Lord over the life of that prodigal son who has left home. Speak the Word of the Lord over those meetings you have to address today, before you even enter the room. Speak the Word of the Lord over those circumstances that you are facing with your staff before you go out to meet with them, and watch what will happen.

Ezekiel obeyed and, as he spoke the Word of God over those dry bones, flesh, sinews and breath came back into the bones and an exceedingly great army stood to its feet. The power of God, released through the spoken Word of God by faith, performs mighty miracles. We've got to start becoming like father Abraham, "who staggered not at the promises of God through unbelief but remained strong in faith, giving glory to God" (Romans 4:20). At the age of 100, with his dear old wife of 90 plus, he spoke the Word of God and they had a beautiful baby son named Isaac born to them.

No matter what your circumstances are today, or what situation you find yourself in, the Lord says to you, "Speak the Word of God over those dry bones," and He will do the rest.

The mercy and grace of God

"For by grace you have been saved through faith, and that not of yourselves; it is the gift of God." – Ephesians 2:8

We need to be reminded that everything we have and are is due to the love of God.

The Bible says in Romans 3:23 that "all have sinned and fall short of the glory of God." No one can claim any righteousness of his own. We owe everything to Jesus. Saint Augustine, that wonderful man of God, said, "Love the Lord your God with all your heart and then live as you wish." What he meant is that if you have been truly saved by grace through faith, then you will live a holy Christian life.

How true it is that we so easily forget from whence we have come. If it wasn't for the grace and mercy that the Lord extended to me, I don't know where I would be today. The Lord took me out of the miry pit, just as he did David. He set me on a rock, cleansed me and gave me a second chance. I can afford to love because He loves me.

What I believe He is saying to us today is that just as we've had that grace extended to us, let us go and do likewise to others. Unforgiveness imprisons us in the past and locks out all potential for change. Forgiveness, however, loosens the stronghold of guilt. Do not get yourself into a predicament of irreversibility. Do not burn your bridges but rather go and make peace with others, freely extending the grace God has given you to others. The Lord says in His prayer, "Forgive us our trespasses as (in the same way) we forgive others who trespass against us."

Make a decision to sort out your problems today, and to ask forgiveness of anyone you have hurt, and the peace of God will overflow your life.

In celebration of mothers

"And many women who followed Jesus from Galilee, ministering to Him, were there looking on from afar, among whom were Mary Magdalene, Mary the mother of James and Joses, and the mother of Zebedee's sons."
— Matthew 27:56

Many of the brave disciples, who had been through so much with Jesus, ran away when He was crucified, but these mothers remained at the cross. How we should thank God for our mothers!

I want to pay tribute to my earthly mother. My mother was a sickly lady but she loved me. Whenever I was ill, I remember her sitting by my bed, sometimes right through the night. She was never impatient with me. I know all about my ancestors from Scotland because of my mother's stories. When I became a Christian, she was very distressed and fearful that I had changed. "Now that I'm a Christian, I love you more than I ever loved you," I reassured her. That day my wife and I knelt by her chair as she prayed the sinner's prayer. From that time onwards my mother was a completely different person. She had joy in her heart and loved the Word of God. We used to have long discussions on scripture. My dad, a tough Scottish blacksmith, only met Jesus after my mother's death and I know that I will see them both again in heaven.

Do you have a mother or father still alive? If you do, visit, telephone or write to them and tell them that you love them. Share the gospel with them if they do not already know the Lord, that He will open the doors into eternity for them. They will be glad you did.

More about mothers

"And Hannah prayed and said: 'My heart rejoices in the LORD; my horn is exalted in the LORD. I smile at my enemies, because I rejoice in Your salvation." – 1 Samuel 2:1

This is a word from a mother who had dedicated her little baby son to the service of the Lord. Samuel grew to become one of the greatest prophets in the Old Testament and is a testimony to the influence of a godly mother.

Today I want to share a light-hearted quotation entitled "When God Created Mothers."

"When the Lord was creating mothers...[an] angel appeared and said, 'What are you doing...? The Lord said, 'Have you read the specifications?' She has to be completely washable, but not plastic, have one hundred and eighty movable parts, all replaceable, run on black coffee and leftovers, a kiss that can cure anything from a broken leg to a disappointed love affair and six pairs of hands, [plus] three pairs of eyes... one pair that will see through closed doors... another pair in the back of her head... and of course, the other pair in the front, so that she can look at a child when he messes up and say, 'I understand and I love you'. I'm so close to creating something close to myself. Already I have one who heals herself when she's sick, can feed a family of six on half a kilo of mince, and can get a nine-year-old to stand under the shower. 'It's too soft,' said the angel. 'But tough!' said the Lord. 'You cannot imagine what this mother can do or endure.' 'Can it think?' said the angel. 'Not only think, but it can reason and compromise,' said the Lord. Finally, the angel bent over and ran its finger across the cheek. 'There's a leak,' the angel pronounced 'It's not a leak,' said the Lord, 'It's a tear.' 'What's it for?' asked the angel. 'It's for joy, sadness, disappointment, pain, loneliness and pride.' The Lord looked sombre and said, 'I didn't put the tear there'."

Thank Jesus every day for your mother.

Finishing the race

"Praying always with all prayer and supplication in the Spirit, being watchful to this end with all perseverance and supplication for all the saints;" – Ephesians 6:18

Perseverance – keeping on keeping on, whether you feel like it or not. The Lord says the Christian walk is accomplished through perseverance – taking the Word of God and holding on to it and not giving up under any circumstances.

One of the saddest occasions I've had in my life recently was to attend a service commemorating the life of a dear sister in Christ who had taken her life. She was a lady in the prime of her life, with a wonderful Christian husband and beautiful children. I was grateful that the Lord had given her an extra three weeks in which she had the opportunity to make peace, first of all with God, and then with her family and loved ones before He finally took her home. What a sad occasion.

The Bible says on more than one occasion in the book of Revelation, "To him who overcomes." We've got to finish the race. The Lord says "continue to run the race with perseverance and supplication for all the saints."

Nothing encourages me more than when a brother or sister in Christ lets me know they are praying for me. We need one another. There have been times when I have stood in the pulpit feeling empty and dry, with nothing to offer, but aware of the prayers of the saints. Those are the times when God has used me the most effectively and a great harvest of souls has come in as I have leaned heavily on Him.

Today my prayer for you is, "Lord, give every reader of this journal tenacity, staying power, courage and strength to press on." Persevere, because the end is drawing near and it will be more than worthwhile when we see Him face to face.

Overcomers

"And they overcame him by the blood of the Lamb and by the word of their testimony, and they did not love their lives to the death." – Revelation 12:11

When the devil comes to accuse you of things you've done in the past, that's the time to declare that the Lord has paid for all your sin by the blood He shed on the cross of Calvary.

The devil does not give up easily. When he comes again to attack you, use the word of your testimony. It is very powerful to declare what God has done in your life, the account of what happened when you came to know Jesus Christ as your Lord and Saviour.

Remember, the Lord Jesus Christ laid His life down for you. He says in John 15:13, "Greater love hath no man than this, that a man lay down his life for his friend." All He wants from us today – for our own sake – is to lay down our lives and give Him first place.

David Wilkerson told the story of Nicky Cruz, a notorious gang leader, in his book *The Cross and the Switchblade*. "Jesus loves you, Nicky," David told him. "Get away from me, Preacher, or I'll kill you," responded Nicky angrily as he ran away, with David Wilkerson running after him. "I'll cut you in a hundred pieces," Nicky shouted, brandishing his flick knife. "And every piece will tell you the same thing – Jesus Christ loves you," David said. That gang leader met God and went on to become a powerful preacher of the gospel.

Remember that the way we overcome the powers of darkness is by the blood of Jesus, by the word of our testimony and by denying ourselves and following Him.

The day of the Lord

"For you yourselves know perfectly that the day of the Lord so comes as a thief in the night." – I Thessalonians 5:2

We must be prepared and ready at all times for the day of the Lord. When a thief breaks into your house, he does not give you advance warning, nor does he announce himself at the front door. He arrives in a flash and the Lord says that's exactly how He is going to come.

The best way to be ready is to spend time with God every day before you do anything else. Before you go out into the fields, to work or university, even before getting the children ready for school, get your heart ready. Repent, make sure that there's nothing in your life that would be offensive to our Lord if He had to come back to take you home today.

A very sad story is told of a gentleman who had a dream that he died and went to hell. He said hell reminded him of a gurgling and bubbling mud hole. Everywhere he looked, people were drowning in waist-high mud. Some were struggling in vain to keep their heads above the mud. He watched a man struggling to wade through the mud, moving from person to person, lifting up people's heads and looking into their faces. "What are you doing?" he asked. The reply shocked him. "I'm looking for the minister who put me in this place," cried out the man.

We need to tell people the truth. We must warn them that unless they know Jesus Christ as Lord and Saviour, they will not go to heaven. We need to snap out of our complacency, indifference and slumbering and be ready, because the Lord is coming like a thief in the night

The coin is in the fish's mouth

"Nevertheless, lest we offend them, go to the sea, cast in a hook, and take the fish that comes up first. And when you have opened its mouth, you will find a piece of money; take that and give it to them for Me and you." – Matthew 17:27

The coin is in the fish's mouth. God has shown us at Shalom Ministries that every time we fish for souls (preach the gospel), the finances come in. Every time we stop fishing for souls, the finances dry up. When Jesus had to pay his taxes to the temple, He instructed Peter to cast out a line. "Open the mouth of the first fish you catch," He told Peter, "You will find the exact amount of money for the temple tax." And it was so.

I suggest today, that if you desire your business to prosper, you need to be obedient to the Holy Spirit. You need to do what God called you to do, namely to preach the gospel. Maybe not verbally, because we can't all be evangelists, but in your daily lives in the business arena, let it be known that your farm, your business and your life belong to Jesus and that every fibre in your body is committed to serving Him. Put Him first, in other words. You will find that you'll never be short of money for anything that you need to do.

Be a soul-winner and God will supply every one of your needs.

Increasing our faith

"Then Jesus answered and said, 'O faithless and perverse generation, how long shall I be with you? How long shall I bear with you? Bring him here to Me.' – Matthew 17:17

The only time that Jesus really got angry with His disciples was when they disbelieved His promises, His power and His ability. When the Lord's disciples said they could not cast out the demon from the epileptic after the Lord had told them exactly what to do, He got very upset with them. I believe it makes the Lord as unhappy to see unbelief in His people as it does to see adultery, murder, and theft.

My prayer for the people of God today is that the Lord Jesus Christ will increase our faith (Luke 17:5). That was the prayer of the disciples too. They said, "Lord, increase our faith." How does faith come? It comes by hearing and reading the Word of God (Romans 10:17). Remember faith is a "doing-word". The way you overcome disbelief is by putting your faith into action.

Do not just speak your faith, but live it. Let it result in action. Trust God and you will see that He is good and faithful. In everything, in every aspect of your life, trust Him and your faith will grow and multiply, bearing a bountiful crop. Ask God to increase your faith daily.

Make your choice today

"And Elijah came to all the people, and said, 'How long will you falter between two opinions? If the LORD is God, follow Him; but if Baal, follow him'. But the people answered him not a word." – 1 Kings 18:21

Elijah was one of the greatest prophets in the Bible. He said to the people of his time, "Let us see who God is. If Baal (the devil) is God, follow him. If Jehovah is God, follow Him." Isn't it interesting that the people were not prepared to commit themselves and remained silent?

People are still chasing after foreign gods. I watched the television last night with a heavy heart as I listened to a man saying that the traditional religions are being revived. Ancestral worship is once again becoming very prominent, he said, as he went on to discuss cosmic forces, appeasing the forefathers, and other cultural issues. My dear friend, cultural issues have nothing to do with the living God. Every one of us has a cultural background. My background is from Scotland. I have a tartan and a clan name of which I am very proud but that has nothing to do with serving the living God.

Elijah knew that and that was why he challenged the people. The 450 prophets of Baal made their sacrifices and nothing happened. The man of God called on Jehovah and fire came out of heaven, consumed the complete sacrifice, the stones, the water and the animals. Then the people fell on their faces and said, "The Lord is God. The Lord, He is God."

What is in your heart today? Do you acknowledge that the Lord is God, or are you looking for another god? The devil is prowling around like a roaring lion in these last days and we can see the results everywhere, especially in the breakup of families.

There is only one God and there is only one Way. His name is Jesus Christ. Make sure you are serving Him alone and you will know the peace that only He can give.

Walking by faith

"Though the fig tree may not blossom, nor fruit be on the vines; though the labour of the olive may fail, and the fields yield no food; though the flock maybe cut off from the fold, and there be no herd in the stalls; yet I will rejoice in the LORD, I will joy in the God of my salvation." – Habakkuk 3:17,18

These two verses, which are also known as a hymn of faith, are very special to farmers because this is so often our experience. When the crops fail and there is no apparent return on our investment, we must put our trust in the Lord. Habakkuk said, "Yet I will rejoice in the Lord of my salvation."

Are you going to walk by faith or are you walking by sight? (2 Corinthians 5:7). Leo Tolstoy said, "Faith is the force of life" and I defy a man to be a successful farmer without faith in God. Faith sees things that are out of sight. Faith takes a basket when it goes to market. Faith says, "He who aims beneath the stars, aims too low." Faith laughs at impossibility. The most beautiful thing is that faith begets faith. The more you walk by faith, the more faith God gives you. The more faith God gives you, the more you please God, because you cannot please Him without faith.

How do you think Noah must have felt building that gigantic ship by faith, in simple obedience to God, when there had never been rain on the earth before? And it still didn't rain – not until his entire family were on board, and the Lord closed the door. Then the rain started falling for forty days and forty nights. That is why God loved Noah so much. He was a man of faith.

Greater works

"Most assuredly, I say to you, he who believes in Me, the works that I do he will do also; and greater works than these he will do, because I go to My Father." – John 14:12

This is one of the most incredible statements in the Bible. Jesus is saying that if we believe in Him, we too will do the same works that He did, and even greater, because He has gone to His Father. He says in verse 14, "If you ask anything in My name, I will do it." Here is a promise that the Lord will honour the spoken word of His servants, by the power of His Holy Spirit.

Theologians may try to explain that away but they argue in vain. You cannot explain it away. Jesus said, "Anything." If you keep his commandments, revival will enter into your soul. Duncan Campbell, who saw a mighty revival take place in the Hebrides on the West Coast of Scotland, said, "The definition of revival is a people saturated with God." When God becomes everything in your life, Jesus says you'll do even greater things than He did. That is quite an awesome statement. Today, spend time with God. Take God's Word literally into your inner being. Meditate, pray, wait on God and then go into the world and do whatever He tells you.

The blessing of obedience

"Behold, to obey is better than sacrifice, and to heed better than the fat of rams." – I Samuel 15:22

The Bible says that rebellion is as the sin of witchcraft, and it is a sad fact that many people of God have fallen through the sin of disobedience. Saul, the first king of Israel, lost his crown because of disobedience and he also lost the anointing of God.

An old hymn says,"Trust and obey for there is no other way to be happy in Jesus, but to trust and obey." Are you trusting God in your life today? Are you believing God to answer your prayers? If you are walking in obedience, He will not let you down. He has never let anyone down but He requires that we be obedient. I know it is not always easy, especially when we see things not turning out the way we think they should. Often we are tempted to make a plan and alter what God has told us to do. It is a big mistake to try to help God. Oswald Chambers says, "After obedience, what? Obedience is the end." There is nothing after obedience. God calls us to obey and He will do the rest.

In Luke 6:46, the Lord says, "Why do you call me Lord, Lord, but you do not do the things which I say?" Do what the Lord has told you to do and you will find that your life will change for the better. Even at the risk of being thought a fanatical person, we must still obey what God tells us to do.

Obedience is what God is calling us to today. Just do what the Lord says and you'll find that your whole situation will change for the better. Then don't be slow to give God all the praise, honour and glory when you see your life starting to prosper.

The people who know their God shall be strong

"...but the people who know their God shall be strong, and carry out great exploits." – Daniel 11:32b

D L Moody was walking down a street in New York one day with a pastor. As they were talking the man of God commented: "The world is waiting and wanting to see what God can do through one man whose heart is totally yielded to him." His words gripped Moody's heart and that night he could not sleep. "Lord," he prayed, "I'll be that man." God used that farm boy to touch the world. He preached to over 100 million people without any computers, films, or satellite TV. Whole trainloads of people followed him from city to city wherever he preached.

Oswald Chambers says, "When we choose deliberately to obey Jesus, He will tax the remotest star and the last grain of sand to assist us with all His Almighty power." The devil uses fear as a weapon to stop believers being used by God. Fear causes paralysis. Unbelief causes doubt, but when someone believes God, there is nothing too difficult for him or her to achieve.

Today, as you go out and face whatever challenge there is in front of you, know that God goes before you, God goes with you and God goes in you. There is nothing you need to fear. William Carey said, "Attempt great things for God and expect great things from God." This English countryman founded the Baptist missionary movement and went to India with his wife and children to move mountains for God.

Do not be fearful of tackling the impossible for the King of Kings, through faith.

Consider your ways

"Now therefore, thus says the LORD of hosts: 'Consider your ways!' –
Haggai 1:5

God records a complaint in the book of Haggai. "You live in panelled houses but my house is in ruins," He says. That is why the heavens are withholding their dew and the earth is withholding its fruit. It is also why you have sown much but reaped little. You eat but are never full – you drink but your thirst is not quenched. You earn your wages but you put it into a bag full of holes.

The Lord says to us this morning, let us consider our ways. Let us put God first, our families second and our ministry third – in that order.

A very wealthy farmer died and left his farm to his son, completely free of debt. The son planted a beautiful crop of wheat but instead of reaping the wheat, paying his expenses and living on the profit, he listened to an investor. This man told him not to pay his income tax but rather to buy a new fleet of tractors. He reasoned that this expense would be totally tax deductible and he got himself into major debt as a result. He planned to buy the fleet on hire purchase and pay it off. What he had not planned on was that the interest rate would skyrocket. As a result, he was unable to meet the repayments and he was forced to file for bankruptcy. Instead of getting his priorities in order, paying the tax man his due, keeping his tractors which were in perfectly good condition and enjoying the fruit of his labour, he lost everything.

The Lord says to you and me this morning, consider your ways. Pay unto Caesar what is Caesar's and pay unto God what is God's. God will do the rest.

Leave it to God

"Casting all your care upon Him, for He cares for you." – 1 Peter 5:7

Are you someone who worries a lot? Are you worried this morning? Do you have a problem with ulcers? Do you have a problem with sleepless nights? Please, stop it today! Worry is a killer! Worry disturbs the peace of mind. Worry provokes people to make unwise decisions.

What is worry? The dictionary says worry is to be anxious or uneasy, especially about something that is potentially dangerous or uncertain. If you belong to the Lord Jesus Christ you need to repent because for a believer, there is nothing uncertain. The future is in God's hands. Worry will cause us to panic. Some specialists are of the opinion that 90% of all sickness is psychosomatic, brought on by worry. The devil is a liar. We need to believe the promises of God today in order to expel that thing called "worry."

One of the most important ways to be set free from worry is to put God in perspective with life. Who are we, and who is God? God IS everything. He is life. There is nothing impossible for Him. In fact, your very days have been numbered before you were even conceived in your mother's womb.

Some of us worry about our children and put tremendous pressure on them to perform well at school. In fact, there are some parents who want their children to do well because they themselves failed at school. Stop worrying and let them do their best. Their best, irrespective of the results, is good enough for God and it should be good enough for us. Stop putting pressure on your wife, your children, your husband. Let's rather commit ourselves to Christ today and make a commitment and covenant to do our best and leave the rest to God. Worry will disappear and evaporate from your life.

The armour of God

"Some trust in chariots, and some in horses; but we will remember the name of the LORD our God." – Psalm 20:7

I have heard many times about people who have shouted out the Name of Jesus in times of extreme difficulty and the Lord has saved them.

The late William Duma, a Zulu preacher from Durban, South Africa, was a small man in stature but a mighty man in the Spirit. He was on his way home one night in his little motor car when he was stopped by gangsters. They had put a big log across the road and when he stopped the thieves ran at him with steel pipes, knives and revolvers. They told him to hand over the keys of his car and were about to kill him, when he looked up at them and said with fire in his eyes, "Do you know who I am?" He spoke with such authority that the thieves dropped their weapons and ran as fast as they could back into the bush. The little man moved the log, got back in his car and drove home safely to his house. He knew who he was in Christ. He knew that Jesus Christ was his Defender, his Lord and his God.

Today, my friend, as you go out, put on the whole armour of God. Your weapon is the Bible, the inspired Word of God. Take up the shield of faith, the helmet of salvation, the breastplate of righteousness. Clad your feet in the shoes of the gospel of peace. Go out rejoicing, covered by the blood of the Lamb, knowing that nothing will happen to you without God's permission.

The secret of contentment

"Not that I speak in regard to need, for I have learned in whatever state I am, to be content." – Philippians 4:11

People are not generally content. They are always striving for something they cannot have. Paul, however, says that he learned to be content whatever state he was in. Whether he was with wealthy or poor people, whether he was rich or poor, hungry or satisfied, he had learned to be content.

People come from far and wide to work at the mission station on Shalom. Some come for a season, others come for longer, but one thing we have realised is that people need to be content within themselves before coming to work here. For example, if someone comes to work in the orphanage and they are expecting to receive a reward from the little children, they will be disappointed. It is not an easy task.

Some desire to come with me to preach the gospel. If their reward is going to be in the response they see when people give their lives to Jesus, they will be disappointed. The people that stay, come here because God has told them to come. They know that their reward is in heaven. Their reward on earth is found in being obedient to the call of God on their lives.

Can you say today that you have learned to be content in whatever state you find yourself? If you cannot, ask yourself, "What am I doing and why am I doing it?"

I trust that you will be able to say, "I'm doing it because the Lord has called me and because of the love and relationship I have with Him. Whether it succeeds or fails is of no consequence to me. What is important to me is that I'm doing what the Lord has called me to do."

That is the secret of contentment.

JUNE

Renewing your strength

"But those who wait on the LORD shall renew their strength; they shall mount up with wings like eagles, they shall run and not be weary, they shall walk and not faint." – Isaiah 40:31

How are you feeling today? Are you feeling weary and out of sorts? The Lord says if you wait upon Him, He shall renew your strength. As a young man, while I was learning to be a farmer in bonnie Scotland, I was sent out with an old tractor driver to collect a load of grass silage. When we arrived at the silage pit we opened it up and with two massive pitchforks started to load the trailer. I was about nineteen years old. The old farm-hand working with me must have been in his late sixties. He was wiry and tough as old boots. I said to him, "Sir, please sit down and let me load the trailer for you." He smiled and said, "Nah, Nah, Laddie, I'll do my bit and you do your bit." With that he took his jacket off and started loading.

The old man would take one forkful – I would take three. Within ten minutes the perspiration was pouring off my face. He never even had a drop of sweat on his. Within twenty minutes I couldn't lift another forkful. When we had a massive load of silage on the back of the trailer, I thought, "Well, thank goodness, that's finished." He said, "No, get on the trailer and tramp it down flat." We tramped the silage until it was a foot high and then started all over again. Halfway through the afternoon he stopped and said, "Let's have a rest." I could hardly move by this stage. He drank his tea, lit his pipe, and after a few minutes said, "Well, Laddie, we'd better get back to work." I was exhausted and he eventually completed loading the trailer himself. That old man knew how to wait and to pace himself. I, as a young man, had no idea whatsoever.

The Lord says to you this day, "Wait upon the Lord and your strength shall be renewed." Do things God's way and in God's time, and you will never tire.

Going in God's strength

"I can do all things through Christ who strengthens me." – Philippians 4:13

When we allow the Lord Jesus Christ to take over our lives, we have a different perspective on things. It is no longer me, but Christ in me, who is going to do the job.

Many years ago I handed over my farming concern to the Lord Jesus Christ because I felt I could not carry on any longer in my own strength. The pressure and the responsibility were becoming too much and I felt that things were coming apart. At that time our farm was very small, without any ministry, school or orphanage. How is it then that we are now overseeing something about ten times as big, if not bigger? We are also writing books and holding preaching campaigns all over the world. How are we managing? The answer is that Christ Jesus has become my strength.

Today, make sure that it is the Lord who is giving you the strength, the vision, the energy to do the job you're doing, and then enjoy it. Draw your strength from Him and allow Him to take responsibility. In other words, it is as if you are driving a car down the road. Stop the car immediately, get out, walk around the other side and get into the passenger seat. Ask the Lord Jesus to drive the car, and do not become a back seat driver.

Do what you can and leave the rest to Christ. You will see the amazing change in your life, your farming concern, your business, and, most of all, in your family.

Satisfaction

"Indeed I have all and abound." – Philippians 4:18a

Isn't this a beautiful scripture? It speaks about someone who is full to overflowing. He abounds and has all.

Satisfaction is something the world craves for. Some of the most dissatisfied people I've ever met are wealthy, famous people. They always want more. I have some farm workers who don't have two brass farthings to rub together and yet they are totally and completely satisfied because they have Jesus Christ as their Lord and Saviour. Satisfaction does not come from worldly possessions, but it comes from within.

I am always impressed by the attitude of a very famous South African rugby player who has become a household name in South Africa. Even when he goes to an important rugby test or function, you won't find him wearing his Springbok rugby tie. He won't be found sitting in the President's box either. He'll probably be outside the crowded grounds, with his two children, watching the big screen with the masses, quite satisfied. That is a man who is fulfilled and does not have to prove anything.

What about you today? Are you striving for recognition? Stop striving and start trusting God like Paul did. Stop always reaching for the stars. Be satisfied where you are and God will promote you in His good time. Then people will see the power of God in you, as they did in Paul. Then you will be able to say, "I have all that I need. I am full and I abound."

Learning from the lowly donkey

"Tell the daughter of Zion, 'Behold, your King is coming to you, lowly, and sitting on a donkey, a colt, the foal of a donkey!'" – Matthew 21:5

Our blessed Redeemer came into Jerusalem, riding a lowly donkey – a colt. He did not come riding a white Arabian stallion, a beautiful military horse. A colt is a young male donkey, not yet broken in. That is a miracle in itself.

We have donkeys on our farm we are training to pull carts to save on the price of diesel. I know from experience that riding a young colt is very difficult indeed. Yet when our precious Jesus got onto a young colt and rode into Jerusalem, there is no record that it tried to buck the Lord off.

An old gentleman, for whom I had the highest regard, used to drive with me into the countryside. Whenever he saw a donkey on the side of the road, he always raised his hat. "Uncle Johannes," I asked him one day, "why do you do that?" He said, "Because that is the animal that carried my Master." My dear friend, have you noticed that every donkey has a cross on its back made up of a line down its spine and one across its shoulders. It is the only animal in the Bible we know of that carried the King of Kings and the Lord of Lords. It is a lowly animal that endures a lot of abuse. It is also extremely stubborn and will do nothing unless it wants to.

Are there lessons we can learn from the lowly donkey? I believe so.

1. Unless the Lord calls us to do something, let us not move.

2. Let us have servants' hearts.

The donkey is a servant. It is prepared to fetch and carry. It doesn't always have to be in the limelight and it had the most privileged opportunity of all. It carried the King of Glory into Jerusalem on its back.

Hungering for the Word of God

" ...and the Word was God." – John 1:1

I've just finished reading the story of a little girl by the name of Mary Jones. This young lady had such a desire to own a Bible that she saved up every penny she could for six years. She was told she could read the Bible at a neighbouring farmer's house in the meantime, if she could learn to read. She made it her business to learn how to read and write, so determined was she to read the Word of God. After school she often walked to the farmer's house and sat in their parlour, avidly reading the Bible. When she was about fifteen years old, she heard there were Bibles for sale in a neighbouring town. She walked barefoot for over one hundred and ten kilometres to buy a copy.

Unfortunately, when she arrived at the minister's house, there were none available. She wept bitterly and the minister was so overwhelmed by her passion that he said, "I cannot but give you a Bible." That Bible is now kept in a glass case in London at the Bible Society. As a result of that young girl's passion to read God's Word, the minister was so moved that he founded the Bible Society, which has provided Bibles for people all over the world.

Do you have such a hunger to read God's Word? My prayer for you today is that God will make that hunger an insatiable one.

If you read His Word daily you will never lose your way in life. It will prove to be your compass and "a lamp unto your feet." (Psalm 119:105).

Learning from the busy ant

"Go to the ant, you sluggard! Consider her ways and be wise." – Proverbs 6:6

As a farmer, I believe the Lord when He says that a fig tree producing new leaves is a sure sign that spring is on its way. The fig tree is symbolic of Israel but the Lord also stressed many other signs pointing to His soon return. Every sign He told us to look out for is coming to pass – among them famine, earthquakes, droughts, floods, pestilence, disease, wars and rumours of wars.

But that does not mean that we need to stop working. If you look in the Bible there is not one scripture that talks about "retirement". Even as I challenge the young men and women to gird up their loins and go into battle for the Lord, I am aware of elderly ladies with their snow-white hair. "You may not be able to get out into the battlefield," I tell them, "but you can pray." I have the privilege of having one of those intercessors in my own ministry at Shalom. I regard Peggy O'Neill as one of our "big guns," because while I'm up in the front preaching, she is in the back praying.

I telephoned a dear old man this morning and thanked him for his encouragement, prayer cover, and financial support in the work we're doing. He said to me, "Angus, I cannot go down the well any longer. I'm too old. But I can stand at the top and hold the rope."

Let us today learn from the ant. Have you ever seen a lazy ant or an ant just basking in the sun? I've never seen a lazy farmer stay on the land for very long. Jesus is coming. Work while it is still day.

God-given authority

"And Jesus came and spoke to them, saying, all authority has been given to Me in heaven and on earth." – Matthew 28:18

Jesus told to us to go out into the world and make disciples and He gave us His authority to do so. Are you using the authority that God has given to you?

When a cow has difficulty giving birth, the first thing we do is get a bucket of hot water and plenty of soap. Then we strip down and soap our arms before putting one arm inside her to free the calf. Sometimes the calf will come backwards, or the head will be pushed back and we have to put it back into the womb in order to allow the head to come out straight. But the most important thing we do is to bow our heads in prayer and ask the Lord Jesus Christ to take control of the calving procedure. Then we give Him all the praise, honour and glory, as the little calf comes shooting out of the mother. When it starts coughing and snorting, we put it down in the straw and allow its mother to clean it. Like a good mother she forgets about all the pain, as she works with her little calf. How we thank God for the authority He has given us in heaven for our daily lives.

Many a time we have stood on the Word of God when a hailstorm has come towards the farm. In the Name of Jesus, we have rebuked the devourer and trusted the Lord to protect our crop. Even this morning you can use that authority. You can start calling those things that aren't into being as if they were, like Abraham, the father of faith.

Let us use the authority Jesus has freely given to us.

Jesus is alive

"He is not here; for He is risen, as He said." – Matthew 28:6

"He is risen," the angel of the Lord told the women who were looking for the body of Jesus.

Where are you looking for the Saviour today? Do you honestly believe He is risen, or do you believe He is still in the tomb? The way some of us act, talk and behave behind closed doors makes one think that we have forgotten that He is risen.

He is alive and in our midst. Everything we do and say the Lord sees and hears. Many of us must mend our ways. We must repent and realise there is no place you can hide from God! If you climb the highest mountain, He is there. If you go into the deepest valley, He is there. If you go under the sea, He is there. If you go into outer space, He is there. If you love the Lord, Christ lives within you.

The Lord reminds us today that His Son has risen from the dead. The God you are praying to this morning is alive. He's well aware of your situation, whether it be on the farm, in the factory or at school. He knows, because He's alive. His promise to you and me is that He will go before us and make a way for us in the wilderness.

Speak to Him today. He is not a statue or a figurine. He is not an idol. He is the only living God and His name is "I AM" – the ever-present self-existent One. He is waiting to hear from you and ready to listen to every word you have to say.

Learning from the humble dove

"Then the dove came to him in the evening, and behold, a freshly plucked olive leaf was in her mouth; and Noah knew that the waters had receded from the earth." – Genesis 8:11

The dove is a very special bird. It symbolises peace. Shalom, the name of our farm, means peace and our logo is a dove. It is a faithful bird, unlike the raven, and it brought back an olive leaf after the great flood to show Noah that there was indeed hope.

Are you and I showing any hope to a dying world? When people tell us that our country is going to the dogs and that there is no hope, are we like the raven that just flies to and fro? Or are we like the dove that brings back an olive leaf and says there is hope, there is another chance, because God is still on the throne?

The dove also symbolises the Holy Spirit. When our Lord Jesus was baptised in the river Jordan and He came up out of the water, the Bible says the Spirit of God descended from heaven "like a dove" upon Him. (John 1:32).

As I am writing, I can hear a dove cooing in the background. What a serene, peaceful sound. I've also been told that the dove only has one partner in life. What a testimony in an age where divorce is the order of the day and a lot of people do not even bother to get married any more. They just shack up together and, when they get tired of each other, they find another mate. We need to learn a lesson from the dove. It is an honourable bird. It mates once only in a lifetime. How are you with your mate today?

Let us go out into the world and be like the dove that brings hope, love, peace and, most of all, the power of the Holy Spirit.

Wisdom and the Word

"Let the word of Christ dwell in you richly in all wisdom..." – *Colossians 3:16a*

It is not education, but the Word of God that makes a man truly wise.

I believe it was Lloyd George, a British Prime Minister, who said, "Education without God makes clever devils!" Today, let me encourage you to let the Word of God dwell in you richly in all wisdom. Those of you who are family people – mothers and fathers – I hope today you took time to read the Word of God with your children before they went to school. If you want them to be wise, remember it is the Word of God and not the fruit of man's intellect that produces true wisdom.

In South Africa, the schools are teaching our children to use condoms in order to avoid getting infected with AIDS. They even hand out condoms to the children to go home and experiment with. Children learn about intercourse when they are hardly old enough to understand what the word means and the result is an increase in immorality. If you sleep with someone you are not married to, you are a fornicator and the Bible says that fornicators are going to hell. Let the Word of God dwell in you richly today. Tell your children that the Word of God says sex is reserved for marriage partners only.

Many people have told me that they have difficulty memorising the Bible. If you feel that way, ask the Lord this morning to refresh your memory. Get a little card and write a memory verse on it. Let the word dwell in you richly and you will find some amazing changes taking place in your life. You will not make so many rash decisions. You will be reluctant to lose your temper as quickly as you normally do and evil thoughts will not find a lodging place in you.

On a short contract

"Set your mind on things above, not on things on the earth." – Colossians 3:2

We live on the earth but we are not part of the earth. We are sojourners, travellers, and citizens of a foreign land. This is not our home. We are passing through and we must refuse to get too settled in this life.

I love my farm with all my heart. My dear wife, Jill, and I developed it out of overgrown bush. We built our little house of wattle poles and mud, dug our own spring for water and cleared the land and ploughed it. We run cattle, grow maize, cabbages, vegetables and timber. We have three dams, a pond and paddocks with beautiful grazing. We run horses on the farm as well. It is a beautiful place. Even as I write, right now, I can hear the birds singing in the trees. But it is not my home! I'm going home to heaven.

I often think about my loved ones who have gone before me – my father and mother, with whom I had the privilege of praying the sinner's prayer, my little nephew, Alistair, who fell off the tractor I was driving and who is waiting for me in paradise, and many brothers and sisters in Christ who have gone ahead. I cannot wait for that great day of reunion. No matter what the government might say, whether it is for or against the farmer, for communism or capitalism, it is no concern of mine. My concern is heaven. I will try, with all of my heart, to be the best citizen I can be on earth, but I am here on a short contract. When my contract expires, I am going home.

How about you?

The tyranny of self

"For you died, and your life is hidden with Christ in God." – Colossians 3:3

When John Wesley, that mighty man of God, was over eighty years old, he was still wrestling with "the lust of the flesh". The flesh is indeed very, very strong. We continue to war against the lust of the flesh all our lives...

God says, "... you died, and your life is hidden with Christ in God." How hard it is for us put the flesh down, to put others before ourselves and to prefer God. But when we can die to self, then we have liberty indeed. Then we can fly like an eagle and do things we never dreamed of because we are no longer concerned about what people think of us or how we are going to fare.

Things like self-centredness, greed, fear of man, shyness, and inferiority become of no consequence and we are only concerned about one thing – the reputation of our blessed Lord and Saviour, Jesus Christ. That is what happened to Peter on the day of Pentecost. He forgot himself. He died to self and lived for Christ and the result was three thousand souls for Christ when he preached his first sermon.

Our biggest enemy is not the devil. It is our own self. Today, ask God to help you die to self and to live a new life, one which is hidden with Christ in God.

Learning from a little lamb

"Behold! The Lamb of God who takes away the sin of the world!" – John 1:29b

I think a newborn lamb must be the most beautiful young animal of all. When the mother has cleaned her little lamb and licked it into a white fluffy ball, it is so lovely and clean smelling that you just want to touch it. It is also the most defenceless animal. Our precious Jesus was referred to as "the Lamb of God who takes away the sin of the world."

I have kept sheep and cattle. If you want to catch a young calf to dehorn, dose or inoculate it, it fights, kicks and makes a tremendous din. A little lamb, though, is totally defenceless. It will stand there and virtually let you do anything to it. It will not even try to defend itself.

Doesn't the Bible talk about Jesus being like "...a lamb led to the slaughter"? A lamb is the only animal that will not put up a fight. It will let you slit its throat without even trying to defend itself. That reminds me of Jesus when He stood before Pontius Pilate. The Bible says He never uttered a word. He was totally defenceless. He died on the cross of Calvary so that your sins and mine could be forgiven.

Next time you see a little lamb, spend time and think about "the Lamb of God who takes away the sin of the world."

Are you a settler or a pioneer?

"The LORD our God spoke to us in Horeb, saying: 'You have dwelt long enough at this mountain." – Deuteronomy 1:6

The Israelites were pastoral people. They did not plough the land or grow crops. When they left Egypt, they were pioneers en route to a promised land. Ask yourself the question today: are you a settler or a pioneer?

We are sojourners in a foreign land. This is not our home! We are simply passing through. The Lord says to us that we must hold lightly to the things of this world. After the Israelites had spent some time at Mount Horeb, the Lord told them to move on.

Do you have any goals for your life, or are you just going to keep going around the same mountain? The Lord says you must go on. There are greener pastures ahead. He wants you to accomplish greater goals for Him. It is time for us to move on and take possession of the big mountains.

One of my heroes in the Bible is Caleb. When Joshua offered him his inheritance he was already over eighty years old and his response was: "Give me the big mountain where the big giants dwell." At Shalom we say if your goal (vision) does not scare you, it's not big enough. May I challenge you today to set goals for yourself that you know you cannot achieve in your own strength, but only by the grace and power of the Holy Spirit in your life? We are more than conquerors through Christ Jesus, who strengthens us.

William Carey, the father and founder of the Baptist Missionary Union, said we must attempt great things for God and expect great things from God. I trust as you leave the mountain you are familiar with, you will go on to greater challenges and higher mountains. God will go before you and He will make a way for you.

Justified by faith alone

"Therefore we conclude that a man is justified by faith apart from the deeds of the law." – Romans 3:28

When I read this scripture verse it takes tremendous responsibility and pressure off me. You see, my friend, it's not what we can do for Jesus, but rather what Jesus can do for us, if we allow Him. The Lord wants us today to trust Him.

When I gave my life to Jesus, I didn't experience any lightning flashes, bells or fireworks. On 18 February 1979, I made a conscious decision to follow Christ. Together with my wife and family, I walked to the front of a little Methodist church in Greytown, South Africa, bowed the knee, and prayed the sinner's prayer. I repented of my sin and asked Him to direct my paths, to lead and guide me. I cast all my cares upon Him that day. When I walked out of the church, I didn't feel particularly different but I knew I was saved and that the Lord had taken care of all my needs.

Three days later I was walking in the beautiful green corn lands on my farm when the penny dropped. I don't ever again have to do anything to find God's approval. I don't have to keep any laws and traditions to make God love me. All I have to do is believe Jesus Christ is the Son of God, that He loves me and died for me and that He is coming back again. Liberty and a sense of freedom flooded my soul Yes indeed, we conclude that we are justified solely by faith. It has nothing whatsoever to do with our good deeds or the law.

Go in peace today, knowing that because you believe Jesus Christ is your Lord and Saviour, your name is written in the Lamb's Book of Life and you have a beautiful future awaiting you.

Witnessing at home

"... you shall be witnesses to Me in Jerusalem ..." – Acts 1:8b

Our God is a missionary God. His sole purpose and objective is to win souls to Himself, to take people out of the grips of Satan and set them free. "You shall be witnesses to me in Jerusalem" means to start at home. That's the hardest place to be a Christian because in your own home, people see the real you.

Is your family saved? If not, make a decision today that you will put their names on your prayer list and pray for them daily by name until God saves them. There is power in prayer. When men work, they work. But when men pray, God works. Prayer is the most powerful weapon a Christian possesses. Someone once asked Billy Graham what the three main contributory factors to his success were as the world's greatest contemporary evangelist. He said, "First, prayer. second, prayer. third, prayer."

Pray for your family. The Lord will use you to win your family to Christ if you will allow Him to. Whatever rebuff comes your way, never fail to respond in love. Whatever sarcasm or accusation is brought against you by your loved ones, bite your tongue, pray for them and bless them. Sooner or later that most powerful thing on earth called love will destroy any bitterness, hatred, envy or anger and your whole household will be saved.

I had the privilege to pray the sinner's prayer with my late dad and mom, two experiences that I will never forget as long as I live. Today my whole family is saved and I praise God for that. Make it your business to start your evangelism at home.

Witnessing wherever we go

" ...and you shall be witnesses to Me... in all Judea..." – Acts 1:8c

I was flying to Cape Town one day and, seated next to me was a beautifully dressed young Indian lady. I really didn't feel much like speaking to her because I was tired and about to speak at a big conference. However, I could sense the Holy Spirit prompting me to be a missionary for Him. "You are going to a big conference to preach to many people," He said, "but there's a person sitting right next to you who needs to hear from you."

I turned and greeted her and she opened her heart to me. She said that she was the manageress of a large shipping company. She had been to Durban to do business and was returning home. As I listened to her, she shared how tired she was, and weary from being up against so much pressure from male chauvinism. When she got home, she had young children and a husband who were also under tremendous pressure. I was able to speak to her very simply and say, "Well, maybe you need to go home and be a mother and a wife and allow your husband to be the breadwinner." Her face lifted immediately and she said, "That's what I've been wanting to do for so long. That's what I am going to do. I'm going to sit down with my husband and tell him what I want to do." With that we parted company. She wrote me an email some time later saying that things were going so much better. Her husband was very happy that they were going to readjust their lives. Salvation had come to that house because she had put her priorities in order as a Christian.

God says, "Go to Judea and preach the gospel for Me." Wherever we are, that is the place to share the good news.

Witnessing at every opportunity

" ...and you shall be witnesses to Me... in Samaria..." – Acts 1:8d

The Samaritans refused to have anything to do with the Jews. They, in turn, were regarded by the Jews as being totally inferior. God tells us to go to the unlovely and to share the gospel with those with whom we would normally not associate.

One of the highlights of my life was the very first man I ever led to Jesus Christ. I was playing Polo Cross. My game had finished and I was standing behind the posts refereeing another game. I think I'd known the Lord Jesus Christ only a few weeks but the Lord had made such a big impact on my life that my face must have been shining with the glory of God. The man standing with me said, "What has happened to you?" I said, "Jannie, I've given my life to Jesus and become a Christian." I was expecting some rebukes and laughter because he, like myself, was a tough country boy. His face went pale and he said to me, "Angus, I'm coming to see you tomorrow afternoon because I want what you've got."

Jannie duly arrived on my farm the next day. We got into my little truck and went down to the "green cathedral" – the cornfields. I took along a little booklet called "The four spiritual laws" because I had no idea how to lead him to Christ. I was a young Christian myself and I didn't even know how to repeat the sinner's prayer. We went through those four spiritual laws one by one. We were laughing and crying together as Jannie found the Lord Jesus Christ as his Lord and Saviour. A short time later he was involved in a car accident and went home to be with Jesus.

Preach the gospel at every opportunity.

Witnessing to the ends of the earth

"... and you shall be witnesses to Me ... to the end of the earth." – Acts 1:8e

The Lord Jesus Christ has called us to take the gospel to the ends of the earth. God has given me my heart's desire and I have the privilege of doing that at the moment. That is why I am so much in love with the Lord Jesus Christ. I am a simple farmer with a very simple education. I remember the first campaign we ever held. I sensed the Holy Spirit asking me, "Can you drink the cup of suffering for Jesus?" "I can by Your Grace," I said. "Are you prepared to be a fool for Me?" "Yes, Lord!" "Are you prepared for people to say all manner of evil about you for My sake?" "Yes, Lord!"

At the fourth question I had to choke back the tears that filled my eyes. "Are you prepared to see less of your family for My sake?" I could only say, "Lord, only by Your Grace." How true those words have been these last years as I have had to leave home more and more. But whoever said that preaching the gospel is cheap? It cost our best friend, Jesus, His very life.

I have put my hand in the hand of God and He has opened unbelievable doors for me. As I write this book, plans are being made for me to go to Australasia, Great Britain, Israel, and Botswana. God is no respecter of persons. He will use anyone who is prepared to trust Him and where He sends you, He equips you. Are you ready today to go wherever He sends you?

Always remember one thing – there is a cost involved.

Deliverance comes from the Lord

"The horse is prepared for the day of battle, but deliverance is of the LORD." – Proverbs 21:31

As a farmer I make as careful preparation as I can but I realise at the end of the day, it's all up to Jesus. I can plant the most beautiful crop – plough the ground, prepare the land, fertilize it, buy the best seed and make sure my tractors are in order – but if it doesn't rain, there is no crop. I can have a crop standing ten feet tall, but if a hailstorm comes over, in two seconds flat it can be wiped out.

"The horse is prepared for the day of battle, but deliverance is of the Lord." Such a true saying! Make sure before you start your day, that you seek the Lord Jesus Christ in everything you plan to do. Without Him it will never succeed. Whether we are preparing for a game of sport, buying or selling property, changing employment, sending our children to another school, or emigrating to another country, we can do the best we know how but, at the end of the day, deliverance comes from the Lord. Put Him first in your decision-making and He will do the rest.

Remember Gideon's army. He started off with thirty-two thousand fighting men and ended up with a mere three hundred. The Lord instructed him to do that so Gideon would not be tempted to touch God's glory and Israel's enemies – the Midianites – would know that it was God who had delivered them. And so it is with you and me today. Our safety comes from the Lord. Do your homework but leave the rest to the Lord Jesus Christ. He has promised to deliver you in the day of battle.

Paid in full

"Blessed is he whose transgression is forgiven, whose sin is covered." –
Psalm 32:1

It is the most exhilarating feeling to be reprieved. Have you ever been to the tax office to pay a large amount of money, only to be told by the tax official, "I'm so sorry, sir, there's been a mistake. You don't owe us anything. In fact, here's a nice cheque for you." David says in the Psalm, "Blessed is he whose transgression is forgiven." It's wonderful to know that God is willing to forgive us for every sin we've ever committed. All He asks us is that we repent and turn away from it.

The Lord also requires us to show the same kind of mercy to those who have hurt us and are in our debt. Are you willing to forgive? You and I have done things of which we are not proud. God has got us off the hook, not once, but many, many times. The least we can do is to forgive those who have sinned against us.

Imagine going out for a lovely meal at a restaurant and being told by the cashier that the bill has been paid in full. You will feel very blessed and thankful to the one who has paid it. Jesus has done that for you and me. He has taken the bills and written in His own blood on each account, "Paid in full." What He has forgiven, He chooses to forget. He asks us to do the same with those who sin against us. "Forgive them their trespasses in the same way I have forgiven you," He commands.

Go out today rejoicing, knowing that He has chosen to pay the full account for you and me. We are in debt to no one for anything, therefore walk in freedom and holiness (the end product of obedience) and you will be blessed.

A little cloud

"There is a cloud, as small as a man's hand, rising out of the sea!" – 1 Kings 18:44a

Elijah, a mighty prophet of God, had prayed and asked the Lord to send rain and break the drought. He sent his servant to see if there was any sign of rain and this was the report after the servant returned the seventh time. "There is a cloud, as small as a man's hand, rising out of the sea."

My friend, when was the last time you prayed to God and asked Him to break the drought in your life? Not only the drought of rain but maybe being unemployed, sick, or depressed. When Elijah's servant told him about the little cloud, Elijah immediately sent him to warn King Ahab that the rain was coming and, indeed, the drought was broken. Today, with satellites and modern weather detectors, we can anticipate when and how rain is coming but it is God who sends it. We have to exercise faith to receive it and Elijah took the Lord at His Word.

The Lord says to you and me today in Matthew 7:7, "Ask and you shall receive." As I am writing, we are experiencing a drought on our farm. On three occasions, we (farm management and workers), have come together and specifically prayed, asking God to send rain. In each case it has rained before the weekend. He is indeed a faithful, miracle working God.

We cannot live without rain and we cannot live without the rain of God in our lives – the Holy Spirit. Let our prayer today be, "Lord, increase our faith" (Luke 17:5). Ask, believing because Jesus said, "Anything you ask in My name I will give to you." (John 14:14).

Ask God to break the drought in your life today.

Reflecting Jesus

"Let all those who seek You rejoice and be glad in You; and let those who love Your salvation say continually, 'Let God be magnified!'" – Psalm 70:4

Is God magnified in your life? Is your salvation demonstrated by your lifestyle so that people recognise it? Does your life testify to the reality of the wonderful news that you are saved, that you belong to Jesus Christ and that if you died today you are going home to be with Him?

Truly, the greatest compliment paid to any believer must be when someone walks up to you in the street and says, "I can see that you walk with God."

Is God magnified in you today? Is the joy of the Lord your strength? When you walk into a room, do you make a difference? Is the fragrance of Jesus evident in your life?

What a challenge for you and me today!

Back to basics

"You shall love the LORD your God with all your heart, with all your soul, and with all your strength." – Deuteronomy 6:5

The basic, fundamental cornerstone of the Christian life is to love the Lord your God with all your heart, with all your soul, and with all your might. Then you can "love God with all your heart and live like you want to", as St Augustine said. You see, if you love God, you will be a godly person and live according to godly principles.

A farmer knows, when he starts battling financially and struggling, that he has got to get back to basics as quickly as possible. There are certain basic fundamentals in agriculture that must be adhered to if one is going to succeed. It doesn't matter how up-market, academic or scientific your farming enterprise may be. For example, no matter how much fertilizer you put on your crop, if there are weeds you will not get a bumper crop. If you don't service your tractor regularly, you will eventually blow the engine, which could cost you half your crop. If you don't pay your farm workers correct wages, the only people you'll attract onto your farm will be the dropouts, thieves and louts who cannot get work anywhere else. Those are basic agricultural principles.

If the Lord Jesus Christ is not the greatest love in your heart, then it doesn't matter if you can speak with other tongues or if you have a healing ministry. How well you can preach the gospel is all to no avail and there will be no lasting fruit. Make sure that your personal relationship with the Lord Jesus Christ is foremost in your life. Have good times of prayer and reading the Word of God and all these other things shall be added unto you (Matthew 6:33). We must get back to basics.

Have you called upon God lately?

"As for me, I will call upon God, and the LORD shall save me." – Psalm 55:16

I like to go up to the mountains as often as possible to hear from the Lord and spend time with Him. I was in the Drakensberg Mountains during December 1994 when the Spirit of God used this scripture to speak to my heart. "As for me, I will call upon God; and the Lord shall save me."

Why is it that when we want an answer we run everywhere but to God? Have you called upon God lately? God will listen to you but He wants you to speak to Him and tell Him your needs so that He can help you out of the situation you find yourself in. That is exactly what the psalmist is saying. He says, "I cry out and I pray to the Lord every morning and at noon and He has redeemed my soul." My dear friend, if God saved the psalmist, why should He not save you?

There is nothing wrong with getting confirmation from fellow Christians concerning decisions you need to make in any area in your life but first go to God and hear from Him. Once you have heard from Him, He will give you as much confirmation as you need from men and women of God you respect. But the first word must come from God.

We have a policy at Shalom Ministries that anyone who desires to work here must first have a distinct word from God. We want to know the scripture, the verse, the chapter and the book before a person is allowed to come because, when the going gets tough, only those people who have the Word of God to relate to, will stand.

Do you have a Word from God this morning for what you are about to do?

Take your problems to the Lord

"But the Lord is faithful, who will establish you and guard you from the evil one." – 2 Thessalonians 3:3

As I am writing, it is a beautiful, rainy, cool morning and I can hear the birds singing. The ground has been totally refreshed. We have just been through two weeks of unbearable heat and watched our corn crop – the main source of our income on this farm – slowly starting to shrink and wilt. We prayed yesterday and asked God to send life-giving rain and last night the Lord granted us close on fifteen millimetres of rain. This morning it is still raining gently. The maize has turned around and is looking like a bumper crop once more.

No matter what your problem is this day, take it to Jesus. Trust in Him and He will bring it to pass because He is a faithful God. He promises to guard us from the evil one.

I defy any farmer to enjoy peace, joy and happiness while he works, without knowing Jesus Christ as personal Lord and Saviour. I know that, if I had not met the Lord when I did on 18 February 1979 I would have either been an alcoholic, or been committed to a mental asylum because the pressure of farming had just become too great. The faithful one, Jesus Christ, has taken all the stress and worry, all the fear and concern out of my heart and has replaced it with joy and love of the land. I enjoy farming and I thank Him today for answered prayer.

The Lord is faithful indeed!

Obedient to our vision

"Therefore, King Agrippa, I was not disobedient to the heavenly vision." –
Acts 26:19

Paul was testifying to King Agrippa about a vision in which the Lord Jesus
Christ spoke to him. The Lord instructed Paul to preach the gospel, to open
the eyes of the spiritually blind and turn the people from darkness to light.
"I was not disobedient to the heavenly vision," Paul told King Agrippa.

Are we being obedient to the heavenly vision that He has given us? There
is nothing I find more encouraging and exhilarating than working with young
Christians but I often find that one of their major problems is that they go
at issues like a bull at a gate but then become tired very easily and
sometimes want to start another venture, without completing the one they
have already started.

Paul said he was obedient to the vision God has given him, that is, to preach
the gospel to the lost. Are you obedient to what God has called you to do?
Or are you looking at pastures you think are greener? If the Lord has called
you to be a prayer warrior, then do it! If He has called you to support the
ministry financially, or to grow food for the hungry, or to pray for the sick,
then do it – and do it until it is completed. Then God will give you the next
project.

Some of us have nothing to do at the moment because God will not give
us another vision until we have completed the one He has called us to.
Maybe this morning we need to get on our knees and say, "Lord, please
forgive me. I'm coming back to the vision." So often we drive up cul-de-sacs,
only to have to turn around, go right back to square one, and start again.
Keep doing what He has called you to do. Be satisfied with that and then
He will promote you to the next degree of vision He has called you to.

The importance of a personal relationship with the Lord

"For I say to you, that unless your righteousness exceeds the righteousness of the scribes and Pharisees, you will by no means enter the kingdom of heaven." – Matthew 5:20

The problem with the Pharisees was that they believed the written Word of God but rejected the Living Word and did not believe that Jesus was indeed the Son of God. Jesus said our righteousness must exceed that of the Pharisees.

The Pharisees kept the sabbath. They paid their tithes in full and lived their lives to the letter of the law. Just like the Pharisees, there are people today who tithe properly, visit the poor, feed the hungry and strive to be obedient to the Bible. What more does God require of them? What the Lord is saying is that unless you have a personal relationship with Him you will never enter the kingdom of heaven. The Pharisees tried to earn their way to heaven by good works and by obeying the law. Jesus says come into relationship with Him first and then, as you walk in obedience with Him, you will obey the law automatically.

How close is your personal relationship with Jesus? Did you speak to Him this morning when you woke up? Do you consult Him in your daily activities? Is He your best friend? Do you have a love relationship with the Lord Jesus Christ? Do you call on Him in times of trouble? Is He your confidante and your chief adviser? If the answer is "no" then, my friend, you are no better than a Pharisee and you will not see the kingdom of God.

You see, the Pharisees knew all about the Bible – the Good Book – but they had never come into a personal relationship with the author of the Book. Do you know the author of the Book?"

Job satisfaction

"Now faith is the substance of things hoped for, the evidence of things not seen." – Hebrews 11:1

Sometimes farmers can be the most negative people you've ever met. I've met farmers who, when the clouds come over say, "Here come the floods." Then the sun breaks through the clouds and they say, "Well, here comes the drought." They are never content and are continually expecting the worst and they often get it.

The Lord wants us to change our mindset. Start to believe the promises of God and refuse to believe the lies of the devil. Faith is the substance of things hoped for. If there is no substance, you cannot expect to get anything. When I put the plough into virgin land and start ploughing for the first time, I believe for a bumper crop. When I purchase cattle at a sale, I believe that they are going to be the best animals I've ever had. Otherwise I would not have bought them.

What have you been thinking about since you got out of bed this morning? Have you been thinking it's going to be a terrible day? Well, my friend, prepare yourself for a terrible day! As for me, I believe it is going to be a great day of opportunity. God is going to open doors for me that no man can close.

Colossians 3:23 says, "Whatever you do, do it heartily, as to the Lord and not to men." When you go to work do it heartily, as unto the Lord. Remember the old saying, "Your attitude determines your altitude." If you are going to work today for the Lord Jesus Christ, you will do it to the best of your ability – and you know something? People are going to notice and praise you and you are going to praise God.

Whatever you do today, do it for Jesus Christ and you will enjoy it. That is real job satisfaction.

Doing the Will of God

"Jesus said to them, My food is to do the will of Him who sent Me, and to finish His work." – John 4:34

If you ask my wife when I am at my happiest, she will tell you it is when I am preaching the gospel of Jesus Christ. God called me to be an evangelist and I am an evangelist-farmer. I can be feeling down, sick, or despondent but the moment I stand on that platform or step into a pulpit and start preaching the Word of God, it is as if fire comes into my very being.

You see, being fulfilled in the work God has called us to is what keeps us going. How often have we heard of healthy working people who have retired and died within a short time, after working for sixty years or more? They retired to sit at home and do nothing, and lost interest in life.

My dear friend, man is composed of body, soul and spirit. When the spirit of a man starts to die, he has nothing left. I heard about an old preacher who was riddled with cancer and yet, every time that man got into the pulpit, he was totally revived and preached his heart out. His meat, his food, was to do the will of God. That's exactly what Jesus said.

Find out what God's will for your life is and do it with all of your heart. That will do you more good than any special food supplements, or any energy-building vitamins. Your energy will come from doing the will of God and finishing your task.

JULY

Things money can't buy

"For the kingdom of God is not eating and drinking, but righteousness and peace and joy in the Holy Spirit." – Romans 14:17

Health, peace of mind, faithfulness at home and joy in one's heart – these are things money cannot buy. The kingdom of God is righteousness, peace and joy in the Holy Spirit. In other words, these are gifts that come directly from God.

My brother Fergus is a golf professional. One day he bought some sports equipment from an elderly wholesaler. The man had made a fortune and was a multi-millionaire, but he was not happy. "It's taken my whole life and cost me my health to make this fortune," he told Fergus. "Now I am spending my fortune on trying to buy back my health and it's not working."

Be sure that you are investing in things that are of eternal value. This world and all it stands for will soon pass away and we can take none of this life's goods with us. "Do not lay up for yourselves treasures on earth, where moth and rust destroy and where thieves break in and steal; but lay up for yourselves treasures in heaven, where neither moth nor rust destroys and where thieves do not break in and steal" (Matthew 6:18–20).

Spend as much time as you can developing relationships, loving one another, preferring your brother and sister to yourself, going the extra mile, and investing in things which produce righteousness, peace and joy in the Holy Spirit.

Guard your heart

"Keep your heart with all diligence, for out of it spring the issues of life." –
Proverbs 4:23

This word from God is more relevant today than ever before because if you do not guard your heart then this corrupt world in which we are living will surely corrupt it. Television programmes and especially the advertisements are leaning increasingly towards pornography and sexual content until you don't know what to allow your children or grandchildren to watch. Every movie seems to have verbal filth, physical violence or sex somewhere in it. Illicit sex and immorality are even creeping into reputable sports and rugby magazines.

We have to guard our hearts because that is where the wellspring of life comes from. The best way to do that is to put on the armour of God every day – to spend time in God's Word and with God's people, thinking and talking about wholesome things. You will become an exception to the rule and people will seek counsel from you as they battle to overcome things like anxiety, depression, fear, bad habits and alcohol and drug addiction.

Romans 10:10 says, "For with the heart one believes to righteousness". That is why it is so important to guard and watch over our hearts and not allow satan to corrupt us from within. I remember reading a billboard at a railway station in Pietermaritzburg that reminded me how subtle the devil is. It said every alcoholic started off as a social drinker.

The Lord says guard your heart diligently for out of it spring the issues of life. Our hearts should always guide and lead us – never our minds.

Standing firm in your faith

" If you will not believe, surely you shall not be established." – Isaiah 7:9b

To a calculating mind, faith is a very hard thing to try to understand. No scientist can adequately explain how Jesus walked on the water. Nor can it be explained in human terms how He was supernaturally transformed on the Mount of Transfiguration and spoke with His Father and the prophets. When five thousand men, plus women and children, were fed with two fishes and five barley loaves – and they collected twelve baskets of scraps afterwards – it doesn't make sense to the human mind. Isaiah says if you do not stand firm in your faith, you will not stand at all. Serving God involves unconditional surrender to His will and Word. Men and women of faith do not question God's Holy Word.

Smith Wigglesworth, a Yorkshire master plumber, was a man of great faith. He had an amazing healing ministry and saw no less than twelve people raised from the dead. How did that happen? He stood firm in his faith and his watchword was: "God said it. I believe it. And that settles it."

Our experience at Shalom has been that the more we believe God, the greater the anointing and the power of God.

Stand on your faith and you will stand forever.

Carried by the Lord

" ...you saw how the LORD your God carried you, as a man carries his son..." – Deuteronomy 1:31

It is wonderful to see a big strong man used to doing hard physical labour, pick up his little child. To watch those big, brown, sunburned, gnarled hands, with rough fingers, gently pick up that little baby – of perhaps three weeks or a month old – and carry the little one close to his bosom is a very moving sight. When I see that my heart melts and I remember how much our Father loves us. He said to the Israelites, "I carried you, as a man carries his own son." How can we possibly not trust in such a wonderful God?

It grieves the Lord when we question whether He is capable of taking care of all our problems. He is more than able to care for our every need and He not only carries us but also protects us as fiercely as any parent.

We have two large bulls on our farm and visitors are usually wary of them because these massive bulls weigh approximately one ton each. I always say, "Don't worry about the bulls, they are harmless. But do you see the cow over there with the young calf? Please don't go near that newly born calf because the mother will attack you." The protective instinct of a parent towards its young is very strong. The Lord says, "Do I not carry you as a father carries his son?"

Know today that the Lord Jesus Christ carries you in His nail-pierced hands, and He will ensure that nothing happens to you without His permission.

Seasoned with salt

"Let your speech always be with grace, seasoned with salt, that you may know how you ought to answer each one." – Colossians 4:6

The Lord is encouraging us to treat each other with much grace, i.e. undeserved loving kindness. Spend a bit of extra time with the Lord today, remembering how much grace He has given to you. Then administer grace to others, loving them in the Name of the Lord Jesus Christ.

Our grace must be seasoned with salt, however. Salt enhances flavour. It also burns when put into a wound. I believe the Lord means that we need to confront some people with the truth and, even if it hurts, it will eventually bring healing. If someone is not working correctly, or behaving inappropriately, we need to confront him or her with much grace, at the same time giving an opportunity to rectify his or her ways. We need to be salty if we are going to be effective. We need to speak the truth. "Sanctify them through Thy truth: Thy Word is truth" (John 17:17).

Make a decision to exercise much grace, seasoned with salt, in all your dealings. Let your yes be yes and let your no be no. You will find that people will respect you for that. Your employees don't have to like you, but they must respect you if you are to succeed in business. Your family should look up to you as an example. They will thank you later on for being salty and speaking gracious words in season.

Hope, patience and prayer

"Rejoicing in hope, patient in tribulation, continuing steadfastly in prayer." – Romans 12:12

This scripture reminds me of a marathon runner, someone who is running a long race. This man paces himself and it makes me think of the character named Christian in "Pilgrim's Progress" by John Bunyan. Christian continued steadfastly on his way home, rejoicing in the hope that he had.

Are you rejoicing today that the end of the race for you – if you are a believer – means heaven? Are you gritting your teeth and going through your time of testing patiently, because you know the Lord will deliver you? He has promised that He will be with you through everything that comes your way and He is faithful to His Word.

Are you continuing steadfastly in prayer? There is power in prayer. Prayer is what gets us through the race. Have you noticed how many senior citizens – godly men and women – spend more and more time in prayer as they get closer to meeting their Saviour? How many great intercessors do you know who are older people? At Shalom our intercessor is close on eighty years old. She prays steadfastly. She is not a physically well woman, but she is a woman of great faith and hope and goes through her tribulations patiently, knowing that God answers prayers. That is how God has told us to walk this road – in hope, with patience, praying continually.

Try it today and see what a difference it will make to your life.

The mark of a mighty man of God

"Humble yourselves in the sight of the Lord, and He will lift you up." – *James 4:10*

Humility is the mark of a mighty man of God. The more God uses a man, the more humble he becomes because he realises he is nothing without God. It is God who promotes, not man. Within five minutes of speaking to a man of God, I can see whether that man is truly God's ambassador, or if he is using God to try to further his own interests.

It is recorded that when Paul Kruger, the Afrikaner leader in the Boer War, was captured and sent to England as a prisoner of war, he was invited to dine with Queen Victoria. This big country farmer sat at the table with the Queen of the British Empire. The table was laden with food in silver and crystal dishes. There were small silver water chalices on the table for each guest to wash their hands in before eating. The farmer, thinking the chalices contained water for drinking, picked his up and drank out of it. The rest of the guests were horrified. While they watched, Queen Victoria picked up her silver chalice and also drank the water in it. My dear friends, that is humility.

The greatest example of humility ever recorded was when our precious Jesus, the King of Glory, took a towel, wrapped it around His waist, filled a basin with water and proceeded to wash the filthy feet of ordinary, common, peasant fishermen, farmers and tax collectors. If you want to be the greatest, He told them, then you must become the least.

Learn to humble yourself. Prefer your brother to yourself, and Jesus will lift you up.

The protection of the Lord

"As the mountains surround Jerusalem, so the LORD surrounds His people from this time forth and forever." – Psalm 125:2

The gladiators of old, who used to fight in the Coliseum in Rome, were men with the ability to fight to the death. They were professional soldiers and lived in towns without walls around them. No one dared come near them. Everybody else scuttled into their walled towns at sundown for fear of bandits and rebel armies, and the big gates would be tightly closed. Not the gladiators. The doors and windows of their homes were never closed. They had no walls around their towns because they were a fearless people. Christians should be exactly like that. We have nothing to fear. As the mountains surround Jerusalem, so the LORD surrounds His people.

In our area many farmers have been murdered in the last few years. God gave me explicit instructions never to go around armed. Some of our farmer friends (and we're not blaming them at all) drive around armed to the teeth. They have automatic shotguns in their pickups and wear revolvers for self-defence. Some of the local Zulu people told me one day that they know why these particular farmers carry firearms. When I asked them why, they laughed and said, "Because they are afraid of us."

Some trust in chariots and some in horses, others hide in the caves, but we will walk securely in the knowledge that the Lord is with us. Forever.

Being an example

"I beseech you therefore, brethren, by the mercies of God, that you present your bodies a living sacrifice, holy, acceptable to God, which is your reasonable service." – Romans 12:1

As a Christian, the Lord says it is your "reasonable service" to present your physical body, your mind, and your spirit, holy and acceptable to God. We must set an example by our lifestyle.

People often come to me for prayer to stop smoking, or for help in controlling their tempers or their filthy language. My dear friend, all you have to do is to STOP. You have to decide that you are no longer going to swear or lose your temper. When you do the possible, God will do the impossible.

I have not sworn ever since the day that I gave my life to Jesus Christ. That is a miracle and it came from God because I asked Him. I had a filthy mouth, as do a lot of farmers before they meet Jesus Christ. God took it from me because it was my desire and my intention to stop swearing. Yes, I've shouted a lot since then but I've never sworn.

The Lord says, "Present your bodies as a living sacrifice." Christians should not dress in a suggestive manner. Remember, your body is a living sacrifice. It's an example. It's an advertisement of how Christians should live.

Make sure your appearance is a good advertisement for the Lord Jesus Christ.

Cleanliness is next to godliness

"Or do you not know that your body is the temple of the Holy Spirit who is in you, whom you have from God, and you are not your own?"
— 1 Corinthians 6:19

The way you dress is very important to a child of God because your body is the temple of the Holy Spirit. Often people will not hear what you say but they will be influenced by the way in which you act and dress. We are supposed to be a living, walking sermon. Please, just because we are farmers or men and women of the land, is no excuse for us to dress in a shabby, unclean manner.

It is a fact of life that what people see on the outside is often what is happening on the inside. As farmers and people of the land, we may have dirty jobs but there is a huge difference between clean dirt and filth.

My late dad worked with steel in his blacksmith's shop, with fourteen-pound hammers and forgers in the fire, all day long. He had the cleanest hands I've ever seen in my life. There was not a speck of dirt under his fingernails. He had hands the size of a baseball mitt, but they were gentle. His fingers had all been broken, but they were clean and manicured at all times.

We do not belong to ourselves any longer. We are "under new management" and we should take care of the Lord's dwelling place at all times, presenting it at its best. Cleanliness is next to godliness.

Walk in the light

"Then Jesus spoke to them again, saying, 'I am the light of the world. He who follows Me shall not walk in darkness, but have the light of life.'"
– John 8:12

If ever this world was in darkness, it is now. The darkness the Lord is speaking about is the darkness of sin, immorality, fear, disease and hopelessness. Our world desperately needs Jesus Christ, "The light of the world."

Robert LeTourneau was bankrupt at the age of forty. He had a small garage and employed a few mechanics. One month he did not have enough money to pay their salaries, but they loved him so much they refused to take anything from him. He got on his knees beside his bed, repented, and gave himself to God, dedicating his business and everything he had to the Lord. From that moment onwards his business turned around.

Robert LeTourneau was the inventor of the turnapull, which is an earth-moving machine – a big scraper – pulled behind a caterpillar. He eventually sold his business and became a multi-billionaire. He was the first businessman in America to fly a twin-engine aeroplane in the 1930s. He used to tithe ninety per cent of his income and keep ten per cent. Still God continued to bless him. His factory covered hectares of land. He sowed large fortunes of money into the mission field and supported mission stations all over the world. This was a man who walked in the light and God blessed him until a ripe old age.

That is the plan God has for you and me. Do things God's way, walk in the light and He will prosper you.

The only way to heaven

"He who believes in the Son has everlasting life; and he who does not believe the Son shall not see life, but the wrath of God abides on him." – John 3:36

The son of one of the farmers in our area was murdered some time ago. My wife, accompanied by our oldest son, went to the funeral. I was away preaching overseas at the time. Jill was very distressed when she told me that the minister stood up in the pulpit and said, "All roads lead to heaven. All we have to do is live a good life and do our best, and we'll arrive there."

Good people don't go to heaven according to the Bible. People who believe that Jesus Christ died for their sin and who receive Him as personal Saviour go to heaven. There are no grey areas when following Jesus Christ. It's either black or white.

There is nothing worse than planting a field of wheat and discovering that half the seed is oats, or planting a field of sunflowers and finding it full of soya beans. There is nothing you can do with a crop like that because it is not compatible. It cannot be mixed together. Jesus says, "You either believe in me or you don't believe in me. If you don't believe in me, the wrath of God will come upon you." The early believers were fed to the lions, crucified, or impaled on stakes, because they would not compromise God's message to mankind.

Our heavenly Father is going to ask us one question only on the day of Judgment. "Do you know my Son? Do you believe that Jesus Christ is the Son of God?" If the answer is "yes," then by grace you'll be saved. If the answer is "no," it doesn't matter what you've done, you are doomed to eternal damnation. There is no other way but the way of Jesus Christ.

Listening to God

"But whoever listens to me will dwell safely, and will be secure, without fear of evil." – Proverbs 1:33

John Wesley was a great evangelist. He travelled all over the British Isles on horseback and literally turned his world upside down.

He didn't start off that way. Even though he was an ordained minister, he had no peace in his heart. He was tormented in his soul because he had not found the truth and entered into a personal relationship with the Lord Jesus Christ. He travelled all the way to the United States of America, preached to the Native American Indians and had no success. On his way home, the ship in which he was sailing was caught in a terrible storm and he feared it would capsize.

The waves were breaking furiously over the deck and, as he watched, he saw a small group of Moravian believers clinging onto the mast, singing hymns and rejoicing in God. They had no fear of evil and were totally secure because they knew God. They were prepared to go to a watery grave, assured that they would meet with the King of kings. This made such an impression on John Wesley that he surrendered his life to Christ a short while later and was mightily used of God.

"Whoever listens to Me will dwell safely and will be secure without fear of evil." Do you have security and freedom from fear? Are you assured that God is in total control of your life? If not, then like John Wesley, seek the Lord today with all your heart and say, "Lord, show me, please, supernaturally, that everything works together for the good of those who love the Lord (Romans 8:28). Give me the faith to believe, irrespective of what happens, that You are in control and I can go out and face this world, knowing that, because I trust in You, I am on the winning side."

14 July

He who wins souls is wise

"And he who wins souls is wise." – Proverbs 11:30b

No matter what profession you are in, you are expected by God to be a soul-winner. Perhaps you feel that you are not called to be an evangelist, but rather a farmer, housewife, lawyer, schoolteacher or whatever. Nevertheless, my dear friend, the Word of God says we are all called to be soul-winners and that he who wins souls is wise.

Paul was a tentmaker by profession. Those who are in secular work often have more opportunities for soul-winning than those who are in full-time employment by the church. During 2003, for example, because I am a farmer I was invited to speak at the Red Meat Producers' Conference in South Africa and I have also been invited to speak at annual general meetings of farmers from time to time. It has been my privilege to speak to farmers across the United Kingdom as well. I love challenging farmers to follow Christ. It is wonderful to see their response as we share the Word of God in love and with conviction.

Ask God to show you someone you can share the gospel with today. Prepare your heart to lead that person to Christ by praying a simple prayer, if necessary. Remember that Romans 10:9 says if we confess with our mouths Jesus Christ and believe that He has been raised from the dead, we shall be saved!

With wings like an eagle

"But those who wait on the LORD shall renew their strength; they shall mount up with wings like eagles, they shall run and not be weary, they shall walk and not faint." – Isaiah 40:31

The other morning I was riding my horse through a forest area onto an open wetland. As I looked up, I saw two beautiful long-crested black African eagles soaring higher and higher into the sky and then swooping down again. They must have been at least six or seven thousand feet up in the air.

I believe the Lord Jesus Christ would have us look at the world today from the perspective of an eagle. We tend to get so involved in our work as we seek to survive from day to day, until we don't know which way to turn. Many of us go round and round in circles, unable to see the wood for the trees. The Lord says to us this day, "Come apart." Sit quietly on the mountainside and look at the whole forest and you will see things with a completely different perspective. If you mount up with wings like eagles, you will see that your situation – which you may regard as a tragedy and an insurmountable mountain – is nothing more than a small molehill.

As those two eagles caught the thermals, the effortless ease of their flight really touched me. They used the wind thermals to their advantage. The Lord wants us to use the wind of His Holy Spirit to our advantage. He promised that He would not leave us fatherless, but that He would send a Comforter. We need to mount up with wings like eagles today and look at our situation from a godly perspective. We will then receive direction and realise that there is nothing that needs to frighten us. If God is for us, who can be against us (Romans 8: 31)?

God uses ordinary people

"But God has chosen the foolish things of the world to put to shame the wise, and God has chosen the weak things of the world to put to shame the things which are mighty." – 1 Corinthians 1:27

Do not despise or underestimate yourself this day. You might say, "I'm just a farmer. What can I do in the kingdom of God?" My dear friend, some of the great patriarchs of the Bible were farmers – for example, Abraham, Adam, Noah, David, Gideon, Saul and Amos. God loves to use the so-called foolish things of this world to put to shame the wise so that no man will touch His glory. It is a great testimony to His power when people say, "That man or woman could never have performed such a miracle. It must be God."

One of the greatest preachers of all times, Gypsy Smith (Rodney Smith), came out of Britain. He was a gypsy and lived in a painted wagon. When he was saved the first thing he did was to buy a dictionary and a Bible, even though he could not read or write. Yet thousands upon thousands heard the gospel through his ministry. One day a lay preacher came to see him. "I don't know what to do any more," he told Gypsy Smith. "I'm totally worn out. I've preached the gospel from Genesis to Revelation. What now?" "Keep telling them what Jesus Christ means to you," responded Gypsy Smith. That was the secret of his own ministry.

Maybe that's all you need to do today as you go about your business. Just keep telling people what Jesus Christ means to you and He will, through the power of His Holy Spirit, use you to bring souls to Himself. Whether you are a housewife, farm worker, factory labourer, or a business executive means nothing to God. God will use the "whosoever" as long as we are obedient and available. Be encouraged.

Count your blessings

"I will bless the LORD at all times; His praise shall continually be in my mouth." – Psalm 34:1

This was a conscious decision that David made. He says, "I will bless the Lord at all times; His praise shall continually be in my mouth," irrespective of his circumstances.

Is that your attitude today? Can you praise the Lord, unconditionally? That is the will of God for you because He is found in the praises of His people. The more you praise, honour and bless Him, the more you will experience His Presence. God is good to His children all the time and it delights Him when we recognise His goodness, even in troubled times. That was Job's testimony. "Even though He slay me, yet will I praise Him" (Job 13:15), he insisted. God blessed him immensely and the outcome of his life was glorious. Read the story in Job chapter 42.

Bless the Lord this morning, my friend, in every circumstance, and see what will happen to your situation. Bless Him, because He has promised He will never leave you nor forsake you. Bless Him, because He promises to be with you even until the end of the earth. Bless Him, because He is yours and you are His. Bless Him, because that situation you are in – that tight spot – cannot last forever. Praise Him continually because He is truly worthy to be praised.

A good way to start the day is to count your blessings. Count them one by one, as the old chorus says. When you start doing that you will find that you have much to thank the Lord for. Bless Him for the sun coming up today, for the birds singing in the trees, for your family, your health, your circumstances. You will find that His praise will continually be in your mouth, and your circumstances will change radically.

Hide God's Word in your heart

"Your word I have hidden in my heart, that I might not sin against You!" –
Psalm 119:11

The wisest precaution to take before we go out into this immoral, volatile, dangerous world is to hide God's Word in our heart. A special word this morning for young people – do what God has told you to do. No more and no less.

To businessmen and women – as you go out to work today it is so easy to bend the rules. Rather render unto Caesar what is Caesar's and unto God what is God's and you will have a happy and prosperous day.

To young students – it doesn't matter what the professor says. If it is contrary to the Word of God, reject it immediately, so that you might become successful and progress in your profession.

To the young sportsman and woman – in order that you might be a winner in the truest sense of the word, hide God's Word in your heart, and you will win – for eternity.

The God of miracles

" ...being fully convinced that what He had promised He was also able to perform." – Romans 4:21

Abraham was known as God's friend because he believed the promises of God. He was "fully convinced" that God would keep His Word.

Are you fully convinced that the Lord is able to take care of every single one of your needs, no matter how big or small? If your faith is weak then spend time with God and read His Word. "Faith comes by hearing, and hearing by the word of God." (Romans 10:17).

Abraham was a wealthy farmer. He succeeded in everything he did because he believed what the Lord said. When he was 100 years old God told him that he would have a son and be the father of many nations, and Abraham believed it.

Are you convinced that the Lord Jesus Christ will perform what He has promised in your life? I'm a simple man and I am convinced that there is nothing too difficult for my God because I have seen Him perform miracles time and time again.

If you are not convinced you are going to reap a bumper crop, don't even plant the seed. If you are not convinced that you are going to finish running the Comrades Marathon, don't start training. If you are not convinced that your family is going to be saved, don't even start praying. But if you are convinced that God is going to answer your prayer, start thanking Him today. If you are convinced that God is going to see you through this time of financial difficulty and you will prosper again, or that He has got the ideal partner in life for you, start thanking Him today. If you are convinced that God is busy healing you of that disease, no matter what anybody has told you, start praising Him and exercising your faith.

The confession of our faith

"Let us hold fast the confession of our hope without wavering, for He who promised is faithful." – Hebrews 10:23

It is very important that we confess our faith, irrespective of our circumstances.

It is easy for me today, as I am writing this book, to hold fast the confession of my faith because, as I walk out the door of my farm office, there is gentle rain falling on the fields on our farm and the maize (corn) crop is standing two and a half metres high. Three days ago it was very hard for me to hold fast the confession of my faith without wavering, because there was no rain to be seen and the corn crop was literally wilting before my eyes.

The Word says, "hold fast" simply because He who has promised is faithful. We prayed, with all our staff, that the Lord would bring rain because without the corn crop there would be no money and therefore no work. We prayed as a body of people, a farming community, and God has honoured us today. The rain is falling gently on my roof as I write this powerful testimony for you.

Do not walk by sight, but by faith (2 Corinthians 5:7) and hold fast, just like the British bulldog. Don't let go. Don't waver. Don't let those legs of yours start getting shaky. God will perform that which He has promised because He is a good God. He is for you and not against you.

Blessings and curses

"Behold, I set before you today a blessing and a curse." – Deuteronomy 11:26

That is the Word of the Lord for us today. He says, "I set before you a blessing and a curse." God has left the choice to us concerning our lives and it is very simple. If we obey His commandments, we will be blessed. If we do not obey His commandments, then we will bring a curse upon ourselves.

People often come to my farm office seeking counsel and prayer. Many times they say, "Why has God done this to me? Why has God taken away my husband from me? Why has God taken my business from me? Why has God allowed this to come upon me?" When we sit down and begin to talk, many of them discover that they have brought a curse upon themselves through slothfulness, mismanagement of money, or lack of discipline in life. I remember giving counsel to a man who said he loved Jesus Christ very much but he still persisted in drinking himself into a stupor time and time again. We warned him that his wife would leave him if he continued to do so. He never heeded our counsel and one day his wife packed her bags and left him.

God sets before us today a blessing and a curse. The blessing comes when we obey what He tells us to do. The curse happens when we make our own plan.

Let us go out into the world today and work to God's plan, obeying His commandments and enjoying the blessings He wants to pour out upon us.

God has no favourites

"Then Peter opened his mouth and said: 'In truth I perceive that God shows no partiality'." – Acts 10:34

The New King James Version says,"In truth I perceive that God shows no partiality."

God has no favourites. He will use the "whosoever" and that is exciting news. You don't have to be a multi-millionaire or a famous personality. You don't have to have an IQ like Einstein, be able to run as fast as Maurice Green, or be as strong as Lennox Lewis. You don't even have to be as great a preacher as Dr Billy Graham. All you have to do is be available.

Perhaps you feel that you are of no use to anyone. You may have gone on pension, and exceeded your "three score and ten years." There is no such word as "retirement" in the Bible. God is still looking for intercessors. Do you realise that Jesus' sole occupation at this very moment in heaven is that of "The Intercessor." He is praying for you and me. Maybe you've just gone through an ugly divorce, or your business has failed. Come to the Lord today in repentance and tell Him that you are ready to do whatever He desires and God will use you again.

What the Lord is looking for is repentance and not remorse. Remorse says, "I'm sorry I got caught." Repentance says, "Lord, give me another chance." God is calling men and women as never before in these last days to do great and mighty exploits for Him, just like Daniel of old.

Rise up mighty man or woman of God, and get back into the fight!

Let your words be few

"Do not be rash with your mouth, and let not your heart utter anything hastily before God. For God is in heaven, and you on earth; therefore let your words be few." – Ecclesiastes 5:2

The other day I heard a beautiful definition of a cynic quoted by a dear friend of mine, Malcolm Gage. He said, "A cynic is someone who knows the price of everything and the value of nothing." There are too many cynics walking around today in this 21st century. They have a lot to say but know little about things of eternal value.

If you don't believe me, just go to a rugby match. My younger son plays first division rugby. He said to me the other day, "Dad, it's amazing how many professional rugby players there are sitting on the sidelines. They know all the moves and exactly what to do, but they've never personally set foot on a rugby field in their lives."

Aren't we just like that? We even try to tell God what to do, forgetting that He is in heaven and we are on earth. We need to start listening more – that's why we've got two ears – and speaking less – that's why we've got only one mouth – and obeying God without questioning Him.

Some tough guys have told me that when they get to heaven one day, they are going to be demanding some answers from God. Oh, my dear friend, those who say that obviously do not know who God is. When we get to heaven, we will be on our faces before the Lord when we hear the mighty voice of our Creator. It will sound like a thousand rivers in full torrent. We will not be asking any questions. We will be pleading for mercy because He is an awesome God.

Our God saves

"Behold, the Lord's hand is not shortened, that it cannot save; nor His ear heavy, that it cannot hear." – Isaiah 59:1

What a beautiful promise from God! The Lord can save us out of any situation and any predicament that we are in because His hand is not shortened or crippled. He is the God who made the sun stand still, adding a day to our calendar so that the Israelites might win their battle (Joshua 10:13).

The Bible says that His ear is not heavy (dull with deafness) so that He cannot hear. He is listening and waiting to hear from you. The trouble is that we are often so busy trying to make a plan and sort things out ourselves that we don't ask Him for help. Our God is a gentleman. He has given us a free will and He will not interfere or intervene unless we ask Him to.

Pray for the lost. Ask Him today to intervene in your marriage, in the relationship between you and your children, in the situation in your country. Ask Him and He will hear. The Lord says in Jeremiah 33:3, "Call unto me, and I will answer you, and show you great and mighty things, of which you do not know (have no knowledge or understanding of)."

Call unto Him today and in expectation and by faith, wait to see the incredible results of your faithful prayers.

The value of a human soul

"For what profit is it to a man if he gains the whole world, and loses his own soul? Or what will a man give in exchange for his soul?" – Matthew 16:26

I used to farm in a Central African country. We had a beautiful farm of three thousand five hundred acres, with a river running down the one boundary. We had barns and sheds, twenty-three workers' houses and a beautiful farmhouse. The farm was ring-fenced and I ran over two hundred and fifty head of cattle there. We also had about a thousand acres of arable land for ploughing.

I sold that farm for what I believed was a good price and we moved down to South Africa. A few years ago I was invited back to the area to preach the gospel of Jesus Christ. My son and I visited our old farm. He was amazed at its beauty. As we were driving out through the gate, he asked me again how much I had sold the farm for. When I told him, he looked at me in amazement.

That country has been ravaged by corruption and, as a result, tremendous devaluation has taken place. The currency is now worth a good deal less than it was when I farmed there. He did a quick calculation. "Dad," he said,"you sold that farm for the equivalent today of one crate of coca cola." I was staggered. Then the Holy Spirit reminded me that the things of this life are so insignificant in comparison to the eternal value of a human soul.

What value do you put on the life of one soul? How do you compare the value of a man who was lost and going to hell but due to your prayers, your love and your testimony, has turned to Christ? There is no monetary value that can be put on the life of a person.

Let us pray that God will give us the discernment and wisdom to put our efforts, time and talents into things that are of eternal worth.

All have sinned

" ...for all have sinned and fall short of the glory of God." – Romans 3:23

There is no one on this earth who is without sin. When you go to church and you see those sanctified looking "pillars" (and sometimes they are caterpillars) sitting in the front of the church, don't think that those are people without sin. The greatest sinners of all are those who tell you that they have lived a good life and never done anything wrong.

Our Lord taught that if you have hatred in your heart for someone, you are guilty of murder, or if you are full of lust you have already committed adultery. If you look at someone's possessions with envy, you are guilty of covetousness and have broken the law of God. The Lord says, "ALL have sinned and fallen short of the glory of God."

The good news is that Jesus is the friend of sinners. He came to save the sick and tormented. Be encouraged today. If there are areas in your life you are wrestling with, confess them to the Lord and allow Him to wash your sins away by the blood of the Lamb. All you have to do is believe that God has forgiven you, repent (which means don't do it again) and start afresh. What a wonderful Saviour we serve. That's why Charles Wesley could write that famous hymn, "My chains fell off, my heart was free. I rose, went forth, and followed Thee."

Praise God for His loving kindness. Praise God for His Son, who has given you and me a new chance this brand new day. Let this be the first day of the rest of your life as you go forward assured that your sins have been forgiven. God has given you another opportunity. Don't waste it.

Serve the Lord with your whole heart

"He who is not with Me is against Me, and he who does not gather with Me scatters abroad." – Matthew 12:30

The Bible says we cannot serve two masters. Either we are going to live our lives God's way, or we are going to do it the world's way. The choice is ours.

James 4:4 says, "Friendship with the world is enmity with God." Whoever makes a friend of the world makes an enemy of God because this world is in rebellion against Him. You have to run your family, your business, your farm and your life according to God's principles. You cannot have your foot in two camps. We, as farmers, know that the most uncomfortable place to be is sitting on the fence.

I always encourage young soldiers to nail their colours to the mast on the very first night that they sleep in their barracks. When it's "lights out," I challenge them to get on their knees in front of all the other sixty-odd soldiers and make a public confession of their faith. The rest of the soldiers might not like them, but they will be respected. The young person who gets no respect is the one who swears, watches blue movies, gets blind drunk one day, and the next day claims Jesus as his Saviour. No one respects a person like that.

Live your life and conduct your affairs according to godly principles at all times and watch God at work in your situation.

Childlike faith

"God is not a man, that He should lie, nor a son of man, that He should repent. Has He said, and will He not do it? Or has He spoken, and will He not make it good?" – Numbers 23:19

Why do people always argue about the Word of God? The Bible says He is not a man – He is God. Men lie but God cannot lie. He cannot be untrue to Himself. What He says stands. He doesn't have to repent (change His mind and go in the opposite direction) because He has not committed any sin.

How much it would simplify our lives if we would concentrate on having childlike faith, believing whatever God says is best for us and for our loved ones, instead of always questioning Him. Imagine an ant trying to question the Lord! We are nothing in the sight of God yet, amazingly, He has created us to be His friends. Let's make a decision today to stop questioning God and start being obedient to His Word.

The Bible says quite clearly that without faith we cannot please God. Faith is believing in something you haven't yet seen, trusting that what God has promised He will do. Our part is to make sure that we have done everything He expects of us – the possible – and He will do the impossible.

Our refuge in the time of trouble

"God is our refuge and strength, a very present help in trouble." – Psalm 46:1

The difference between God and man is that man often leaves you when trouble comes. God, however, says He will be present and He will be your help in times of trouble, no matter what the circumstances. That is why I love God so very much.

When you walk in the world, you think you have many friends, but the moment trouble comes they tend to vanish away like the morning mist, leaving you sadly disillusioned. When you are a prosperous businessman, a champion sportsman, a successful model or beauty contestant, you have lots of friends. When your business goes under, you don't make the team, or you are no longer physically attractive, suddenly the friends of the world just seem to evaporate, don't they? Before I became a Christian I had many social drinking friends. When I stopped drinking alcohol, overnight I had few friends left. Jesus says, "I am your refuge and strength. I am with you especially in times of trouble." You can depend on Him.

There is a beautiful poem called "In His Footsteps." It speaks about a man walking in difficult territory. At one stage he could see only one set of footprints in the sand and he cried out, "Lord, where were You when the going was tough?" The Lord said, "Those are My footprints. I was carrying you."

Let Him be your source of strength if you are going through a time of trouble today and remember, He will never leave or forsake you (Hebrews 13:5).

When two become one

"For this reason a man shall leave his father and mother and be joined to his wife, and the two shall become one flesh.'" – Matthew 19:5

I was privileged recently to conduct a wedding in the foothills of KwaZulu–Natal. The chapel was a reconditioned cowshed and it reminded me that our Lord Jesus Christ was born in a stable. The bride came in five minutes late, as tradition requires, looking beautiful with her bridesmaids and flower girl. It was a wonderful time as this couple made their covenant in the sight of God. It was a glorious afternoon. There were cattle in the paddock, the birds were flying amongst the trees and we truly felt the presence of the Holy Spirit.

This is God's way. A man must leave his father and mother and be joined to his wife in holy matrimony. Then the two shall become one flesh. "Partners" (two people shacking up together) is not scriptural. It is sinful according to the Word of God. To be married in the sight of God, to exchange rings, to make a commitment to love and cherish one another through sickness and health is truly a most beautiful thing.

If you are not married, let me encourage you to be patient and wait for your husband or your wife, if that is the will of God for your life. God always gives the best to those who leave the choice with Him. If you are married, recommit to your marriage and thank God for the partner He has given you.

The secret of abundant life

"Most assuredly, I say to you, if anyone keeps My word he shall never see death." – John 8:51

People all over the world are running to and fro trying to find the way to peace, purposeful living and eternal life. If only they would realise that the answer is found in the Bible.

The Lord says if you keep His Word, you will never see death. By that He means that you will not go to a lost eternity but you will have life eternal, starting now and continuing forever. You do not have to wait until you die to experience the power of eternal life. It affects every area of our lives positively. You see, God has got a pattern for you and me. All He asks us to do is follow that pattern and then we will avoid much suffering and pain.

God says keep His Word, and your marriage will never die. He says, "Husbands, love your wives. Wives, submit to your husbands. Children, respect your elders. Parents, don't antagonise your children." If we live God's way, then we will have the most beautiful family relationships and they will grow from strength to strength. God says that we are not to sleep with another person until we are married to them. Obeying His word will avoid death, pain, suffering, misunderstandings and heartache.

Let us make a quality decision today to live our lives God's Way and to obey His Word. That is the secret of enjoying the abundant life promised by Jesus in John 10:10.

AUGUST

Running with purpose

"They shall run and not be weary ..." – Isaiah 40:31c

Some of the world's greatest runners are still fit and full of energy when they cross the finishing line. Why don't they easily grow weary? Because they train regularly, eat correctly and get enough sleep. The Lord says, "If you wait upon Me, you will never grow weary." If we spend time in His Word, in meditation, prayer, praise and worship, we will find ourselves supernaturally energized as we approach the finish line. My dear friend, we are living in the last days. The race is going to intensify and speed up, and only those who know how to pace themselves in the Lord Jesus Christ will finish strongly.

As Christians – as sons and daughters of the living God – we have got to cross that finish line at full speed. As we grow older in the Lord we should grow stronger. The dictionary says the word "weary" means causing fatigue or tedious (boring). When we wait upon the Lord, we will not get bored or become fatigued. A long-distance marathon runner has told me that one of the biggest pitfalls runners face is losing concentration as they start to become weary. The race becomes tedious, they become fatigued, and they lose sight of the finish line.

That will never happen to you if you have a living relationship with the Lord Jesus Christ. In fact, if anything, you should run faster at the end than you did at the beginning. Train hard by spending time reading the Word of God, eating the Word of God, sleeping the Word of God, speaking the Word of God, and running with the Word of God in your heart.

God bless you today as you go out, running with purpose, with the finish line in sight.

Putting Christ first

"He must increase, but I must decrease." – John 3:30

The greatest prophet that has ever been born, John the Baptist, spoke these words.

John the Baptist was Jesus' cousin, and yet he could say that Jesus must increase and he must decrease. Jesus said of him that he was the greatest man ever born from the womb of a woman. Why is that? I believe it is because John was a humble man, one who preferred God to himself.

Do you put the Lord first in your business, on your farm, your enterprise and your family? Is it more important to you what people think about the Lord than what they think about you or your reputation? Do you govern your affairs in such a way that people can see that you prefer the Lord to your own comforts? John the Baptist did. He said, "I must decrease so that He may increase."

I firmly believe that when Christians start to act like John the Baptist, we will have absolute revival. A man of God said we would have the greatest revolution in history if only fifty per cent of Christians, who claim to have committed their lives to Christ, would turn and begin to follow Jesus properly like John the Baptist.

Preaching the gospel in season and out of season

"But as we have been approved by God to be entrusted with the gospel, even so we speak, not as pleasing men, but God who tests our hearts."
— *1 Thessalonians 2:4*

There is a distinct difference between a son and a hireling. A hireling works for a wage. A son works for his inheritance. A hireling is often a clock-watcher; starting and finishing work on time, seldom doing more than he has to. Sons, on the other hand, usually put their watches in a back pocket and continue with their work until the day is done. That is especially true in farming because it is not a job, but a way of life. Paul says, "We have been approved by God to be entrusted with the gospel, even so we speak; not as pleasing men, but God, who tests our hearts."

Paul was not a hireling. Therefore, when he walked on this earth, he didn't preach the gospel for a wage, nor to please men. He preached the gospel because he was a son of God. We need to be reminded that God has called us to preach His gospel in season and out of season, twenty-four hours a day. There are no "after hours." He has entrusted the gospel to you and to me and we must share it in obedience to His command.

God is testing your heart today. If you fear Him, rather than man, then speak the truth with all of your heart so that people's lives may be changed forever. You and I are accountable to God for what we have done with the gospel of Jesus Christ. Do not say that the preaching of the gospel is up to the evangelist, teacher or pastor. Never forget that Paul was a tentmaker, a working man like you and me.

Preach your sermon today, even if it is by your lifestyle only, but preach it until He comes.

Loving our neighbours

"For all the law is fulfilled in one word, even in this: You shall love your neighbour as yourself." – Galatians 5:14

In farming, we are dealing not only with economics but with the elements and every aspect of life, and it is a wonderful thing to have good neighbours.

Just before South Africa's general election in the early 1990s, we experienced some horrific farm murders and it was an encouraging thing to experience the way in which the farmers stood together during this severe time of testing. A telephone call or an alarm sounding at any time of day or night had the neighbours arriving within minutes

The Lord says you shall love your neighbour as yourself. We also have responsibilities to one another, as neighbours. There's an old farm saying, "A good fence makes a good neighbour." If you don't keep your fences up, your cattle and livestock will stray onto your neighbour's farm and cause trouble, especially when they graze his beautiful prime wheat or the maize harvest waiting to be reaped.

When God asked Cain where his brother was he said, "Am I my brother's keeper?" The answer is, yes, we are. We are responsible for one another. In fact, the Lord says that the whole law is fulfilled when we love the Lord and love one another. We need to look after each other. It's a commandment from God! How far do we go? Jesus says in John 15:13 "Greater love hath no man than this, that he lay down his life for his friends." We have to go all the way.

Preaching the gospel

"Woe is me if I do not preach the gospel!" – 1 Corinthians 9:16b

To preach the gospel is more than an obligation. It is the very life within me. Is that how you feel?

Paul says, "If I preach the gospel, it's nothing to boast about, for necessity is laid upon me." That is how it should be for every believer. It should not be an effort to tell people about your best friend, the one that you love the most. In fact, Paul says, "Woe is me... I am undone... I am unhappy if I do not tell people about Jesus Christ."

People might say you are "over the top." Well, so be it. How were you the day that you first fell in love with your wife? I am sure you could not stop yourself from telephoning her, writing to her, thinking about her and telling everyone about her. Well, so it should be when you fall in love with the King of Kings.

What is preaching? According to Smith Wigglesworth, "Preaching is the Word of God, the Word of power, coming burning hot out of the living mouth of a believing man." By that definition, each and every one of us should be a preacher.

I am at my happiest when I am preaching the gospel. I can talk all day, literally until the cows come home, when I am speaking about our precious Lord and Saviour, Jesus Christ. I never tire of speaking about the King, because I love Him so much. "Woe is me if I do not preach the gospel."

Contentment

"Not that I speak in regard to need, for I have learned in whatever state I am, to be content." – Philippians 4:11

Howard Hughes was once one of the most powerful men in the United States of America and he was known to be a recluse. He held the world record for flying around the world in an aeroplane. He was a man who had done everything and been everywhere, yet he lived in total obscurity. A good looking man, who weighed something like two hundred and thirty pounds, he was married to a succession of famous film stars, yet he died weighing less than a hundred pounds. He was a man totally discontented with his lot in life.

Paul says he had learned the secret of contentment. The psalmist prayed, "Lord, don't make me so rich that I forget You, and don't make me so poor that I have to steal." That is a good prayer.

It is time to stop complaining and thank God for what we have. Let us be content with our lives and stop comparing our lot to others. My wife and I live in a house that we built out of wattle and daub when we first arrived in South Africa. If you compare that with the homes in the expensive parts of Johannesburg or Durban, we would probably be regarded as peasants. However, if you compare us with the millions of people who live in little cardboard shacks in the squatter townships of South Africa, then we would be regarded as extremely wealthy.

Be content with what God has given you and, most of all, be thankful that your name is written in the Lamb's Book of Life. Be thankful that you know Jesus Christ as your Lord and Saviour, for "what shall it profit a man if he shall gain the whole world and lose his soul? (Mark 8:36)."

Be still

"Be still, and know that I am God" – Psalm 46:10

One of the most difficult things to do in the twenty–first century is to be still. Turn on your television and you will see a screen with about ten different channels, all happening at the same time. As you sit there trying to select a channel, your eyes go from one picture to another, until you find yourself racing round the screen, not knowing which button to press.

The Lord says, "Be still, and know that I am God." Why did Jesus go up the mountain so often? Many times His disciples looked everywhere for Him, but He was not to be found because He was being still. He was spending time with His Father, listening to His voice, hearing what was expected of Him and what He had to do next.

So often we forget who God is, because we do not spend enough time with Him. The Bible says that those who know their God shall be strong and carry out great exploits (Daniel 11:32).

You can measure the mettle of a man by the time that he spends with God.

Saved by grace alone

"... all our righteousnesses are like filthy rags..." – Isaiah 64:6

Many years ago there were orders of monks who used to wear horsehair shirts in their attempt to put the flesh down. They whipped and starved themselves to try and bring the flesh into subjection to the spirit but it never worked.

The Lord says all our efforts are like "filthy rags" in His sight. He wants us to come to Him just as we are, with all our problems and inadequacies, lay them at the feet of Jesus and let Him restore, renew and strengthen us. We have to prove nothing to God. He knows us better than we know ourselves, because He created us. He just wants us to love, acknowledge and honour Him, to speak up for Him if necessary, but most of all not try to earn respect or a place in the kingdom of Heaven.

It is so easy, once we have walked with the Lord for a number of years, slowly but surely to start feeling that possibly we have earned a few points in God's estimation because of the righteous life we have tried to live. It doesn't work like that. It is by grace alone – God's totally underserved favour – that we are saved. The Lord says that the first shall be last and the last shall be first in the kingdom of God. None of us can ever earn our way to heaven by good works. Let us thank Him today for His gracious loving-kindness and so great a salvation.

The joy of giving

"And remember the words of the Lord Jesus, that He said, 'It is more blessed to give than to receive.'" – Acts 20:35

Paul said that he did not wish to be a burden to anyone but supplied his needs – and those of the people who were with him – with his own hands. We have many young people at Shalom who have a desire to go into Central Africa into unreached areas to preach the gospel and we encourage them to do so. We also encourage them to become "tent makers," to be men and women who will use their own hands and abilities so as not to put pressure on weak or poor people who have barely enough food to feed themselves.

We are to preach the gospel at all costs but there are many ways of doing so. One way is by giving not only Bibles or food and clothing to the poor, but by showing the love of Jesus Christ in a tangible way. It is more beneficial to give a man a fishing hook and teach him how to fish than to give him a fish; or to give him some seed and teach him how to grow a crop of wheat, rather than give him a loaf of bread.

The Lord said it is more blessed to give than to receive. It is so easy to write out a cheque to appease your conscience. It's much harder to teach someone how to drive a tractor, milk a cow, raise chickens or read and write. What ability or trade do you have? What is your profession? What about using it to help the poor?

Perhaps we need to sit down today and take account of what we are actually doing and giving – not of our money but of ourselves. God is going to ask us one question when we arrive home in heaven: "What did you do with what I gave you?"

Live for the moment

"This is the day the LORD has made; we will rejoice and be glad in it." –
Psalm 118:24

I was challenged by the motto of a private school I spoke at recently: "Carpe diem" (seize the moment). That is the Lord's challenge to us today. Yesterday is gone forever. Some people live in the past. Others are always talking about the future. Jesus says live for the day. "This is the day the Lord has made and we will rejoice and be glad in it."

Let's go out today with a positive attitude. Be like Joshua and Caleb, who came back from the Promised Land with a good report. "It's a land of milk and honey," they said, while the other ten spies groaned, "It's a land of giants."

Thank God for the weather. Praise Him for opportunities to make a difference in our world. When people see you coming, let them look forward to some good news from you, rather than have them avoid you like the plague because you are always complaining.

When people say to us, "I suppose you are expecting another good crop this year," we respond: "Yes, praise be to God. We're thanking Him for it and rejoicing in His goodness." When others tell us that they are cutting back because of the price structure, or the rand/dollar exchange, or inflation, we say, "We're doubling up. Jesus said, this is the day that He has made, so it must be a good day and we're going to give it our best shot." With that kind of attitude you cannot lose.

Enjoy the day the Lord has given you. Expect the most from it and that is what you will receive. Expect nothing and that's exactly what you'll get. Thank Him and praise Him and be glad in it. Tomorrow you may be in heaven!

Watching our words

"In the multitude of words sin is not lacking, but he who restrains his lips is wise." – Proverbs 10:19

My wife and best friend, Jill, often says to me, "Angus, let your words be few, because one day you may have to eat them!" Jill does not speak off the cuff as I do. She thinks before she speaks.

A word spoken in anger or on the spur of the moment, is like a down (goose feather) pillow shaken out and scattered on a windy day. Trying to catch those feathers and put them back into the pillow is as impossible as reclaiming words that have been recklessly spoken. They're out and you can never bring them back. You can tell that person a thousand times that you're sorry, you didn't mean it and you said it in the heat of the moment, but it's done! There is on old saying, "Sticks and stones may break my bones but words will never harm me," but it is totally misleading. It's the direct opposite. Sticks and stones can break your bones, but they can be repaired and healed. Words, however, can never be taken back.

Someone who speaks a lot normally gets himself into big trouble and will say things he or she will regret. That's why the Lord says, "In a multitude of words sin is not lacking." A wise person (like my wife) restrains her lips so that she doesn't have to keep apologising.

Be careful what you say today and you will find that your day will go well. Count to ten before you vent your frustration. Ask yourself, "Would Jesus say that?" If the answer is "No," don't say it. "Death and life are in the power of the tongue and those who love it will eat its fruit." (Proverbs 18:21).

Being the fragrance of Christ to our world

"Therefore you shall be perfect, just as your Father in heaven is perfect." –
Matthew 5:48

The Lord expects us to be God-fearing people. It is not acceptable to say, "Well, that's just the way I am and I can't change." You can change; furthermore you must change, because the Lord said so. We can do all things through Christ Jesus who strengthens us (Philippians 4:13).

When you spend time with someone, you tend to become like him or her. If you had to spend a lot of time with Dr Billy Graham, you might become interested in evangelism. Or if you had the opportunity to spend time with Albert Einstein, you might become fascinated with mathematics. In the same way, if you spend much time with your heavenly Father, you will become a godly person.

This is a time when the Lord commands us to come apart and be separate, shunning compromise and striving for the perfection of our Lord. We need to socialise with people who love the Lord so that we can become more like the Lord Jesus Christ, a beautiful fragrance wherever we go.

There are many church leaders who have no credibility with the world because they are dabbling in politics, or collaborating with the New Age philosophy, or some other kind of liberal theology that permits homosexuals to live together, condones pornography and encourages sin. We will not be amongst those but continually strive to be perfect as our Father in heaven is perfect. When people want to differentiate between light and darkness, they will know to whom they should come.

God's people

*"Then I will say to those who were not My people, 'You are My people!'
And they shall say, 'You are my God!'"* – Hosea 2:23b

What an honour for God to say, "That person belongs to Me. He is my son. She is my daughter." God says today that you are His people, if you love Him with all your heart.

It is also an honour when people recognize us as God's people. I was speaking at a campaign in the Eastern Cape of South Africa, in a small farming town called Komga, when a dear brother in Christ paid me possibly one of the greatest compliments I've ever received in my Christian walk. He said, "Angus, I see you as a companion of Jesus." That touched me so deeply I wrote it in the flyleaf of my Bible. If he had said, "You are a great preacher," or "You are a greatly gifted man," or anything else, it would not have touched me.

Can you say today, "Lord, you are my God"? Or do you serve many different gods? The Bible says that you can only serve the one true God, because our God is a jealous God. If you really want to be effective for Him you need to acknowledge Him solely as your Lord and God. You cannot serve two masters and expect Him to call you His people. If you want to be a companion of Jesus Christ, you cannot serve ancestral spirits and at the same time acknowledge Jesus Christ as Lord. Ancestor worship is very much part of the Zulu culture, a people I love dearly. So much so, I am known as a Zulu with a white skin. But when we become Christians, we cannot worship our ancestors or follow our own cultures any more (where they are unbiblical). Our culture is that of a Christian.

The Lord says, "You are my people." Can you respond today and say, "And you are my God"?

Overcomers

"Who is he who overcomes the world, but he who believes that Jesus is the Son of God?" – 1 John 5:5

Even as I write this book, the United States of America, with the assistance of Britain, has declared war on Iraq. North Korea, the whole of Australasia and the Far East are in turmoil. The AIDS epidemic is sweeping our beautiful continent of Africa and millions of people are dying. There are little children in our children's home who are victims of AIDS, immorality is the order of the day and people are just living together for convenience sake. Who is he who can overcome this? Only he who believes that Jesus Christ is God! The only way to overcome depression, despair, fear and distress is to know the one who says, "I will never leave you nor forsake you – I will be with you until the very end of the age."

You can do all things through Him who strengthens you. It is in Jesus Christ that we can remain optimistic, focused, and winners. People around me are selling farms and emigrating but we are buying farms and developing. We don't have any reverse gear in our make-up. One of my greatest heroes, David Livingstone, said, "I'll go anywhere, as long as it's forward." We are going forward. Our destination is heaven. While we are here on earth we are living life to the fullest and enjoying every aspect of life, because we know that if God is for us there is no man that can stand against us.

Make a decision today to believe that Jesus is the Son of God, and cast your every care upon Him because He cares for you (1 Peter 5:7). Go out and make the most of your day. Every time you hear a negative report, confess that Jesus Christ is the Son of God and that He makes us more than overcomers

Walking without fainting

"They shall walk and not faint." – Isaiah 40:31d

Dr David Livingstone, a true man of God, spent four years in Africa on his first expedition. He walked from Cape Town to the Victoria Falls, then to the West Coast at Lobito Bay on the Atlantic Ocean. From there he walked back to Central Africa. He followed the Zambezi River right down to Quillmane on the Indian Ocean and caught a ship back to bonnie Scotland. There were many times when he was sick and nearly perished. During his expeditions he was mauled by a lion, had malaria more than sixty times, and was very often hungry, thirsty and tired. He suffered all kinds of physical discomforts, yet he carried on. He never gave up. He had a single purpose – to see that Christianity came to Africa. Because of that, even when his body grew weary, his spirit kept strong.

"They shall walk, and not faint." Who shall walk and not faint? Only those who spend time with the living God. Are you feeling faint? Do you feel as if you want to sit down at the side of the road and stop? The symptoms, my dear friend, are very easy to recognise. You've taken your eyes off the Lord Jesus Christ and you have forgotten the call on your life.

He is the only one who can give you sufficient strength to walk today, so stop trying to do it on your own. Repent, and put your hand back in His. Allow Him to walk with you, renewing your strength constantly so that you will not faint. Soon you will reach your destination – heaven itself.

Our treasure

"For where your treasure is, there your heart will be also." – Matthew 6:21

George Muller started an orphanage in Great Britain many years ago. Ten thousand children were cared for at the cost of over six million pounds, though he never asked for a penny. The work was a faith venture. When asked why he had started the orphanage, he said, "I want to show the world what God can do through one ordinary man who decides to believe the promises of Jesus." The objective of the orphanage was not the children, though he deeply loved them, but to magnify the name of Jesus Christ. The Lord was his treasure.

It's very easy to find out where someone's treasure lies. After just a few minutes of conversation, it will become evident. A rugby fanatic will talk about his team, a farmer will speak about cattle, but a child of God will share how much the Lord means to him because that's where his heart is. Where is your treasure? If you are playing sport, growing crops, or striving to be champion farmers in order to magnify God, that is a wonderful thing. But if your objective is to magnify yourself, then my dear friend, you are in trouble.

The Bible says that a man's eyes are the window of his heart and they give away his treasure. His eyes will flash with interest when you speak to him about things that he treasures in his heart. Conversely, when you speak about the Lord Jesus Christ to an unbeliever, you often see something like a blanket come over his eyes. Because he is blind and cannot see spiritually, he becomes uninterested, unless the Holy Spirit brings him under conviction.

Where is your heart today? Remember, if you put the Lord Jesus Christ first and make Him your treasure, all of these other things will be added unto you (Matthew 6:33).

No weapon formed against you shall prosper

"No weapon formed against you shall prosper, and every tongue which rises against you in judgment You shall condemn. This is the heritage of the servants of the LORD, and their righteousness is from Me," says the LORD." – Isaiah 54:17

This is the inheritance of the children of the Lord. God says our righteousness is of Him, not of ourselves. We are protected through the blood of Jesus Christ and the Lord will receive no accusations against us.

Some people are afraid to go out in case they have an accident, make a mistake, or do something wrong. We, as the servants of God, should never feel that way. We go out knowing that the Lord goes before us and that He has put his guardian angels around us. When we make mistakes, we repent, confess, say we're sorry and press on, assured that there is no condemnation for us in Christ Jesus (Romans 8:1). The Christian has such a tremendous advantage over an unbeliever because our confidence is in the promises of God. We know that He who has begun a good work in us will complete it until the day of Jesus Christ (Philippians 1:6).

We are contemplating making our first film at Shalom and we believe that many souls will come to Christ as a result. We are planning to increase our children's home to accommodate up to one hundred and fifty children, and to increase the capacity of our school. We are also planning to take our "Seed Sower" Gospel Truck from Cape Town to Jerusalem, with thousands of Bibles on board. We hear many negative voices raised against us, and if we listened to them we would achieve none of these things. We do not receive those words because God has promised that no weapon formed against us shall prosper.

As the old saying goes: "Only one life, 'twill soon be past; only what's done for Christ will last." Do not be intimidated by unjust words, criticism or the judgment of others.

Thankfulness

"In everything give thanks; for this is the will of God in Christ Jesus for you." – 1 Thessalonians 5:18

Are you giving thanks to God in everything that is taking place in your life at the moment? If not, the Word of God encourages you to do so.

The Lord doesn't say we have to give thanks for everything but rather in everything. If you are going through a time of testing, you don't have to thank God for the tribulations but you can thank Him that He will see you through them.

One of the greatest tragedies that I've ever experienced in my life was when my little nephew, whom I loved so dearly, was riding on a tractor with me and fell off. I rode over that little boy and he died in my arms. I didn't give thanks to God for what happened but I thanked God in the situation that He would see me through. He did, and I've lived to tell the tale. I don't believe that God caused the accident but I believe that, through the accident, God has worked many mighty miracles. That little boy's whole family – my brother, his wife, and the rest of their children – have come to know the saving grace of Christ.

So we give God thanks in everything. When we go through traumatic times, whether it be floods or drought on our farms, we thank Him in it, confident that He is going to see us through. And you know, He always does. Thank the Lord this morning for everything that has happened through and in your life. Believe that "all things work together for the good of those who love the Lord and are called according to his purpose." (Romans 8:28).

The God of the impossible

"The things which are impossible with men are possible with God." – Luke 18:27

Our God is a miracle-working God. I can testify to that from personal experience. Just a few months ago we held a huge gospel campaign in Northern Zululand, South Africa. We used a five-thousand-seater tent. Some believed that it was too large and we would not be able to fill it but they reckoned without the God of miracles. We spoke to over fifty thousand people during the campaign and more than ten thousand decision cards were handed in over the eight nights. With God, nothing is impossible!

All the Lord requires is that we give Him the opportunity to show that He can do anything. We called the campaign: "Jesus, the Healer." Some Christians took offence when they saw the advertisements. "How sure are you that Jesus is going to heal the sick?" they asked. I said, "Very sure, simply because nothing is impossible with God." We saw people getting out of wheelchairs and walking and I am not talking about one or two, but many. We saw deaf ears unstopped and blind eyes opened because our God can do anything.

What does the Lord require from us? He requires simple, childlike faith. He requires us to ask Him, in the way a child asks a parent. He has promised to answer us and He will perform mighty miracles in our lives, if we will believe. There is nothing that is impossible for our God. The day you say it can't be done, that's the same day the Lord says, "I can do it."

Take those situations – those mountains you can't get over and those valleys that are so deep that you can't get through them – to God today.

Sound the alarm

"Blow the trumpet in Zion, and sound an alarm in My holy mountain! Let all the inhabitants of the land tremble; for the day of the LORD is coming, for it is at hand:" – Joel 2:1

We need to blow the trumpet in Zion and sound an alarm. We need to tell people that time is short – Jesus is coming.

I designed a banner for one of my campaigns. It had a photograph of a watchman seated in a tower, holding a trumpet. His job was to look out for the enemy and to sound the alarm. The sad thing about the picture was that the watchman was sound asleep and the enemy was already at the gate. In fact, some of them were coming over the wall. The inhabitants inside the walls of the castle were sound asleep too. They were depending on the watchman to warn them of impending danger.

We are living in perilous times. It doesn't matter what part of the world I go to – whether it is Zimbabwe, New Zealand, Australia or the British Isles – people everywhere are suffering from stress and I constantly hear of bankruptcies, depression and even suicide. The Lord says we are to blow the trumpet. We need to sound the alarm. People are being called home every single second of the day. We have one obligation – to remind them that the day of the Lord is at hand and that their lives must be in order when they meet Jesus.

Are you blowing the trumpet, my friend?

Obedience

"But why do you call Me 'Lord, Lord,' and do not do the things which I say?" – Luke 6:46

Jesus Christ must be Lord of all, or He is not Lord at all. If we acknowledge Him as our Lord and Saviour, He must be supreme in our lives.

One thing that so often saddens me as I mix with people of the world is that they will seldom mention the name of Jesus, except as a swear word. Yet, on Sunday mornings those same people will be dressed up to the nines and look as pious and holy as anybody else. After church, they don't want to hear any more about Christianity. In fact, when you speak to them about the Lord during the week they rebuke you.

The Lord says, "Why do you call me Lord and you do not do the things which I say?" "Oh," some say, "I don't have to keep talking about Jesus to prove that I'm a Christian." Why should you not want to? I cannot help but talk about Jesus. He is the main subject of my conversation, because He is everything to me. He is my Lord.

Let us pray daily for courage and strength that we may boldly acknowledge Jesus Christ as Lord of our lives, so that we will not be like Peter, who loved the Lord and yet denied Him three times before the cock crowed even once.

True freedom

"Therefore if the Son makes you free, you shall be free indeed." – John 8:36

Janis Joplin, the famous pop star who is believed to have died from an overdose of drugs, sang in one of her songs, "Freedom is just another word for nothing left to lose." That is so sad.

The freedom that we are talking about today is not that kind of freedom at all. It is the freedom that comes through bowing the knee and accepting Jesus Christ as Lord and Saviour. It is the freedom of an eagle, when it soars up into the high thermals and screams with joy even when it sees storms coming because it fears nothing.

It's a freedom that makes a challenge an exciting adventure. It's a freedom that breaks the yoke of death, failure and destruction. It's a freedom that God gives us so that we know we need never fear failure, death, or disgrace because everything we do and say is in Him. He is a champion, a winner.

Today go out and use that same freedom Christ has given you to set free captives held by the devil, assured that "if the Son makes you free, you shall be free indeed." (John 8:36).

God is love

"And now abide faith, hope, love, these three; but the greatest of these is love." – 1 Corinthians 13:13

In His Footsteps by Charles Sheldon is a book that touched my life deeply. In it the writer talks about a pastor who dressed up as a tramp, posing as an out-of-work printer. He went to the houses of his own parishioners (very wealthy people), begging for food, shelter and employment and was absolutely horrified at the response from many of the "outstanding pillars" in his church. Sadly, this comes as no surprise. Mahatma Gandhi was quoted as saying that he would have had no problem following Jesus Christ, were it not for His followers. He was put off by the lack of love he saw in many Christians. That man could have changed the destiny of the world if he had become a Christian.

If we prophesy, lay hands on the sick and they recover, but we do not walk in love it means little to the Lord. The Bible says we must be known by our love. It was the love of God that brought us to Christ. It was because of love that God allowed Jesus to be crucified on the cross of Calvary for sinners like you and me. He commands us to shed that love abroad to our world. Anything else makes us like clanging cymbals, noisy and worthless.

Get on your knees before you go to work today and ask the Lord to show you someone you can love tangibly, as well as with expressions of kind words and encouragement.

Chosen by God

"You did not choose Me, but I chose you..." – John 15:16

You thought that you chose God, didn't you? God said you didn't choose Him, He chose you. He chose you out of millions and millions of people. Why? We won't know until we get to heaven, but what we do know is that He has chosen and appointed us to work for Him. Spend time on your knees, praying and reading the scriptures until you hear from God about the special task He has for you.

Jesus chose us just as He chose the twelve disciples. He wants us to make an impact on our world, starting where we are living, telling people about the Son of the living God. Many times the evil one tells people that they are of no use to anyone, but that is a lie from the pit of hell. The Lord says He has chosen and appointed us to bear fruit – to be productive. Don't be afraid to share the good news wherever you go. He has a habit of not choosing the high and mighty, the well educated or the famous. Instead He chooses the nobodies, young and old, who are prepared to say, "Yes, Lord, I will go."

Rise up this morning, mighty man or woman of God, and know, because you've been chosen and appointed, that the Lord is going before you. Wherever you put your foot, you will be victorious in Christ. Trust Him for opportunities to speak to others. The Bible says that wise people lead others to Christ. Go out and preach the gospel, pray for the sick and be an ambassador for Jesus.

Abiding fruit

" ...that your fruit should remain, that whatever you ask the Father in My name He may give you." – John 15:16

Are we producing fruit? If not, we have no right whatsoever to ask God for anything in His Name. In the Book of Hosea, the Lord talks about His House being a shambles, while the homes of professing believers are beautifully built. Little has changed. There are still believers who give the Lord only their change – their leftovers. Business, pleasure and everything else comes first in their lives.

The Lord says, "If you ask my Father anything in my name He'll give it to you – if you are producing fruit." What kind of fruit? The Bible speaks about the "fruit of the Spirit" – attitudes of love, joy, peace, long suffering, kindness, goodness, faithfulness, gentleness and self-control" (Galatians 5:22,23). There is also the fruit of soul winning, tithes and offerings, and spending quality time alone with God. These are not phases or fads but something that remains. The Lord says when your fruit remains then you may ask your Father anything in Jesus' name and He will give it to you.

Our prayer today is, "Lord, make us fruitful so that when we pray You will hear our prayers. Amen."

Seek the Lord and live

*"For thus says the LORD to the house of Israel: 'Seek Me and live'." –
Amos 5:4*

Many people have been to visit me over the years, seeking direction for their lives. Some are young people looking for direction as to what profession to go into. Others are men and women who have retired and don't know what to do with the remainder of their lives. The Lord says, "Seek me and live." If Christ is Lord of your life, you will be content and fulfilled in every thing you do and the Lord will give you life abundantly.

Since I committed my life to Christ on 18 February 1979, my life has been totally transformed and I can honestly say that I am living in the fullness of Christ. I never experienced that as an unbeliever. Before I became a Christian, I travelled all over the world. I was a "wild, colonial boy." I rode horses in Australia for a living, picked pineapples, milked cows and stacked bricks. I lived in Scotland for two and a half years working as a coal-heaver, delivering coal to people's houses, and cutting wood. I went to agricultural college, then returned to Africa and worked on farms in Zambia and Swaziland. In all that time I never really lived – I simply existed. Since I found the Lord, my life is completely fulfilled. It has been an exciting adventure as I have preached the gospel in just about every part of the world. I have lived in hovels and in palaces, dined with kings and with prime ministers but nothing can compare to the joy of seeing people coming to Christ and being healed in body, soul and spirit.

Put Jesus first in your life, and He will transform it in ways you never dreamed possible. God is a good God. He is for us and not against us. Trust Him. Seek Him and live.

Rejoicing in tribulations

"And not only that, but we also glory in tribulations, knowing that tribulation produces perseverance." – Romans 5:3

Are you rejoicing in your tribulations? Samuel Rutherford, a great Scottish preacher said, "Grace withers without adversity" and "The devil is but God's master fencer (swordsman) to teach us to handle our weapons."

I've never yet met an anointed man or woman of God who has not been through tribulation of some degree or another. Every single preacher, every man or woman of faith that God has used has a testimony of going through the fire of affliction. That is why Paul says we glory in our tribulations because the Lord uses them to build character.

If you have been going through a tough time lately, rejoice, for surely God has a plan for your life. I always say to my children that no matter how many mistakes we make or how tough it gets, as long as we have learned a lesson from it, no experience is wasted. If you have been learning well the lessons that God has been teaching you through adversity, then you will be a better person for it. Remember, God will not allow you to be tempted above that which you are able to handle. (1 Corinthians 10:13).

Arthur Attwell said, "There never yet was a drought that did not end in rain." I can honestly tell you from personal experience that the more severe the drought, the more blessing the rain is and the more it is appreciated when it comes.

Today, thank God for every situation that you are in because He is teaching you lessons you will never forget!

Listening to His voice

" ...Behold, to obey is better than sacrifice, and to heed than the fat of rams." – I Samuel 15:22b

Pastor William Duma, the famous Zulu preacher from South Africa, was a man who loved to obey God promptly and, as a result, God used him most powerfully in ministry. He had a renowned healing ministry and was even known to have raised the dead.

One day he was travelling on a very crowded bus. People were squashed in tightly, their luggage, suitcases and crates of live chickens tied to the roof. The engine was screaming as the bus flew though the sugar cane fields of Zululand, dust rising thickly in the air. "Get off this bus," the Holy Spirit said to him. He was in the middle of nowhere it seemed, but the small bespectacled man stood up immediately and pulled the emergency cord.

The driver slammed on the brakes and people fell forward as the bus came to a screaming halt. "Why did you do that?" the driver screamed. "Because God told me to get off," replied the mild pastor. "Are you insane?" shouted the driver, pushing him violently off the bus and taking off again at top speed, leaving William Duma stranded in the middle of the sugar cane fields. My dear friend, that bus went round the very next corner and had a head-on collision with a truck. The seat Pastor Duma had occupied was crushed beyond recognition. He would have been killed instantly if he had not obeyed God.

Today, if the Holy Spirit prompts you to do something, however silly it might seem, just do it. Be obedient to what His voice tells you, without question.

Turning the other cheek

"But I tell you not to resist an evil person. But whoever slaps you on your right cheek, turn the other to him also." – Matthew 5:39

A young Christian man of about nineteen years of age joined a professional regiment of fighting men. In his barracks were about sixty men, who had seen action all over the world. Their sergeant was a particularly tough man. He had been a professional soldier all his life, had tattoos on his arms, a filthy mouth and a serious drinking problem. One evening he was out drinking with some of the soldiers. On their return, they found the young soldier on his knees beside his bed, praying. They mocked the young man and shouted abuse at him. The sergeant took off his hobnailed, steel-capped army boots and threw them viciously at the young soldier, hitting him on the back of his head. One of the boots cut his head, which started to bleed profusely. With that the sergeant passed out in a drunken slumber.

Early the next morning the sergeant awoke and the first thing he remembered was that he had thrown his boots at a young Christian soldier the night before. He wondered where they were and as he looked down, he saw them standing side by side, perfectly polished and gleaming. Realising that the young Christian had done this in spite of the abuse he had suffered, that man broke down and wept. He went and sat next to the young man's bed and said, "Son, tell me about this Jesus of yours. I also want to follow Him."

Today, turn the other cheek. Go the extra mile. Be Jesus to that person or that situation in which you find yourself and the Lord will give you the victory.

Seeking first the kingdom of God

"But seek first the kingdom of God and His righteousness, and all these things shall be added to you." – Matthew 6:33

A minister who had a great influence in my life as an young believer was running a number of churches. He was also studying for a degree in theology. I remember him saying on one occasion that he lacked opportunity to prepare for the exam he was sitting later that day. When I asked him how the examination had gone, he responded positively. "How did you get your answers?" I asked. "Oh," he laughed, "A bit of divine cheating! The Lord gave me the answers."

I firmly believe that, if we put God first in our lives, He undertakes for us and I have experienced that many times in my farming career. I remember having to send a herd of beef calves to the sale yards at the wrong time of the year when the prices were at their lowest. But we needed the money, as times were hard. When our animals came up for sale, they got top prices. It was quite extraordinary. All praise and honour goes to Jesus. Similar experiences have happened to me time and time again in my life.

It doesn't matter what you are doing. You don't have to be the most brilliant farmer or the best student in the world. You don't have to be the best engineer or businessman – what you have to be is dedicated to Jesus. He will never let you down. He will be with you even until the end of the age.

The truth sets us free

"Lead me in Your truth and teach me, for You are the God of my salvation; on You I wait all the day." – Psalm 25:5

Every morning on our farm we start the day with praise, scripture reading and prayer. We have declared that the truth will be spoken on our farm – and nothing else! We are fundamentalists at Shalom. We believe the Word of God from cover to cover to be the words spoken directly from heaven and we will not deviate from its truth. We deal with many Zulu people who are steeped in ancestor worship and witchcraft and we categorically state that there is no other God but the God of Israel. That is what the Lord said too. Tongue in cheek He says, "If there are, can you please tell me, because I don't know of any other God."

In these last days, we need to be outspoken when it comes to the truth, because it is only the truth that will set people free. This business of "Live and let live" and "All roads lead to heaven" is nothing short of heresy. My dear friend, if you were to go to a country like Iran today and try to hand out Christian tracts on the street, you would be arrested, put in gaol and possibly lose your life. How sad then that Christians who do not suffer such persecution in our own nation (which is supposed to be a Christian nation), do not have the courage to stand up and say that Jesus is the Way, the Truth and the Life. When we will not stand up for the truth, we become insipid and lukewarm, a condition the Lord despises. (Revelation 3:16).

Make a stand for Christ today. Do not be ashamed of the gospel. Jesus is not ashamed of you.

SEPTEMBER

The preserving power of God's truth

" Let Your loving kindness and Your truth continually preserve me." – Psalm 40:11b

I am privileged to travel extensively, preaching the gospel. I speak to all kinds of people but I especially love speaking to young people. Their hearts are pliable and soft and are searching for the truth.

David says that God's truth continually preserves him, clearly showing him what is right and what is wrong. We need to speak the truth, especially to our young people. We must warn them that sexual relationships outside of marriage are fornication and sinful in God's sight, pornography is from the devil, sleeping with a partner of the same sex is an abomination to God, and rebellion – disobeying their parents or their superiors – is like witchcraft.

Are you telling your young people the truth? Or are you just going with the flow because you are afraid of upsetting the status quo? We need to draw a line as Joshua did when he said: "Choose for yourselves this day whom you will serve... But as for me and my house, we will serve the LORD." (Joshua 24:15).

I challenge you today to take a stand for Christ. Tell your children: "We are not having any pornography or foul-mouthed videos in our home. We are not allowing you to sleep with your girlfriend or boyfriend in this house. We are not allowing blasphemy." Yes, it will cause a lot of ructions, but your children will thank you one day for standing up for the truth and preserving their lives.

Strangers in the earth

"I am a stranger in the earth; do not hide Your commandments from me."
— Psalm 119:19

Do you feel totally isolated today, as though you don't have a friend in the world? Are you perhaps the only Christian in your family and you feel ostracized by your loved ones? You are not the only one who has ever felt like a stranger. That is exactly how the psalmist felt.

We no longer have common ground with the world because we are strangers in the earth. We are travellers passing through. The commandments of God that keep us walking in righteousness are the same commandments that separate us from the world. That is why Jesus said we should rejoice when people say all manner of evil about us for His Name's sake.

My oldest son was very excited because he had been chosen to become an officer in the army while he was doing his national service. He worked diligently, was physically very fit and has a good IQ. Yet, at the last moment, he was thrown off the course. One of his friends told me that he believed it cost him his commission because my son was not prepared to compromise, watch blue movies and spend time in the bar or use filthy language. He was not popular. He was not "one of the boys." So he became a two-striper, a corporal. One thing I do know – Jesus must have rejoiced in heaven because that young man was prepared to go the whole way for Him.

How about you and me today? Are we strangers in the world? If Jesus came back today to call His Church home, would He recognise you as a stranger in this world, or would He see you as very much part of the world?

Walking worthily

"That you would walk worthy of God who calls you into His own kingdom and glory." – I Thessalonians 2:12

The way a man walks through life can tell you many things. The man who has carried a heavy burden all his life will walk with rounded shoulders. A young man who has plenty of money and influence and has never worked for anything, often struts around like a fighting cock. A servant of the Lord, on the other hand, will walk uprightly in the power of God, but humbly so as not to offend, always looking to see where he can help someone else.

I met a young man recently who had come all the way from Cape Town to Durban in order to compete in a national canoeing competition. He is the son of a very wealthy farmer in the Cape and God is abundantly blessing them. Their crops and fruit are magnificent. The prices are good and they are making a lot of money. "Angus," he said, "God is surely blessing us for a reason. I want to sow the profits back into the lives of poor people." His walk is worthy of God.

Are you walking worthy of God? Is "your walking doing the talking?" Or are you a Christian in word only? It is important that we do not just tell people we love them but that we show them by our attitudes and actions. As James the Apostle said, "I will show you my faith by my works." (James 2:18). Our lifestyle must line up with our preaching.

We need to walk humbly before God, knowing that everything we have and everything we are is only because of the grace of God. There is no room for arrogance or self-righteousness. May our walk today be found worthy of the great God whom we serve.

God's telephone number

"'Call to Me, and I will answer you...'" – Jeremiah 33:3

I was a brand-new Christian, not even six weeks old in the Lord, when I experienced the power of God's telephone number. We were burning firebreaks on the farm when the fire jumped into a forest area near my boundary with the property of a massive international timber company. The wind was blowing and the fire was fierce. I jumped in my pick-up truck and raced to the house so fast that the tailgate literally ripped off the back of the vehicle. "Call the neighbours," I shouted to my wife. "Ask them please to come and help." I was desperate.

The neighbouring farmers rushed over and we did all we could to contain the fire. Massive water tankers poured thousands of litres of water onto the fire but we could not put it out. Eventually, the farmers had to leave and I didn't know what to do. If that fire jumped into the neighbour's plantation, I knew it would cost me everything I had.

"Do you think it will rain?" I asked my driver. He looked at me in surprise. "The rainy season is over," he said. "Look up in the sky. There are no clouds." "Well," I said, "I have just become a Christian and I am going to pray."

I closed my eyes and prayed and immediately a clap of thunder shook the air. My legs turned to jelly. The face of the Zulu driver went pale and he was speechless. With that the north wind stopped blowing and a gentle south wind started to blow. Half an hour later the rain fell and doused the fire. For the next two days it rained gently until that fire was put out completely.

We serve a God who answers prayer! Have you called out to Him today? Why not do so right now?

Known by the fruit of our lives

"Can a fig tree, my brethren, bear olives, or a grapevine bear figs? Thus no spring yields both salt water and fresh." – James 3:12

Do people know you by your fruit? Do they recognise you as a believer by what you say or by what you are? There are some people who profess to be Christians but the fruit of their lives contradicts their confession. "They profess to know God, but in works they deny him..." (Titus 1:16).

Many years ago I was working on a farm in New South Wales, Australia. They had a local rodeo show at the agricultural field and I was fascinated. I had never seen bull riding or bronco-busting and my own attempt at riding a bull lasted less than two seconds.

I saw men dressed as genuine cowboys, complete with Stetsons, fancy belts and buckles, checked shirts and cowboy boots with spurs. I was impressed. I thought these must really be the champions. When it was time for the competition to start, however, these men were so under the influence of alcohol they could hardly get on their horses, never mind stay on them. They had all the equipment, but they were definitely not bronco-busters!

Just before the competition ended, I noticed a young man drive up in his truck, dressed in a pair of jeans and a shirt. He paid his money, got his number, and sat on the stand waiting for the announcer to call out his name. When he mounted the horse assigned to him, he rode it like a champion and was declared the winner to thunderous applause. He collected his prize, got back in his pick-up and drove straight back to his farm. That picture has never left my mind.

As Christians, we must be like that. Not talkers, not just looking the part, but allowing people to see Jesus Christ in us by the fruit of our lives.

A new creation in Christ

"Therefore, if anyone is in Christ, he is a new creation; old things have passed away; behold, all things have become new." – 2 Corinthians 5:17

Charles Duke walked on the moon. He had done most things that a man could wish for in life. First of all, he was selected to be a fighter pilot. Then he was chosen out of the squadron of fighter pilots to be a test pilot. After that he was selected to be an astronaut. He flew to the moon in one of the most powerful machines ever created. When he landed on the moon he drove the most expensive four-wheel drive buggy ever built by man.

But, he said, the day that he gave his life to the Lord Jesus Christ, all of those experiences paled into insignificance. When he met the man from Galilee, the Creator of heaven, earth and the moon, and accepted Jesus Christ as his personal Lord and Saviour, it was the most awesome experience he had ever had in all his life.

Have you had that experience? Have you ever asked Jesus Christ to be your Lord and Saviour? If not, why not do it today? Just pray this prayer with me: "Dear Lord Jesus, I repent of all my sin. I acknowledge that I can do nothing without You and today I commit my life to You as my Lord and Saviour. I will serve no other God but You and I thank You for dying on the cross of Calvary for a sinner like me. I thank you, Lord, that after three days You were raised from the dead and are seated in heavenly places and I, too, though I die, will live forever. Thank You for saving my soul. Amen."

Tell the first three people you meet this morning, irrespective of who they are, what you did today.

The gospel

"And He said to them, 'Go into all the world and preach the gospel to every creature'." – Mark 16:15

It is said that the greatest evangelist in any fellowship is the new Christian who has just given his life to the Lord. So it was when we had a campaign in the Orient Theatre in East London some years ago. Young Chantal (I think she was only about sixteen) gave her life to Jesus. Ten minutes later, sitting in the gallery in the auditorium, she said to her mother, "There's someone outside who needs Jesus. He's a fisherman."

The Orient Theatre is built right on the beach and young Chantal walked outside onto the sand. There were three fishermen fishing from the beach that night. She asked the first one, "Do you need Jesus?" "No," he replied. "Do you need Jesus?" she asked the second fisherman. "No." She turned to the third one and asked him the same question. "Yes," he said, "I do." She brought him into the auditorium where I was preaching. The man was in his oilskins, fishing rod in hand, when he accepted Jesus Christ as Lord and Saviour.

How many people have you spoken to recently about Jesus? Maybe you need to do it today because someone may be waiting for you to share the good news. Chantal had known the Lord for only a few minutes and she was instrumental in leading her first soul to Christ. You can do the same thing. Do it today and don't delay!

No condemnation

"There is therefore now no condemnation to those who are in Christ Jesus..." – Romans 8:1

During a gospel campaign in the Eastern Cape some time ago, I was sitting on a sand dune, spending time alone in prayer and waiting on God for the message for that evening. As I was meditating on the Word, a man walked up and started speaking to me. He was very well dressed, but didn't look too strong physically. I started talking to him about the things of God and he opened his heart to me. He was very ashamed of himself, he said, because he had been living an immoral lifestyle and had contracted AIDS. I asked him if he knew Jesus and he replied that he did, but he needed reassurance that the Lord had forgiven him his sins. The Word of God is such a beautiful and powerful weapon against the devil. When we believe it, the Word brings hope and life. I shared Romans 8:1 and I John 1:9 with him and he went away rejoicing, assured that his sins had indeed been forgiven and determined to live for God.

Are you feeling condemned this morning? There is no need. Confess your sins to the Lord and believe that He is faithful and just to forgive you and to cleanse you from all unrighteousness, according to I John 1:9. Remember, Jesus is the only one who can forgive sins because He paid the supreme price for sin. He was the "Lamb that was slain" for your sins and mine.

Today, whatever it is that you have done, do not hesitate to ask God for forgiveness and you too will go on your way rejoicing – not because you are a good person, but because you serve a good God.

Meditating on the Word of God

"This Book of the Law shall not depart from your mouth, but you shall meditate in it day and night, that you may observe to do according to all that is written in it. For then you will make your way prosperous, and then you will have good success." – Joshua 1:8

In these perilous times in which we are living, when so many decisions have to be made, we need to spend much time in God's Holy Word. As the Lord told Joshua, we need to meditate on the Word of God literally day and night so that the Lord can make our way prosperous and we can have good success. Joshua did exactly that. He was a man of the Word and, as a result, he was able to perform great miracles and exploits for God.

A missionary in China led a Chinese man to the Lord and there was great excitement in the missionary's heart as he carried on with his travels. A few months later he returned and enquired how the new convert was doing. "How is your new life coming along?" he asked him.

"Well," replied the believer. "It seems as though there are two dogs fighting within me – a black one and a white one" (representing good and evil). "Which one is winning?" asked the missionary. The new convert replied, "That depends on which one I'm feeding the most."

What are you feeding your spirit man at this moment? If you are feeling downhearted and depressed, dirty and ugly, maybe you have been feeding the "black dog" too much and today you need to make a quality decision to concentrate on feeding your spirit man the undiluted Word of God.

Broken and contrite hearts

"The sacrifices of God are a broken spirit, a broken and a contrite heart; these, O God, You will not despise." – Psalm 51:17

A rough, coarse railway worker, who swore and blasphemed the name of the Lord incessantly, was gloriously converted. He told his friends he would never swear again and they were astounded at the change in him. Then an accident happened in the shunting yard. A train was reversing and this believer was directing the driver. Somehow or other his hand jammed between two carriages as they coupled up and was totally crushed. He screamed and swore loudly, the first time since his conversion.

Everyone rallied around to assist him but when they tried to put him in the ambulance, he stopped them. With tears running down his face, his bloodied hand literally hanging in tatters, he knelt down in repentance and asked the Lord to forgive him for blaspheming. Then he climbed into the ambulance and was taken to the hospital.

I firmly believe the only difference between Peter, the big fisherman, and Judas Iscariot, was that Peter repented of denying his Lord, and Judas did not. Judas dealt with his sin his own way and ended up hanging himself. The Lord says to you today that it doesn't matter what you've done. If you confess your sin, He will forgive you. Jesus will never turn away a broken, contrite heart.

Revival

"Will You not revive us again, that Your people may rejoice in You?" – *Psalm 85:6*

There are many wonderful stories about the great Welsh Revival. Can you visualise a court room with the accused standing in the dock, pleading with the judge to send him to jail because he is a sinner and deserves to be punished? And the prosecutor pleading with the judge to please be lenient with this man and give him another chance, while the jury are singing Amazing Grace? Oh, for those days again – when public houses and bars closed down because they had no customers; policemen made up quartets and, instead of arresting people and trying to keep the peace, went up and down the streets, singing hymns. A little Shetland pony stood dumbfounded while a big Welsh miner, tears running down his cheeks, pleaded with the pony to please pull the wagon. Oh, my friend, that revival would come to us today!

If ever we needed revival, it is today. Everywhere we look people are downcast and downhearted. Oh, that we might have revival like the days of the great Welsh Revival, when whole towns and communities were changed by the power of the living God. Pray today that God would revive, first of all your own soul, then your family, community and country.

The Lord says to us in 2 Chronicles 7:14, "If My people who are called by My name will humble themselves, and pray and seek My face, and turn from their wicked ways, then I will hear from heaven, and will forgive their sin and heal their land." Let us really start to fast and pray earnestly that God will bring revival to our nation.

Attitudes

"But why do you call Me 'Lord, Lord,' and not do the things which I say?" –
Luke 6:46

Alexander the Great, while conquering the world, found himself in the battlefield one day and came to a hospital tent. There were people lying all over the place. Many had lost limbs, some had been blinded, and others had terrible head wounds. A young man sat in the corner in an obvious state of shock, but there was not even a mark on his body and nothing appeared to be wrong with him physically. The great warrior walked up to this young man and asked him his name. "My name is Alexander," he replied. Alexander the Great looked him right in the eye and said sternly, "Either change your attitude or change your name."

The Lord is saying the same thing to us today. How sad it is to hear someone talking about the things of God after a powerful church service, and then to meet that same person, perhaps a week later on a Saturday afternoon at a game of rugby or at some other sporting occasion, and see him drinking alcohol, smoking, and swearing. We cannot serve two masters. We must either change our attitude or change our name.

The Lord says that, if we are going to call Him Lord, then He must be our Lord in all situations and circumstances, and we must portray the personality and character of Jesus Christ in every situation in which we find ourselves.

Holiness

" ...You shall be holy, for I the LORD your God am holy." – Leviticus 19:2b

As a believer, I have been redeemed by the blood of the Lamb and set apart for the glory of God. I enjoy having fun and joking but I think it is a very dangerous thing to do that from the pulpit or when you are representing the Lord Jesus Christ. When you are sharing the Word of God, it is no time for "a laugh a minute". The Word of God is about life and death and has nothing to do with comedy. Jesus gave His life so that you and I could live. There is a place for revelling and playing but there is also a place for giving God full reverence.

It particularly grieves me to hear people talk about "the man upstairs" or about "my buddy," especially while sitting in a church service with their feet draped over the back of a chair, shirt unbuttoned to the waist. My friend, He is a holy God and we must respect Him accordingly. Yes, He's a personal God, but we must treat Him with much reverence.

I love the comment made by an early Highland preacher from Scotland who said, "Bring me a God all mercy but not just, bring me a God all love but not righteous, and I will have no scruple in calling him an idiot of your imagination!" There is no such God. There is no convenient God for your conscience. God is God. He has made laws, commandments and statutes and they are to be kept. He requires you and me to be holy just as He is holy. Let us go about our business with reverence, giving Him all the respect that He so richly deserves.

Christ in us, the hope of Glory

" ...Christ in you, the hope of glory." – Colossians 1:27

The church is not a building or a beautiful cathedral, such as one sees in Europe. When you enter those cathedrals you often find them absolutely empty! Sometimes you have to pay in order to gain access to them because they have become tourist sites. People walk around with their sandwiches and cold drinks, while looking at the stained glass windows and gazing at the beautiful lawns outside and the magnificent sculptures.

Jesus does not live in a building. He lives in the heart of a believer. It is Christ in us that makes the church. We have to take care of our bodies because the Lord tells us that our body is the temple of the Holy Spirit.

The church of Jesus Christ can never be eliminated or destroyed. As an early believer said, "They may kill me if they please, but they will never tear the living Christ out of my heart." The believer's blood is the seed of the church. The enemies of Christ may destroy churches and burn Bibles, but they will never stop the church of Jesus Christ, because He lives in the hearts of people. He doesn't live in an institution or an organisation. He lives in a farmer's heart. He lives in a housewife's heart. He lives in the heart of a little boy or girl. We are the church.

An expensive purchase

"For you were bought at a price..." – 1 Corinthians 6:20a

Oliver Cromwell, the Puritan leader, was known as the iron man of England. One day an officer in his army committed a serious offence and was subsequently sentenced to death. The officer's wife, who loved her husband dearly, appealed for her husband and asked that Oliver Cromwell have mercy on him. However, the sentence was already confirmed and she was told that he was to be executed at six a.m. the next morning. When the bell rang, the firing squad would shoot him.

Very early in the morning, the wife climbed up the bell tower. As the elderly bell ringer rang the bell faithfully at six a.m., she put her hand between the bell and the gong and it was crushed into a bloody pulp. The firing squad was unable to hear the chimes and so they did not shoot the officer. The wife came down from the tower, her hand in a bloody mess, went up to Oliver Cromwell and appealed for her husband. The iron man cried, and released him because she had paid the price.

You and I were also sentenced to death, because each and every one of us is a sinner. However, the man from Galilee put His own body on the line so that we might be forgiven and receive eternal life. Let us never forget the supreme price that was paid for us by the Lord Jesus Christ and let it motivate us to live for Him.

Listening to God

"' ...you shall not cross over this Jordan." – Deuteronomy 3:27b

One of the saddest stories in the Bible is that of the incredible and mighty man of God, Moses, who had done so much for God and His people and yet, right at the very end of his life, he did not listen to God. If you remember, God told him to speak to the rock so that water would come out and quench the thirst of the Israelites in the desert. Moses had become angry at the people's continual complaining. He did not listen to God, but struck the rock twice with his stick. His disobedience cost him and he was not allowed to proceed across the Jordan River into the land of milk and honey.

Are you listening to God this morning? If God has told you to do something, do it! God will bless, honour and prosper you, but only if you obey Him, even if it doesn't sound logical in your estimation. When Jesus called Peter to walk on the water, Peter did not question God. When Elijah the prophet told the widow to make him a cake with the last bit of flour and oil she had, it did not make sense. She did it anyway and God blessed her. When God told Gideon to send thirty-two thousand soldiers home and keep only three hundred, that didn't make sense either but he did it and God gave him the victory. When God told Abraham to sacrifice his only son – Isaac – that he'd waited one hundred years for, he listened to God and he is one of the few men in the Bible who is called "God's friend."

Do you want to be God's friend today? Then LISTEN to what He is telling you through His written Word and DO it.

The altar of God

"Then Noah built an altar to the LORD..." – Genesis 8:20

After the great flood, when God preserved Noah, his family and the animals, the first thing Noah did when he came to land was to build an altar to God. Men and women of God through the ages have done a similar thing.

Do you have an altar – a place where you come before God daily and offer up sacrifices of praise and thanksgiving? Do you have a family altar where you, your spouse and children spend time with God before you go out to face the day? Do you have an altar with your staff in your workplace?

I held a campaign in the Little Karoo, in the Eastern Cape of South Africa. After preaching a message on holiness one Sunday morning, people responded to the altar call, weeping as they came. I saw a grandfather, tears running down his face, holding his grandson in his arms as they came forward to commit their lives to Jesus Christ. Two elderly ladies wept unashamedly in each other's arms. I discovered afterwards that they hadn't spoken to each other for forty years. A wife knelt alone and it wasn't long before a big, strong, darkly-tanned farmer, an ex-provincial rugby player, walked slowly to the front and knelt beside her.

What a place! The altar of God! Do not neglect your altar today before you go out into the world.

The incredible love of God

"Greater love has no one than this, than to lay down one's life for his friends." – John 15:13

During the war, while that infamous bridge known as "the bridge on the River Kwai" was being built, the prisoners of war were under tremendous pressure. The Japanese were not kind to their prisoners and worked and starved them until they were literally skin and bone, and many died as a result.

One day a contingent of prisoners came in from their afternoon's work. They put their shovels in the storeroom and stood to attention as the Japanese officer addressed them. A Japanese soldier informed the officer that one shovel was missing and the officer threatened to shoot every prisoner if no one accounted for the missing implement. He loaded his rifle and took aim when, suddenly, a man took two steps forward and stood at attention, shoulders back, head lifted high. "I did it," he said. The officer was so angry that he beat the man to death. He was still lying there in a pool of blood when the soldier came running out of the storeroom again and apologised to the officer. There had been a miscount, he said, and all the shovels were accounted for. One man had died for his friends. That event had such a profound effect on all the other prisoners of war that at the end of the war there were no reprisals made against the Japanese guards.

Remember today that Jesus Christ took two steps forward for you and me. Totally innocent, He laid down His life so that we could live forever. All we have to do is acknowledge Him as the Son of God, repent of all our sins and thank Him for His incredible love for us.

Pray without ceasing

" ...pray without ceasing," – 1 Thessalonians 5:17

The power of prayer is an incredible weapon of warfare for the Christian.

One year we planted one hundred and fifteen hectares of seed corn (maize) literally in the dust, because we believed God instructed us to do it. We were praying for desperately needed rain when a dear friend of ours, Harold Kohler, came to visit and spent the weekend with us. As we shared a time of prayer, he prayed, "God, send rain to show us that You still answer prayer." In the middle of the night, the skies were clear and the stars were shining brightly. One cloud passed over our farm and, suddenly, the rain began to fall. Eleven millimetres of rain (just under half an inch) fell within a few hours. The next day, one hundred millimetres (four inches) fell and filled all our dams, so that our cattle had water to drink.

Do not give up praying! The Bible says, "Pray without ceasing." Never stop praying. Keep thanking God for that miracle in your life that is coming, that healing, that financial provision you desperately need. Keep on praying, because God answers prayer.

Victory over death

"For to me, to live is Christ, and to die is gain." – Philippians 1:21

A famous Scottish missionary, James Chalmers, preached the gospel to the South Sea Islanders (as they were known), many of whom were cannibals. He said boldly, "I am immortal until my work for the Lord is done on this earth."

Believers should never be afraid to die. Psalm 139 tells us that the Lord allotted our days before we were conceived in our mother's womb. All we have to do is live godly lives, do what we can for the furtherance of the Gospel here on earth and be ready at all times to face the King of Glory. We do not know the time or the hour, but we do know for sure that God knows. If God knows, that's good enough for me and I trust for you as well.

For Paul, his life was all about Christ. When he died, he knew he was going home to be with Jesus in heaven. You could not frighten that man with death or anything else. The good news is that, if we know Jesus Christ as our personal Lord and Saviour, we're going home to be with Him in glory forever.

Jehovah–Jireh, the Lord our provider

"And my God shall supply all your need according to His riches in glory by Christ Jesus." – Philippians 4:19

I love George Muller, that great man of faith who built the orphanages in Bristol, UK, and cared for thousands of children by faith. When he was offered a pension scheme in his twilight years, he said, "Please give it to someone else. I couldn't possibly accept it. The Lord has looked after me all these years. He's not about to let go now."

Surely that's how we should be. We must do our best, take precautions, make sure our children are well cared for, and live life to the fullest, in the confidence that the Lord is Jehovah–Jireh, our Provider. He is the one who knows how to take care of all our needs in this life and the next. The day the Lord calls us, we are going home and no one is going to change that.

If we can trust Him for eternity, we can trust Him to take care of all our needs right now.

Victory over death

"O Death, where is your sting?" – *1 Corinthians 15:55a*

When the first martyr in the New Testament, Stephen, was being stoned, he cried out, "Lord, don't hold this sin against them." The Bible says that he then fell asleep (died). I believe with all my heart that the Lord gives us the grace to live and He gives us the grace to die. We need fear nothing.

I heard a beautiful account from a lady, Joyce Everitt, who lives in Dornach, right up in the north of Scotland, further north than Inverness. She told me about a Christian leader who was being hunted because of his faith in Jesus Christ. He was very afraid that he would let the Lord down because he knew that they would eventually catch him. He would sit down in his little croft at night, light a candle, put his finger in the flame and hold it there as long as he could in order to try to get used to the pain. He was afraid that he would let the Lord down once he was caught. Eventually he was caught and ultimately burned at the stake for his faith. That man never flinched at all. As he was being burned at the stake, he sang hymns while the fire consumed him. He never let his Master down.

So be it, Lord, with each one of us believers. In the face of great trials and tribulations, give us, as we know You will, the grace to live for Christ and also the grace, if needs be, to die for Christ.

Getting our priorities right

" ...For I am a stranger with You, a sojourner, as all my fathers were."
— Psalms 39:12

We are sojourners, travellers, passing through this life. We are here for seventy years and, if God sees fit, maybe an extra few years after that. We are not to get too comfortable. Yes, we are to work hard and do the best we can with what God has given us but we must never imagine that we are here forever. Indeed, life is but a vapour. Here today and gone tomorrow.

Malcolm Muggeridge said, "The greatest disaster that can befall any born-again Spirit-filled Christian is to feel at home in this world."

Today, before we leave home or go about our work, we need to get our priorities in order. We need to realise that everything we are doing will be left behind when God calls us home. The only thing that will be going to heaven will be our spirit. Everything else will remain. We must put our emphasis and priorities in the right order: God first, then our family, and then our work.

The desires of your heart

"If you ask anything in My name, I will do it." — John 14:14

In 1993 I was invited to preach the gospel of Jesus Christ in bonnie Scotland, the home country of my parents. God supernaturally provided for me and I ministered there for three months. Indeed, we serve a very mighty God.

Secretly I had a desire to own a kilt — the traditional dress of the Scotsman — in the green, black and red colours of the Buchan clan. Kilts are very expensive so I asked the Lord for one, believing in faith.

I had been in Scotland about six weeks and was invited to speak at a Wednesday night church meeting. A man came up to me at the end of the service while I was praying for the sick, and said, "Laddie, don't go away. This morning the Lord told me to give you something." About an hour later he came back into the church, carrying a coat hanger with a drape over it. My heart nearly jumped out of my body, because I knew exactly what was under that drape. I said, "Sir, what is your name?" He replied, "My name is Robert Buchan" (which is my name). I took the drape off and there was a kilt, complete with sporran, belt, dress jacket and kilt pin. I was absolutely ecstatic. This man was exactly the same size as me and it fitted me perfectly. I still have that kilt to this day.

There is nothing too hard for God. There is nothing that He will not do for you, if you ask Him in faith and love Him. That kilt was not an essential. It was just a desire of my heart. Psalm 37:4 says, "Delight yourself in the Lord and He shall give you the desires of your heart."

First solitude, then service

"And in the daytime He was teaching in the temple, but at night He went out and stayed on the mountain called Olivet." – Luke 21:37

We must hear from God before we get involved with the things of the world. That is why our quiet time in the morning is so vitally important. Many a farmer, especially the dairyman, will tell you they haven't got time early in the morning. My dear friend, you cannot afford not to have time. You have to get up earlier. It is in the solitude that God will give you direction for your day. First solitude, then service. Remember neither is complete in itself. Each one enriches the other. In solitude God ministers to us. In service we minister to Him and, obviously, to others.

It's first the mountain, then the ministry. We must hear from Him first. The Lord has promised that He will teach us all things, but we also need to get out there and do it. It's very important not to get fixated on one or the other. We can't stay on the mountain all day like Peter wanted to do when Jesus was on the Mount of Transfiguration. We have to come back down to the valley and get stuck in, roll up our sleeves and get our hands dirty. Once we are weary, we go back up the mountain and hear more from God. So the cycle continues until Jesus takes us home to be with him in heaven forever.

Sharpen your swords every morning (your sword is the Word of God), and then go into the world and do the work God has called you to.

New beginnings

" ...old things have passed away; behold, all things have become new."
– 2 Corinthians 5:17b

James Calvert, a great missionary, was sent to the Fiji Islands to preach the gospel to the cannibals. The ship's captain was reluctant to let the small missionary party off the ship at one of the islands and he pleaded with James Calvert. "Please reconsider. These people will possibly kill you." The man of God responded, "That is not an issue with us because we died before we came here."

The greatest miracle in life is when the "old man" dies and the "new man" is born. It is a supernatural thing but the newborn believer still needs to grow in grace and the knowledge of Jesus Christ. I saw this little snippet printed somewhere: "There is no growth without challenge, and there is no challenge without change." We need to change and to go on from glory to glory. We need to keep on trusting Jesus if we are to be beneficial in the kingdom of God. In order for that to happen though, the "old man" has literally got to die. Old habits, old ways must make way for new ways – God's ways.

Yesterday is gone forever. We must be prepared to grow today, to be challenged by God and to change, knowing that we can do all things through Christ who strengthens us (Philippians 4:13).

God is working

"For I consider that the sufferings of this present time are not worthy to be compared with the glory which shall be revealed in us." – Romans 8:18

Be encouraged by this little poem that I found tucked away. I don't know who the author is, but he or she is obviously a person of the land. Irrespective of what you are going through today, know one thing – that God is working through your circumstances to make you a better person for the eternal life which lies ahead of you.

> The farmer ploughs through the fields of green,
> And the blade of the plough is sharp and keen,
> But the seed must be sown to bring forth grain,
> For nothing is born without suffering and pain –
>
> And God never ploughs in the soul of man,
> Without intention and purpose and plan,
> So whenever you feel the plough's sharp blade,
> Let not your heart be sorely afraid.
>
> For, like the farmer, God chooses a field
> From which he expects an excellent yield –
> So rejoice though your heart is broken in two,
> God seeks to bring forth a rich harvest in you.

(Author unknown)

Learning from nature

"Behold, how good and how pleasant it is for brethren to dwell together in unity!" – Psalms 133:1

When believers dwell together in the spirit of our Lord Jesus Christ, we can be likened to the geese that fly overhead in V-formations. I can assure you that it is not for decorative or any other purpose that they fly in that particular formation. It is because in unity they can cover so much more distance. The experts say they can gain seventy-one per cent more flying range if they fly in a V-formation as a whole flock than if one bird flew by itself.

If we have as much sense as a goose, we will join in formation with those who are headed in the right direction, homeward bound to heaven. We can learn so much from God's creation. While flying geese honk to encourage those up front to keep up the speed. When a goose gets sick, wounded or shot down, two geese drop out of the formation and follow their fellow member down to the ground in order to help and provide protection. They stay with the disabled goose until it either heals or dies, then they join another flock and continue towards their destination.

One word stands out from their example and that is "unselfishness." When the lead goose gets tired, he moves to the back of the formation and another goose flies up to the point position. Surely, as believers, that is how we must be. When we see one of our brothers or sisters today tiring, we need to take up the point position and keep leading until they are strengthened again.

Every time you look up to the sky and you see a V-formation flying over, remember that the Lord Jesus Christ has called us to press on together. The Bible says that one will chase a thousand but two will chase ten thousand.

Watching our words

"For God has not given us a spirit of fear, but of power and of love and of a sound mind." – 2 Timothy 1:7

We are walking advertisements to the world and people tend to judge Christianity by the way you and I behave. That is why we must be careful at all times to walk by faith, to walk in love, and to stand on the unshakeable Word of God, especially as times get harder.

Charles G Finney, that great revivalist who lived in the late 1700s wrote: "Now, Christian, do you ever consider how horrible your conduct is in the eyes of an unbelieving world? They know what promises your Father has made, and they see by your anxiety and worldly-mindedness how little confidence you have in these promises. They witness your foreboding and worldly spirit, and think in their hearts, 'These Christians know that God is not to be trusted, for as a matter of fact, they have no confidence in His promises.' How can you, in any way, more deeply wound the Christian faith than by this unbelief, and worse still, more fully and certainly dishonour God? It is a most shameful declaration in the most impressive manner possible, that you believe God to be a liar."

Today, let us watch over our vocabulary and be very careful that we do not become ambassadors for the devil by the negative way in which we speak. Let our speech be positive, full of faith, glorifying our God in everything we do and say.

Soldiers of the cross

"No one engaged in warfare entangles himself with the affairs of this life, that he may please him who enlisted him as a soldier." – 2 Timothy 2:4

Who enlisted you and me as soldiers of the cross? None other than the Commander Himself, the Lord Jesus Christ!

Our instructions are that we are to keep away from becoming entangled in the things of this world, which only hamstring us and make us ineffective. All we do must be done as unto the Lord. We must not allow ourselves to be enticed by shortcuts or smooth roads that lead to eternal damnation, such as stealing, lying, false accusations, debt, dishonesty, ungodliness. We are rather to concentrate on the things that a good soldier of the cross would use, namely truth, honesty, reliability, discipline, obeying the law of the land, working hard, humility, prayerfulness, loving-kindness and being humble in all things. If we live this kind of lifestyle, we will be pleasing to our God and the results will become evident in our work and home situations as God prospers us.

Let us determine to live God's way from today onwards, turning our backs on the system of this sick and dying world. Then we will be in a position to pray for the sick, set the captives free, heal the broken-hearted and proclaim the acceptable year of our Lord Jesus Christ.

OCTOBER

The gift of God

"For by grace you have been saved through faith, and that not of yourselves; it is the gift of God, not of works, lest anyone should boast." – Ephesians 2:8,9

It always saddens me to see young children trying to win the approval of their parents by sporting or academic achievements. The parents should love their children irrespective of results or what team they play for, purely because they are their offspring.

God loves us like that. There is nothing we can do to make Him love us any more, and there is nothing that we can do to make Him love us any less. When we strive, it is not for God's affection or a place in heaven, but to live holy lives because we want to be good ambassadors for Him. We want to be good witnesses and show the world that there is only one way and that is through Jesus Christ, our Lord and Saviour.

No matter what we have achieved for God, what great works we have done, or how hard we have worked for the kingdom of God, it is by grace alone that we are saved, not through good works or any righteousness of our own.

The ark in our homes

"But I will establish My covenant with you; and you shall go into the ark; you, your sons, your wife, and your sons' wives with you." – Genesis 6:18

I really believe in these last days that God is calling us to make an ark out of our homes, our farms and our businesses. We must raise up a standard so that those we influence will find a place of refuge from the storms of life. Our employees, our children – and their children – need a place of sanctity and sanity, where they can live in peace and harmony, in a world that seems to be losing all control.

I believe that as the storms of life increase, these "arks" of ours will become sanctuaries where people will come and rest and I encourage you to set a standard of excellence. Do not allow drunkenness and revelry, but let your environment become a place where people freely receive counsel, healing, deliverance and peace.

Ask God today to give you His peace, so that people in a dying world will be drawn to you, giving you an opportunity to present to them Jesus Christ, our Saviour and Lord.

Reaping bountifully

"But this I say: he who sows sparingly will also reap sparingly, and he who sows bountifully will also reap bountifully." – 2 Corinthians 9:6

John Wesley wrote, "Gain all you can, save all you can, and give all you can." He made forty thousand pounds sterling from the books that he wrote and gave it all away. That was a lot of money in those days. What about you and me? Let us sow generously. The more we give, the more we receive.

I have a picture in my prayer room of a fish with a coin in its mouth. My wife drew it for me. The caption says, "The coin is in the fish's mouth." In other words, whatever we do, let us do it with all of our hearts and trust God for a good return so that we can reinvest finance into the kingdom of God. Let us refuse to look at the clouds of doom and gloom or be governed by the circumstances of this world. Let us rather do what God has told us to do – sow generously and expect to receive generously.

Remember, God said we are the head and not the tail. We are overcomers. "Blessed shall you be when you come in, and blessed shall you be when you go out." (Deuteronomy 28:6).

God wants to bless us so that we can bless the Kingdom, both financially and spiritually; but we must do it God's way, on His terms and His conditions. Let's be a blessing today wherever we go. Let us be known as people who have a hotline to heaven, whose farms are always rained on, who have connections in heavenly places, and who will help the poor. Let us never become proud, but remain humble, in everything, giving God all the glory, the praise and the honour.

The nearness of God

"For what great nation is there that has God so near to it..?" –
Deuteronomy 4:7a

Those who love the Lord Jesus Christ with all their hearts have become the children of God and, as John says, have been grafted into the vine. We are God's people and we belong to the nation of God. How blessed are we, Moses says, that we have a God who is so near to us. Do you realise how close God is to you this morning? He is living inside your very heart. All He wants you to do today is speak to Him, tell Him your needs and your desires, your fears and your worries and He will undertake for you.

Sometimes I have desperately needed spares for a tractor, or something urgent, and rushed to the store at the last moment, asking the Lord to please find a parking place for me and He has done it. God is interested in little and big things. On other occasions, when we've been caught in the grip of drought and asked the Lord Jesus Christ to release rain on the farm, within twenty-four hours the rain has arrived.

He's a wonderful God, never too busy looking after the things of this world that He does not have time for us. He does. He is concerned about our needs and desires and He's a good Father. As long as we walk in righteousness and holiness before Him, He will hear and answer every single prayer we ask of Him.

Our God is alive

"If you ask anything in My name, I will do it." – John 14:14

Yonggi Cho is the minister of probably the largest church in the world. I believe at the last count it was something like 800,000 people. When he started off in a small tent with a congregation of about four or five members, he began to pray very specifically. I remember reading once that he asked God for a bicycle – not just any bicycle. He prayed for a maroon-coloured bicycle with cable brakes and even specified the make. God gave him exactly what he asked for. He loves to do that.

The Lord gave me a vision to take His Word from Cape Town to Jerusalem. As I spent time with Him, He gave me the specifications, colour and type of the truck, including the capacity and size. I prayed very specifically about that and today that truck stands outside my farm office door. Every time I see it, I thank the Lord for answered prayer.

He's a God who is very near to us. Speak to and have fellowship with Him today. He desires to be your friend and your confidant. He longs to give you advice through His Holy Word and peace in your heart. How blessed we are that our God is not some stone image or figment of our imagination, or a statue in a far-off country. Our God is alive and living in our hearts and the greatest news of all is we are going to see Him face to face, very soon.

Our God is a holy God

"For God did not call us to uncleanness, but in holiness." – I Thessalonians 4:7

The Lord tells us very clearly in His Word that we must abstain from sexual immorality. We must live a sanctified life, refusing to submit to the lust and passions of the flesh. The Lord says He wants us to be a holy people.

It is becoming increasingly difficult to live for God, because we live in a world that has few standards left, where anything goes, and honour, integrity and the Word of God carry little weight. In South Africa we do not even open our Parliament with the Word of God anymore, lest we embarrass those from other faiths. We are continually apologising for our faith in God and that is why we have no power or authority.

Do you know that unbelievers respect a holy person? They may not like to do so, but they acknowledge sincerity and genuine holiness. Herod respected John the Baptist even though the prophet had rebuked him publicly for living a life of adultery. It broke his heart when he had to give the order for John to be beheaded. People respect holiness and they will seek out holy men and women for counsel in tough times.

Let holiness of life be our watchword.

Make a covenant with your eyes

"I have made a covenant with my eyes..." – Job 31:1

The "eye gate" is very powerful and Job knew that. He determined in his heart to focus his eyes on the Lord. We should learn from his example.

Be careful what you allow to come into your life – what material you read, films you watch, conversation you keep and friends you have – because all of these things will influence your life. If you let the wrong things in, sooner or later you will find yourself caught up in the tentacles of sin. Make a covenant with your eyes.

Cry out to God this morning to change your heart. Repent before Him. Get rid of all those ungodly magazines lying around your home. If that television is a stumbling block and source of temptation, get rid of it. The Bible says that if your eye is causing you to sin, pluck it out in order that you might save your life..

Our God is a holy God. Remember that at all times. He only uses holy people to do His work – not gifted people or people who have lots of natural talents.

Entertaining angels unawares

"Do not forget to entertain strangers, for by so doing some have unwittingly entertained angels." – Hebrews 13:2

The story is told of a young soldier who had been away fighting in Vietnam. He called his parents from San Francisco. "I am coming home,' he said, "but I have a favour to ask. I want to bring a friend home." "Sure," they replied, "We would love to meet him." "There is something you should know," their son said. "He was hurt pretty badly in the fighting. He stepped on a landmine and lost an arm and a leg and has nowhere else to go. I want him to come and live with us."

There was silence for a moment. "You don't know what you're asking. Someone with such a handicap would be a terrible burden. We think you should just come home and forget about him. He'll find a way to live on his own." At that, the son hung up and his parents heard nothing more from him. A few days later, they received a call from the San Francisco police who advised them that their son had died after falling from a building. The grief-stricken parents flew to San Francisco and were taken to the city morgue to identify his body. To their horror they discovered that he had only one arm and one leg.

The Lord wants us to love people with the same unconditional love that He has for us. So be very careful today who you refuse to welcome into your home. You may be entertaining an angel unawares.

The fire of affliction

" ...I have tested you in the furnace of affliction." – Isaiah 48:10b

Are you going through the fire at the moment? Are things tough in your life? Take courage, believer, God has chosen you and is testing you in the furnace of affliction.

His word is like a soft shower, dampening the fury of the flames. It is like an asbestos suit, against which the heat has no power. Let poverty, affliction or sickness come – God has chosen us. When we need comfort, the Son of Man is with us in the furnace. He is a friend who sticks closer than a brother. Even though we do not see Him, we feel the pressure of His hands and we hear His voice. Do not fear, Christian, Jesus is with you in all your fiery trials and He will never leave anyone He has chosen for His own – especially in the furnace of affliction. Take His hand and follow Him wherever He leads you. The safest place is in God's perfect will. Now, if His perfect will for you at the moment is in the furnace, then that's the place to stay. He will ensure that not even the smell of smoke will be on your clothes; neither will a hair on your head be singed.

Go out today with joy in your heart knowing that if God goes before you, you have nothing to fear. Work hard. Do whatever your hand finds to do and before you know it you will be out of that furnace giving thanks to God for his loving, miracle-working power.

Celebrate life

"This is the day the LORD has made; we will rejoice and be glad in it." –
Psalm 118:24

I enjoyed a beautiful reading by Gregory M. Losig-Nont and I want to share it with you.

"Today when I awoke I suddenly realised that this was going to be the best day of my life ever. There were times when I wondered if I would make it today, but I did. And because I did, I'm going to celebrate. Today I'm going to celebrate what an unbelievable life I've had so far. The accomplishments, the many blessings and, yes, even the hardships, because they have served to make me stronger. I will go through this day with my head held high and a happy heart. I will marvel at God's seemingly simple gifts, the morning dew, the sun, the clouds, the trees, the flowers, the birds. Today none of these miraculous creations will escape my notice. Today I will share my excitement for life with other people. I will make someone smile. I will go out of my way to perform an unexpected act of kindness for someone I don't even know. Today I'll give a sincere compliment to someone who seems down.

Today is the day that I'll quit worrying about what I don't have and start being grateful for all the wonderful things that God has already given to me. I'll remember that to worry is just a waste of time because my faith in God and His divine plan ensures everything will be just right. And then tonight, before I go to bed, I'll go outside and raise my eyes to the heavens. I'll stand in awe at the beauty of the stars and the moon and I will praise God for these magnificent treasures. As the day ends I will lay my head down on my pillow. I will thank the Almighty, the Lord Jesus Christ, for the best day of my life and I will sleep the sleep of a contented child, excited with expectation because I know tomorrow is going to be the best day of my life ever."

Walking a lonely road

" ...I called him alone, and blessed him and increased him." – Isaiah 51:2

Abraham, a farmer of note, had to leave everything and set out to an unknown destination. God called him to walk a lonely road.

Those who desire to become godly men or women, striving to follow after righteousness, will be called to walk a lonely road – just like a ploughman. Picture in your mind an old-fashioned plough being pulled by two huge Scottish Clydesdale horses, as the ploughman holds the plough steady. A flock of birds circles overhead, waiting to pick up all the tasty food being turned up with the soil. But that ploughman is in the field on his own. He is not there with fifteen or twenty other ploughmen. Ploughing is a lonely job. I know, I've done plenty of ploughing myself.

I read an article once about a celebrated Scottish nobleman and statesman who said that he was "ploughing his lonely furrow." The article went on to say that whenever God required someone to do a big thing for Him, He sent him to a lonely furrow first. He called him to go alone.

You may be the loneliest person on earth as you walk closely with the Lord but, when you do, you will also become aware of the chariots of God and then you will forget your loneliness. There's a beautiful little verse that reads, "The soil is hard and the plough goes heavily. The wind is fierce and I toil on wearily. But His hands made the yoke! Ah, wonder – that I should bear His yoke. It is enough, if I may but plough the furrow, for the sower to sow the seed." (Author unknown)

So, my dear friend, if you have taken hold of the plough, hold on until the field is finished.

Peacemakers

"Blessed are the peacemakers, for they shall be called sons of God." –
Matthew 5:9

Are you a peacemaker or a peace lover? A peace lover just goes with the flow. He keeps quiet and does what he is told. But a true Christian has to have an opinion – God's opinion. There is no such thing as a Christian who hasn't an opinion. We have to make a decision to believe God's Word and speak up when necessary.

I love this quotation by Professor Thomas F Torrance (a retired Scottish theologian and teacher). "Wherever Jesus went... He became the centre of tense and bewildering questioning, in which the lives and thoughts of men were torn wide open. The gospels are so deeply implicated in this upheaval that they are the media through which Jesus continues to be the centre of volcanic disturbance amongst men."

Why is it that we get so distressed when we speak the Word of God and are met with strong reaction? We should expect it. When I first started preaching, I used to get terribly hurt if people walked out of the service, especially if they were men of the cloth. The Word of the Lord cuts deep and we must be prepared for all manner of evil to be said about us when we preach the gospel of Jesus Christ.

We have to stand firm. I remember a campaign in East London where a heckler sat in the back seat of the indoor stadium. He wore cowboy boots and a Stetson, and clutched a quart of beer in his hand. Every time I spoke he interrupted, heckling and trying to upset me. He hated the Word of God. What a joy to hear some weeks later that this same drunken man had bowed his knee and given his life to Jesus Christ.

Never retreat. It is only the gospel of peace that brings genuine peace.

The power of the Word of God

"For what does the Scripture say?" – Romans 4:3a

The Word of God is controversial because it calls people out of darkness into God's glorious light. The Word of God is the truth and the truth can be very salty. If someone has a festering wound caused by filth and the dirt of this world and you pour salt into that wound it causes intense pain, but it is also a healing process.

In other words, if two unmarried people are living together in a sexual relationship, they are fornicators according to the Word of God. If two people of the same sex are sleeping together, they are doing something that is an abomination in the eyes of God, and the Word of God must be shared with them in love. When people are not being paid correctly for a day's work, they are being defrauded. When a man does not love his wife, or is not looking after his children correctly, speaking God's Word into the situation can cause you to be unpopular. Jesus said, in Luke 6:23, "Rejoice in that day, and leap for joy! For indeed your reward is great in heaven, for in like manner their fathers did to the prophets."

Do not compromise the Word of God. The moment you do that, it takes all the power and anointing out of it and people will not be convicted to change. We are not called to be everybody's friend. We are called to be the messengers and the servants of our Lord and Saviour, for His sake first and, secondly, for the sake of our loved ones. Be strong and very courageous today. Go out and do that to which God has called you, without fear.

Return to the Lord

" ...Return to Me, says the LORD of hosts, and I will return to you." –
Zechariah 1:3

Many years ago, during the 1800s especially, all farmers and their families ceased work on the sabbath day. They took their wagons and headed for the local church. There they would spend their whole day in the presence of God. Their services were long, full and joyful. They broke bread and shared Holy Communion, meeting later to discuss all kinds of things. They had wonderful fellowship together as families. Some came from long distances, often travelling at night in their determination to be in the Lord's house.

Let's get back to God and put Him first in our lives. It is the Lord who keeps the family unit together and makes the nation strong. How sad it is to see parents both having to hold down a job in order to make ends meet. To live in a world where everything is fast food and fast forward and there is just no time to be together as a family.

Let us return to God, just like our forefathers did, so that He can return to us. Don't be so concerned about the profit margin or the so-called "wasting of a whole day." Our heavenly Father chose to rest one day in seven. You'd better believe it my friend. This coming Lord's Day let us not neglect to take time to worship together.

The Lord says to us today that if we will return to Him, He will return to us.

Peace

"For He Himself is our peace." – Ephesians 2:14a

This world is longing for peace, but cannot find it because true peace is found only in the Lord Jesus Christ. He is our peace. I have met so many men and women who have acknowledged the truth of that, yet have not made their peace with God. "As soon as I've paid off my farm I'll serve the Lord," say some. Others are waiting until their children graduate or they have done this or that but the truth of the matter is that the peace of God that we are all striving for is not even found in Christian service. It's found only in Him. He is our peace. Whether you are serving the Lord in ministry or working in secular work, whether you are at school or a pensioner, that peace is yours only if you look to the Lord Jesus Christ. He says in John 14:27 "Peace I leave with you. My peace I give to you; not as the world gives to you do I give you."

Find your peace through the Lord. You won't find it going for a jog, riding a horse or even spending time in fasting and prayer. It's found in Jesus Himself. He is the only source of peace in this world. Peace is the blessed assurance that Jesus Christ is with us always, in every situation and every circumstance. I heard a man say once that he would rather be in a two-metre sailing boat going around Cape Horn with ten–metre waves blowing and a howling hurricane with Jesus at the helm, than in an ocean liner on a calm sea without the Lord.

The peace of Jesus comes upon you when He is in control of your life.

Get back to the Bible

"My soul clings to the dust; revive me according to Your word." – *Psalm 119:25*

Are you feeling today as if your soul is clinging to the dust? The Lord says that He will revive you according to His written Word.

There is nothing like the Word of God to revive our hearts. I have found that the Word of God has kept me alive in times of tremendous need and great distress. It encouraged me when I had to bury my father. It strengthened me when we had the most unbelievable drought and it seemed that all was lost. When I thought I was going to lose my youngest son and the doctors said he was only a stone's throw away from death, it was the written Word of God that revived me. There is nothing to compare with the power of the supernaturally anointed Word of God.

Without the stabilising influence of the Word of God, we often find ourselves in a roller coaster experience. One minute we are up in the air, and the next we are down in the dumps. One minute we are eating dust and the next we are on the mountain top. It is only the Word of God that can revive and keep us strong.

Today, get back to the Bible. It is medicine for your very soul.

Grace and strength in the time of trial

"...we ourselves boast of you among the churches of God for your patience and faith in all your persecutions and tribulations that you endure."
– 2 Thessalonians 1:4

The following appeared in a cattle magazine and I want to share it with you. "I asked for strength – and God gave me difficulties to make me strong. I asked for wisdom – and God gave me problems to learn to solve. I asked for courage – and God gave me dangers to overcome. I asked for love – and God gave me troubled people to help. I asked for favours – and God gave me opportunities. I asked for prosperity – and God gave me brain and brawn to work. I received nothing I wanted – I received everything I needed. My prayers have been answered."

We all have to work hard to put bread on the table. It's an honourable thing to persevere when times are hard, and especially when we do so with joy and without complaining. Many people have come to Christ because they have seen Christians going through tribulations and hardships with joy and perseverance, a strong testimony to the reality of God in their lives.

The Lord knows what is best for us and we can trust Him. I love to sit with an old farmer on his veranda, quietly sipping a cup of coffee and listening to him sharing his stories about times of testing. You can see by the wrinkles on his face (that tell their own story) that the man has been through much hardship, trial and tribulation. But he is also a man who has met God through the hardships of life and has mellowed and learned wisdom. His life story encourages me.

Don't ask God to take you out of the fire today. Rather ask Him to give you the grace and strength to walk through the fire with Him.

Speaking to the heart

"Speak comfort to Jerusalem..." – Isaiah 40:2

For many years I grew crops of maize that were used for seed. It required a large team of workers to remove the flowers of one variety of corn and leave the flowers of the other. Many a time, because of the hot and blustery weather, the corn that I'd planted in sections would come in too fast and we would end up having to deflower a very large area. That meant working much longer hours and was very hard work.

I grew seed for a company under contract and the inspectors often visited the farm. Sometimes they demanded that the lands be cleaned again. On days like that we had often worked since the early hours of the morning until the late afternoon and everyone, including myself, was exhausted. I tried everything to persuade the staff to help, but they were not interested. Even the offer of extra money did not motivate them. But when I spoke to their hearts and told them that if we did not do it, the crop would be condemned – we would have no work, no farm, and nowhere to go – they responded every time.

The Lord exhorted Isaiah to "Speak comfort ("speak tenderly" N.I.V.) to Jerusalem...." i.e. speak to the heart of Jerusalem. You will never lead a man to Christ through an argument. God wants us to reach their heart.

The power of passion

"Then I said, I will not make mention of Him, nor speak anymore in His name. But His word was in my heart like a burning fire shut up in my bones..." – Jeremiah 20:9

Jeremiah was terribly persecuted for preaching the Word of God. Once he was put into the stocks in the city square and people threw rotten vegetables at him, publicly humiliating him because he was a preacher. He was mocked, scoffed at and found himself in danger many times. One day he had had enough. "That's it!" he told the Lord. "I will not make mention of Your Name again." But in the next verse he says, "There is a fire in my bones which constrains me to preach the Word of God."

Paul said the same thing. "Woe is me if I do not preach the gospel" (1 Corinthians 9:16). It is the love of Christ that constrains us to preach the gospel because the Lord has touched our hearts and changed us forever.

That same love will reach others also. Share the Word with passion from a burning heart and God will touch their hearts too.

Kept by the power of God

"But the Lord is faithful, who will establish you and guard you from the evil one." – 2 Thessalonians 3:3

When we make the altar call in our campaigns, we believe in challenging people to come forward and make a public confession of their faith. I believe it is important to declare our faith publicly. But sometimes people worry about those confessing Christ. "We know that man," they say. "He is evil, a drunkard, a thief and a womaniser. He won't last. Monday night he will be back in the pub."

This scripture reminds us that God is faithful, well able to establish and guard us from the onslaught of the evil one. We should never judge people, because God alone is the Judge of mankind. The power and anointing of the spoken Word of God changes lives. It changed mine and I'm sure it can change yours. Let's not write people off so quickly. God took a man by the name of Saul of Tarsus and changed his life forever in a moment of time. The murderer of Christians became a minister to Christians.

Let us thank God for His faithfulness and His promise that He will guard us against the evil one and see us through to the end.

The faithfulness of God

" ...she judged Him faithful who had promised." – Hebrews 11:11

A woman, almost a hundred years old, was promised by God that she would be the mother of a nation as numerous as the stars in the sky and the grains of sand on the seashore and she chose to believe God. Our God is faithful and Abraham and Sarah gave birth to Isaac in due time.

The crop on our farm was taking tremendous strain because it had not rained for about ten days. We had just been through an incredible heatwave with temperatures soaring above thirty degrees. This farm is the backbone of our ministry. The Lord has used it as the platform for the launching of the gospel into Africa and indeed to many parts of the world.

The maize was drooping terribly as I cried out to God for rain. Two nights later a heavy mist came over the farm followed by thunder. Forty millimetres of rain fell within ten minutes and as I watched, I thanked God for his faithfulness.

We have a small irrigation system on the farm, which pumps sixty thousand litres an hour from a borehole. Our sprays go on night and day to irrigate a small patch of cabbages about one hectare in size and another hundred and seventy hectares of intensely planted corn (maize). In less than five minutes our heavenly Father opened up His eternal irrigation system and completely irrigated that whole crop. Those corn plants are standing like soldiers in a row. The cobs are getting heavy and starting to lean outwards. God has done it again!

He wants to meet your need but He asks that, like Sarah, you will judge Him faithful who has promised that He will undertake for you.

The Bible, God's unshakeable truth

"In the beginning was the Word..." – John 1:1

We need to take the Word of God to heart, literally. There is nothing in this world we can depend on, apart from the Word of God. The world is full of uncertainty but the Word of God remains steadfast and true. The "Living Word" (the Lord Jesus Christ) and the "Written Word" speak with one voice.

If you are walking in righteousness and holiness and God has given you a promise, you can believe it. When you stand in the presence of God it is by grace (undeserved loving kindness) alone but you may humbly remind the Lord of His promise because He always honours His Word. The Lord says, "Seek first the kingdom of God and His righteousness (holiness) and all of these other things (the crops, the income) will be added unto you." (Matthew 6:33).

Take the Word of God at face value today. What has God said to you? What promises has He made to you? Spend time on your face before God, reading and meditating on His Word and listening to His voice. And then stand firm on God's unshakeable Word, the Bible.

A quiet life

" .. that you also aspire to lead a quiet life..." – 1 Thessalonians 4:11a

One of the things that I find endearing about my wife Jill, is her quiet, tranquil, peaceful spirit. Our children love to spend time with her. People talk to her because she listens.

Do you have a quiet spirit? Are you living a quiet life as the Lord commands? I believe that our Saviour, Jesus Christ, when He walked on this earth, had a quiet spirit. When people came into His presence, the hustle and bustle of the world seemed to be shut out. When He sat down at the well with a woman, His quiet spirit allowed her to share what was in her heart.

A quiet spirit does not mean that we do not work hard and diligently. It comes from spending time in His presence and listening, so that God can speak through us to others. We get so busy that we can't see the wood for the trees. But if we live a quiet life, we can sit on top of the hill and see the whole forest and know exactly where we are going, instead of running around in circles. Dr Billy Graham says in his memoirs that many of the invitations he accepted were unnecessary. We run around too much. We need to sit down more.

Let us obey this commandment of God today and lead a quiet life so that we can be more effective for the kingdom of God.

Minding our own business

" ...to mind your own business..." – *I Thessalonians 4:11b*

David, one of the greatest kings in Israel, minded his own business. When Saul lost his anointing, David did not challenge him. Saul tried to kill David out of jealousy but he refused to retaliate and hurt God's anointed. He did not consider it his business.

Do not be tempted to touch God's anointed. Pray for the servants of the Lord but mind your own business. God does not need you or me to sort out His business for Him.

I have two sons and two spiritual sons working with me. My two sons are in agriculture. One of my spiritual sons is an up-and-coming evangelist, the other is a pastor/teacher/counsellor and is running our fellowship at home base. I have to remember that God has called me into an international healing and evangelism ministry and I have to mind my own business, assisting them only as a consultant, advisor and father figure.

I know a farmer in the southern-most tip of the continent of Africa. He was disappointed when his sons said they did not wish to farm but rather export wild Cape flowers. When I had the privilege of preaching down there a number of years ago, they had the biggest industry in town. They were employing more people than any farmer in the district. All because their father was a wise man, minded his own business and allowed his sons to get on with theirs.

Let us learn to mind our own business and stop interfering in areas we know nothing about. Make a decision today to stick to the call God has put on your life, whatever it might be, and work at it with all your heart. That is the secret of success.

Working with our own hands

" ...work with your own hands, as we commanded you," – I Thessalonians
4:11c

Paul led by example. He was a "tentmaker" by trade and I am sure that his
tents were well made, without flaws or blemishes. He was a man of high
principle who worked very hard. That is what gave him the right to speak
in the marketplace.

Many people try telling others how to farm when their own farms are a
disgrace. They hold forth about running businesses, when their own are on
the point of bankruptcy. That is not what God expects from us. We must
work hard with our own hands and be a good example as a believer.

I've never yet met a leader who leads from behind. Do not be one of those
who tell others to go out into the world and lead souls to Christ until you
are doing it; or tell husbands and wives to love one another, while you have
no time for your own spouse. Do not tell your children to obey you if you
will not obey your boss. Lead from the front. Lead by example. Never
despise the line of work God has called you into. If He has called you to be
a doctor, a teacher, a lawyer, or whatever, be the best. Work hard with your
hands.

Living godly lifestyles

" ...that you may walk properly toward those who are outside, and that you may lack nothing." – I Thessalonians 4:12

These last few days we've been talking about lifestyle – leading a quiet life, minding our own business and working with our own hands. Paul says, "So that you may walk properly toward those on the outside", ie unbelievers.

It is very disheartening to hear a message on Sunday from a powerful speaker, only to discover on Monday that his business is on the brink of collapse, his marriage is in serious trouble and his family is in total disarray. How encouraging it is, on the other hand, to enquire after someone's whereabouts in a local farming district and to get this kind of response. "Oh, John Brown, the local preacher? What a good family man. You won't miss his farm. It's one of the best in the district because he's such a good farmer." Walking properly towards those on the outside gains their respect.

The Lord adds, "that you may lack nothing." When we live godly lifestyles, even people on the outside – unbelievers – will come to our assistance because they respect us. Unbelievers do not have to like us but it is most important that they respect us, otherwise we will never be able to minister the gospel of Jesus Christ to them. That is what Paul is saying here. Godly lives produce the fruit of the Spirit – love, joy, peace, long-suffering, kindness, goodness, faithfulness, gentleness and self-control. You do not have to be a drunkard, womaniser or thief to find acceptance from people on the outside. The truth is that they do not really respect people like that. You have to work hard, live sober lives and have something to share with them that answers their deepest needs. We have to point them to Jesus.

Expect God's blessing today

"For I know the thoughts that I think toward you, says the LORD, thoughts of peace and not of evil, to give you a future and a hope." – Jeremiah 29:11

Our God is a GOOD GOD. How deeply it must grieve Him when we accuse Him of punishing us or doing all sorts of evil things in our lives. My dear friend, the Word of God says clearly that the Lord has thoughts of peace and not evil toward you, to give you a future and a hope. God is for us, not against us. If we have good thoughts towards our children to give them a good future, how much more does God have towards us? He wants our businesses, farms and homes to prosper and our careers to blossom because He has our best interests at heart.

Some of us allow the devil to walk into our back door and cause chaos in our homes – and we blame it on God. God has given us principles in His Word to live by. He has given us His Holy Spirit as our personal counsellor and if we obey the prompting of the Holy Spirit and stand on the Word of God, trusting the Lord in everything, we will succeed. The world will come to us for counsel, guidance and direction and we will become leaders in our respective fields, because that is what God has ordained us for.

Remember, our God is no man's debtor and neither should we be. God has told us that we will be lenders and not borrowers. We need to get that mindset in our hearts and believe that God means good for us and not evil. He means success for us and not failure because He is a good God.

Seeking the Lord

"And you will seek Me and find Me, when you search for Me with all your heart." – Jeremiah 29:13

When people tell me that they cannot hear from God, I encourage them to spend time waiting on God. Jesus went up the mountain alone in order to hear from His Father. Paul said, "We will give ourselves continually to prayer, and to the ministry of the word." (Acts 6:4).

If you want to hear from God, you have to spend time in His Presence. You have to search your own heart at the same time to make sure that there is nothing in your heart that is restricting God from speaking to you. Our God is a holy God and He loves to speak to those who genuinely want to hear from Him.

Jacob wrestled with God all night and would not let go until God blessed him. Elisha refused to let Elijah out of his sight until he heard from God and received a double anointing. Moses said he would not move until God reassured Him of His continued presence

Some of us are running to and fro, going to conferences, watching videos, listening to tapes, but neglecting to read the Word of God and spend time on our knees, waiting to hear from God for ourselves. Cancel your appointments and take the day off, if necessary. Determine not to move until you have a direct, clear-cut Word from the Lord, confirmed through His written Word and His peace in your heart. Others may confirm that Word but you need to hear from God first.

The Lord has promised that if you seek Him, you will find Him. If you search for Him with all your heart, He will reveal Himself to you. Nothing is too big or too small for His attention.

Is Christ first in your life?

"Yet indeed I also count all things loss for the excellence of the knowledge of Christ Jesus my Lord, for whom I have suffered the loss of all things, and count them as rubbish, that I may gain Christ" – Philippians 3:8

Paul was a member of the Sanhedrin, the very elect of the Pharisees. He called himself a Hebrew of the Hebrews, from the tribe of Benjamin. When it came to zeal, nobody persecuted the church as thoroughly as he did. But, he says, his background and family history were as rubbish when compared to Christ.

Solomon, the wisest man who ever lived, said, "Vanity, vanity, all is vanity." There is nothing in this life worth living for outside of Jesus Christ. "For what will it profit a man if he gains the whole world, and loses his own soul?" (Mark 8:36).

Some of the humblest men I have ever met are men who have incredible pedigrees, but have met with Jesus Christ. Jim Elliot, a young man who died a martyr's death in the Amazon Jungle at the age of twenty-nine was president of the his university's Student Union and its wrestling champion. He told his mother to put all his diplomas, degrees and trophies in the attic out of sight because they meant nothing to him when contrasted with the things of God.

What are we putting first in our lives today? Can we say that everything we are and have achieved is nothing in comparison to the joy of knowing Christ? That is all the Lord Jesus Christ required of the rich young ruler. But he could not release his money and put God first. In keeping everything, he lost everything. God will not take second place.

Ask yourself a sincere and honest question today: is Christ first in your life? If the answer is no, then lay your treasures at the foot of the cross. Putting Jesus Christ first is the key to living a life of purpose and of fulfilment.

Disciplined living

"But I discipline my body and bring it into subjection, lest, when I have preached to others, I myself should become disqualified." – I Corinthians 9:27

The Word of God commands us to live a disciplined lifestyle lest, when we have preached the gospel to others, we should find ourselves disqualified.

This is very important because one of the major discouragements from following Christ is the hypocrisy people often see amongst believers. Divorce, for example, is very prevalent in the church today. The Lord Jesus Christ is specific on the subject – He says He hates divorce. Christians are called to work through issues together. Another example is alcohol. Paul told Timothy to abstain from strong drink if he wanted to be a strong leader. "Sipping Saints" are no testimony. How can we minister the gospel to an alcoholic when we are drinking alcohol ourselves? We are called to discipline our bodies and bring them into subjection.

Good athletes train hard. They watch their diets and work on their physical strength. They get up early and run long distances. We have to do the same. We need to read the Word of God daily and get it into our inner man in order to stand up against the filth that gets thrown at us daily.

We've got to be good soldiers, fit and well trained. Our weapons must be sharp. We must be aware of the devil's tactics. We must be careful that we are not unevenly yoked, because our partners, whoever they may be, if they are unsaved, will pull us down. Compromise in the street will result in loss of power in the pulpit.

Let us make a decision today, like Paul, to bring every area of our lives into subjection to the Word of God that we may be good examples to those on the outside.

Making every punch count

"Therefore... I fight: not as one who beats the air." – I Corinthians 9:26

Have you ever observed professional boxers and seen how scientifically they fight? There is not one ounce of excess fat on their torsos. Boxers run long distances every day just to get their stamina up. They spend hours hitting punch-bags and sparring with sparring partners. Many of them train for months – and even years – because they want every single punch they throw to count.

Paul says that he does not fight as one who merely beats the air. Everything he does has to find its mark. Time is of the essence, my friend. We cannot keep on going round in circles. We must fight the good fight with everything that we have in us. It's not good enough to say, "I'm just doing what I can". We have to do our best for the Lord Jesus Christ. We've got to stop being amateurs and become professionals because we are living in a critical time. Every minute counts. We are walking advertisements for Jesus Christ and are constantly being watched by the world.

How does a Christian train? We train through fasting, prayer, meditation, reading and memorising God's Word. Also by making time for fellowship, Bible Study and living a godly lifestyle so that we may not be people who simply "beat the air."

Wherever the Lord Jesus Christ went, He either caused a riot or a revival. If He is so much part of your life, then the same thing should be happening to you. Let's stop beating the air and start landing the punches, straight and square on the devil's jaw. Let's be good fighters today for the Lord.

NOVEMBER

Letting God be God

"And he (Moses) said to them, "Hear now, you rebels! Must we bring water for you out of this rock?" – Numbers 20:10

It is very foolish and dangerous for a Christian to touch God's glory. We do that when we try to take the place of God and do things for Him in our own strength.

The Lord had told Moses very distinctly to speak to the rock in order to give water to the people. Moses, however, struck the rock as he shouted: "Must WE (speaking on behalf of himself and his brother Aaron), bring water for you out of this rock?" Moses was only a representative of God and he stepped out of line the moment he took matters into his own hands. Moses lost his anointing and God said, "I cannot use you any longer. I will now use Joshua to take the people into the land of milk and honey."

We need to be so careful that we do not attempt to take on the role of God when it comes to people's lives, especially those for whom we are responsible. We are never permitted to take the place of the Lord Jesus Christ in their lives. Many greatly anointed servants of God have come short because they presumed to touch the glory of God. We need to watch words like "I," "me" and "mine." Let us rather use words like "we" and "ours," always conscious that we represent the Lord Jesus Christ. "Jesus says" – not "my will" – should be our standard. Dr Billy Graham said that tremendous spiritual power was released every time he quoted scripture and added "Jesus says."

Let us ask the Lord to give us the strength to be His ambassadors only, remembering that He alone is God and we are just men. What He says is important, not what we think and feel. Never touch God's glory.

Standing firm

"Therefore let him who thinks he stands take heed lest he fall." – 1 Corinthians 10:12

Do you know that if you are on your knees, you cannot fall? The safest place to be is in constant prayer. The most dangerous place to be is when one becomes proud, arrogant and puffed up. When God starts to pour out His blessings upon us, we need to remain very humble. When you're at the top, it is easy to fall down. Ask any man in a race. He'll tell you the best place to be is in second place. The guy in front is usually in a very precarious position. When we think we are ahead, we need to be most on our guard.

When the great revival broke out in Dundee, Scotland, Robert Murray McCheyne was greatly used of the Lord. He was a humble man and said, "Rather than have been an instrument of the Lord, all I was, was an adoring spectator." John the Baptist said, "I must decrease so that He can increase." If that is your attitude today, you have nothing to fear. Keep humble, close to Jesus, and He will lift you up. Then you will succeed and not fall.

It is very important to have friends you can be accountable to. We have a team at Shalom that I am continually submitting to. Because they love me, they will share with me when they feel I may be starting to err in my ways. My wife, more than anyone else – the one who loves me the most – is very careful to see how I stand, lest I fall. She hates flattery of any description, lest the head starts to swell. No matter how many people give their lives to Christ, she will always say, "God was good today," because, in fact, it was God, was it not?

Be careful how you stand today. In everything, give God the glory.

Decisions

"Multitudes, multitudes in the valley of decision!..." – Joel 3:14a

I remember reading a little snippet once, which said that if Christopher Columbus had turned back, no one would have blamed him but no one would have remembered him either. A person who cannot make a decision is remembered by no one and is of no consequence to anyone.

The Bible tells us that there are multitudes in the valley of decision. As believers, we have the privilege of receiving guidance from the Lord and we should therefore be people of decision. People respond to that because there is a sense of security, especially where your children are concerned.

Many years ago, my oldest daughter was given a part in a high school skit organised by some students. My wife refused to allow her to participate and she was not very impressed but the decision had been made and we stood firm. The next day she came home from school, put her arms around her mother and thanked her, as the skit had caused a good deal of trouble. She was spared the embarrassment because her mother had made a decision she didn't particularly like at the time but was now grateful for.

Decisions have to be made every day. They are important because they can alter our destinies forever. Never make life–changing decisions, without seeking the Lord's face and receiving guidance from His Word.

More about decisions

" ...For the day of the LORD is near in the valley of decision." – Joel 3:14b

There is nothing more off-putting or aggravating than asking someone to do something and they say they will come back to you but never do. Eventually, we lose confidence in those who cannot make decisions. As leaders of our homes, businesses, communities, churches and fellowships we need to be in a position to make decisions, and the only way that we can do that is by knowing the heart of God. Many children have no respect for their parents because they do not have the courage to make and stand by their decisions. Children who aspire to great things, and children who have confidence, are children who know their boundaries because their parents make decisions.

It is decision-making time, especially in the light of the Lord's soon return! Are you going to take responsibility for your household? Are you going to run your business on godly principles? Are you going to tithe faithfully? Are you going to attend the House of God regularly for worship and fellowship? If God says we need to take one day in seven to meet together, then we must make the decision not to work on Sundays unless there is a crisis.

Peace and joy always follow a definite decision. The most uncomfortable place in the world is to be seated on the fence, especially a barbed-wire fence. Ask any farmer. I love that old English master plumber, Smith Wigglesworth. He said, "God said it; I believe it; that settles it."

When you need to make a decision, go to the Word and do what it says. You might not always be applauded or showered with flowers but your decision will reap a great harvest because God's Word never returns void.

Wisdom

"If any of you lacks wisdom, let him ask of God, who gives to all liberally and without reproach, and it will be given to him." – James 1:5

Wisdom comes from God. Man's wisdom, in God's eyes, is foolishness and, as the one-time prime minister of Great Britain, Lloyd George said, "Education without God makes clever devils."

We desperately need God's wisdom in these last days. The Lord has already made His plans and He will tell us what to do – if we ask Him. His thoughts are far beyond ours and in God's arithmetic, two and two make seven. He says clearly in His Word that if we lack wisdom He will give it to us, not sparingly, but liberally – plenty of it.

As a young man I farmed in Central Africa in Zambia. I later moved to KwaZulu–Natal, South Africa. Different growing conditions, different insects, different weather patterns were confusing, so I went to my neighbours and asked for help. I never told them what I knew about farming but kept quiet, ate the meat, spat out the bones and thanked them. They taught me much and I was able to be a successful farmer. That doesn't make me clever. It just means that I listened carefully to the counsel given to me by experienced farmers. Why is it that people are so reluctant to ask God for wisdom?

There is a sad story in the Bible of a young ruler who, when his father died, immediately fired all the old advisors and replaced them with his young friends. They advised him badly and his rule ended in disaster. The people rose up against him and stoned his representative to death when he was sent to collect taxes. He never took the counsel of his father's elders and, as a result, paid the ultimate price.

Are we taking God's counsel? All we have to do is ask for it and He promises to give it to us liberally.

Distractions

"But Martha was distracted with much serving..." – Luke 10:40

Do you remember the two sisters of Lazarus, Mary and Martha? Mary sat at the feet of Jesus and listened to His counsel, while Martha was busy with much serving. We can get so busy – even doing the work of the Lord that we forget the Lord of the work.

I know of a farmer in Central Africa who employed a large labour force but he insisted on dipping his cattle for ticks himself. The farm workers sat on the fence and watched him running around like a madman, trying to get the cattle into the dip, because he did not trust anyone else to do it. It sounds like absolute foolishness, but how many of us do just that? The Lord says to us today, "Come aside and rest a bit. I want to talk to you."

If you are someone who is so busy that your life has become a rat race, you are in trouble. The devil loves to take advantage of tiredness. You will lose your joy and your sanctification as you find yourself shouting, swearing, and misbehaving, and eventually you will lose everything. The Lord says to you and me today, "Stop being distracted by so much serving and start hearing my still, small voice speaking to you."

When I go on campaigns, I love to spend the day alone with the Lord because I don't want to be distracted. I'm about my Father's business and I have to hear what He has to say to me. There's nothing more exhilarating than to step into the pulpit and know exactly what God wants me to say.

Do not allow yourself to be distracted. Focus on what God has called you to do. Do that – no more and no less – and your life will be very fruitful.

Bearing one another's burdens

"Bear one another's burdens, and so fulfill the law of Christ." – Galatians 6:2

Many years ago a young man rode across South Africa on horseback, looking for work. All his worldly possessions were in a rucksack. He passed through a farm gate and, as he rode away, he saw someone approaching so he turned around and opened the gate again. "I really appreciate what you did," said the stranger. "I'm the owner of this farm. Any man who is prepared to go out of his way to help a stranger is a man I'd like to have working for me." Eventually that young man inherited the farm. It all happened because he bore the burden (a very little one) of a man who was riding behind him.

As Christians, we must not pass by those in need, or look the other way when they ask for assistance. When we help others, God undertakes to bless us. We cannot out-give God. Our God is a giving God – that is His nature – and that is how He wants us to be.

Remember the widow with the small quantity of oatmeal and oil? She sacrificed the little she had to meet the needs of the prophet, Elijah, and as a result, her needs were supplied until the drought was over. That is how God works. We should never help somebody because we want something in return but because Jesus told us to bear one another's burdens. Today, seek those whom you can bless and help, and whose burden you can lighten.

Giving God the glory

"But God forbid that I should boast except in the cross of our Lord Jesus Christ, by whom the world has been crucified to me, and I to the world." – Galatians 6:14

St Francis of Assisi visited a small village in Italy and the parents of a dreadfully handicapped baby pleaded with him to pray that their child might be healed. He declined politely. "If I do this and God heals the child, you will try to worship me," he said. Eventually, after much persuasion and tears, he agreed. His heart broke as he looked at that little twisted body and began to pray. The power of God healed the child instantly and the crowd were ecstatic. They began to dance and sing for joy but when they looked for the man of God, he was gone.

Many people have asked me to pray for their hands, desiring that they would be used to heal the sick. I always tell them, "I won't pray for your hands, but I will pray that God will give you a heart of compassion for sick and suffering people." That's the kind of heart Francis of Assisi had.

Never glory in anything that God has done in and through your life. Glory only in the Lord Jesus Christ. It is through the Lord that the world has been crucified to us, and the accolades of this world are of no interest to the believer. Our reward is in heaven. Whatever gifts God has given you – whether you are the best farmer in the district, the best sportsman, nurse, or doctor – always give all the glory to Jesus.

Promotion

"Then we who are alive and remain shall be caught up together with them in the clouds to meet the Lord in the air. And thus we shall always be with the Lord." – 1 Thessalonians 4:17

For a believer, death is not something to fear, but rather something to look forward to. Many of us however, according to the Word of God, will not die before we see the Lord Jesus Christ. We are a band of "cloud watchers," constantly watching for the return of the Lord, who has promised that we will meet Him in the clouds.

Time is marching on. Promotion is at hand for every single person. The question is: are you prepared for the journey that lies ahead? Or are you so engrossed in your worldly assets that, if the Lord came today, you would not be in a position to leave because you have not tied up your affairs. Hold lightly to the things of this world. Set your goal and vision on heavenly things and be ready in season and out of season. Keep short accounts with God and man because you never know when that day will occur. It might even be today!

Ensure that your travel documents are in order, i.e. that you do not have anything against anyone, that there is no sin in your life, and that you are acknowledging Jesus Christ as Lord and Saviour.

Do not be afraid of change

"To everything there is a season..." – Ecclesiastes 3:1

Change is inevitable and comes like the seasons, whether you like it or not. While I am writing, we are in the middle of summer in KwaZulu–Natal, South Africa. The rain is pouring down, the crops are looking superb, and the cattle are sleek and fat. Soon we will be going into autumn and getting ready to harvest the crop as winter approaches.

It is a most pitiful sight to see a person who is not prepared to accept change. I know a farmer who would not release his farm to his son for fear of losing control. By the time the old gentleman was ready to let go, the son was no longer interested. He had killed any desire that the young man had in him.

Don't be afraid of change. If God is bringing you into a new season, rejoice. I'm so excited about releasing my responsibilities on the farm to my sons so that I can get on with the new dimension God has called me to. I feel like an African fish eagle soaring high above the Zambezi River, screaming at the top of my voice, "I am free indeed, and I thank You, God, for releasing me because in my own carnal nature I could never do it."

We have to be prepared to release what we have in order to change, or we will die – spiritually, mentally and physically. Be prepared to change and put your hand in the hand of God, who never changes.

Betrayal

" ...So Absalom stole the hearts of the men of Israel." – 2 Samuel 15:6b

One of the saddest stories in the Bible is that of Absalom, the beloved son of King David. He was an evil young man, who betrayed his father and tried to take the kingdom of Israel from his father by deceit. Absalom sat at the city gate and intercepted people who came to seek counsel from King David, telling them that he knew a better way. How do we deal with betrayal?

An elderly farmer and his wife came to speak to me one day. They were weeping bitterly. "Please pray for us," they said. "We are farming with our son and we are losing money steadily. We believe that our own son is stealing from us."

Those we love are often in the best position to betray us. Others seldom get close enough. David prayed for Absalom right to the end. He never took revenge or touched a hair on his head, yet Absalom died a fearful death. Jesus never attacked Judas Iscariot either, and he ended up hanging himself. Praise God there is forgiveness. Peter repented and God forgave him.

If you are feeling betrayed today – perhaps by your own spouse, your children, or spiritual family – then pray for them. Stand fast and make sure you do not measure out fire with fire but love them with the love of the Lord. God will vindicate and protect you and you will come out on top. God is our advocate and our protector.

Lastly, remember one thing – and this is good news – Jesus Christ will never betray you or me.

Finishing the race

"But none of these things move me; nor do I count my life dear to myself, so that I may finish my race with joy..." – Acts 20:24a

It is important to finish what we start. Many of us have great ideas and expectations and we tell the world what we are going to do, but often do not finish strong. In fact, many of us just don't finish. In a race, few remember the runners who started well, but everyone remembers the first man to cross the finishing line. Paul says that nothing moves him, except to finish the race strong for Jesus.

I have seen new farmers start with passion, excitement and zeal, and then lose interest. When the crop reached knee-high, the grass and the weeds were the same height. Instead of reaping a bumper crop, they reaped only a mediocre one because they did not finish the job correctly. The Lord says we need to finish the race.

It's not always about age. David Brainerd, a mighty man of God, was twenty-four years old when he completed his race, finishing strong. Robert Murray McCheyne was twenty-nine years old.

Sadly, there were many who did not finish their race and bailed out halfway. Today they are no longer serving God. Do not be one of those! Ask God to increase your faith and make you a good finisher. Ask Him to help you raise your expectation because he who aims beneath the stars aims too low. When faith goes to the market it takes a basket and laughs at impossibility. A man of faith never looks behind him and there is no reverse gear in his vehicle. Press on to the mark of your high calling. Be done with lesser things. Be known as a good finisher.

Telling it like it is

*"For I have not shunned to declare to you the whole counsel of God." –
Acts 20:27*

It cost Paul when he spoke the whole truth, the counsel of God. He was beaten, stoned, whipped and thrown into jail but that did not stop him. It must not stop us either.

We need to tell it like it is. Of course, we must speak the truth in love – but remember, when you tell the truth, it *is* love. Compromising the Word is not love. If someone is on his way to hell, love demands that we tell the truth and spare him or her the agony of an eternal fiery death. The problem today is that too many believers fear man instead of fearing God.

Let us speak the truth, no matter what it costs. If someone working with you has a foul mouth, tell him that you do not want to hear that kind of language any more. Warn those living in adultery that they are hell-bound, unless they quit. Tell drug addicts and alcoholics that there is a way of escape from the clutches of evil. You may become unpopular but at least you will sleep well at night.

As Gypsy Smith said, it takes a live fish to swim against the current and a dead one to flow with it. Be a live fish today for Jesus. Be salty. Be different. Declare the whole counsel of God and give people the opportunity to find peace with God.

Perilous times

"But know this, that in the last days perilous times will come:" – *2 Timothy 3:1*

The Lord warned us that perilous times will come upon us in these last days and it is happening. The devil is blatant and his followers are just as blatant. To be a "gay" person today, for example, is almost the "in" thing. It is tragic, but we must confront evil in love and with the Word of God.

I went overseas on a preaching tour not so long ago to a first world nation. When they heard what is happening in Africa with AIDS, violence and lawlessness, they said to me, "Go back and fetch your wife and family. Come and stay with us." I responded, "I can't wait to get back home. In Africa we know who is for Jesus and who is against Him. But the enemy you are fighting in your nation is very subtle. Your battle is against apathy, compromise and indifference. Our enemies are in our face and we know where we stand."

Be sure that you know who you are, where you are going and which army you are fighting in. There is no neutral place on this earth. We must fight in God's army, armed with the Word of God and standing firmly on its principles. Moses made his choice. He took a stick, drew a line in the dust and said, "Those who are for the Lord, come across to this side. Those who are not for the Lord, stay on the other side." That day all those who stayed on the other side perished as the earth opened up and swallowed them.

In these last days, we too have to draw the line and say, "This far, devil, and no further. I am not allowing myself to be subjected to the filth and sub-standards of this world. I am standing firm on the Word of God in these perilous times."

Keeping our eyes fixed on Jesus

"I have fought the good fight, I have finished the race, I have kept the faith." – 2 Timothy 4:7

Some people are quick to say that fiery trials or tribulation are the result of sin in your life. If your crop is not a bumper one, all your cattle are not fat, you have an overdraft, and your tractor has just packed up, there must be a problem with your faith, they insist. If that were the case, why did Paul, one of the greatest evangelists who ever lived, say, "I have fought the good fight?" Why did he have to fight if we are supposed to just "name it and claim it?"

I believe in the Word of God and I stand firmly on it but I am fighting the fight of my life. I am determined to finish the race at all costs. Like Paul, I want to be able to say at the end, "I've kept the faith." My passion is biographies and autobiographies and I have read many of them. I have noticed that every person God has used mightily has suffered. They have all fought the good fight and run their race to the end and God has seen that they persevered and won the victory crown.

Do not let the accuser of the brethren, the devil himself, discourage you because you are going through a fiery trial today. Know one thing! Many mighty men and women of God have gone through the same trial before you, and many will go through it after you. The Lord says – grit your teeth, keep your eyes fixed on Jesus and press on. Keep on running in a forward direction. Be like Job who said, "Even though He slay me, yet will I still trust Him" (Job 13:15).

Fight the fight. Run the race. Keep the faith – and God will do the rest.

Avoiding foolish talk

"But avoid foolish and ignorant disputes, knowing that they generate strife."
— 2 Timothy 2:23

I had been out in the fields all day and came home tired and dusty. My eldest son was still studying at university and he was chatting to his mother in the kitchen, enjoying a cup of coffee. He looked clean, shaven, well-dressed and relaxed.

I glared at him. "It's costing your mother and me a lot of money to put you through university. You have to work hard." One thing led to another and my wife tried to reason with me but I was in no mood to listen. Eventually, my son walked out of the kitchen and went to his room. Jill was furious. That night we did not pray together. I got into bed with a self-righteous attitude. "I'm the boss in my home," I told myself.

The Holy Spirit started to minister to me in the darkness and convict me for my bad attitude. I had to get out of bed, go to my son's room and wake him up. "son," I said, "I'm very sorry for hurting you. I had no right to say what I said. I am proud of you." I came out that room feeling like an eagle. I was free. I asked forgiveness from God, went back and gave my wife a big cuddle and asked her to forgive me, which she did.

My dear friend, if you've done something like that today, rectify it immediately and watch what you say. The Bible particularly says, "Parents, do not antagonise your children" (Ephesians 6:4).

A form of godliness

" ...having a form of godliness but denying its power. And from such people turn away!" – 2 Timothy 3:5

This verse makes me think about churchgoers, rather than prostitutes, alcoholics, drug addicts and witch doctors. People who have a "form of godliness," but deny its power are those who go to church because it's the social thing to do. For them, going to church is like belonging to a club. These kinds of people shy away when we start to talk about the manifest power of God, divine healing, salvation, holiness and commitment.

The greatest enemy of our Lord Jesus Christ is religion. Ask the Lord this morning to put a fire in your soul, lest you become lukewarm, negative and passive – just going through the motions. If Jesus Christ is not a reality in your life today, get on your knees and ask Him to become your personal Lord and Saviour. Take a good look at your life. If you have been negative, critical and cynical, ask God to forgive you. Start believing that He is a miracle-working God – the One who is all-powerful and can do anything you ask Him, if you only believe (John 14:14).

Our God answers prayer. We've seen the sick healed when we anointed them with oil and prayed the prayer of faith. We've seen an east wind blow a hailstorm away. We've seen mealies (corn) come out of dry ground. We've seen Him keep the rain out of the stadium during campaign meetings when it was pouring all around.

Don't shut Him out of your life with religion – a form of godliness without real spiritual power.

Watching our words

"But shun profane and idle babblings, for they will increase to more ungodliness." – 2 Timothy 2:16

The Bible exhorts us to be careful that we do not get caught up in useless, time-wasting conversation. Make sure especially that you are not part of any gossip. When someone comes to you and says, "I shouldn't tell you this, but...," stop them immediately. What normally follows are rumours and scandal, ungodly and unbecoming conversation for a Christian. Let's rather talk about godly things and build one another up in the Lord with wholesome and useful conversation.

Chattering and talking about things that have no value, teasing and goading one another always start so innocently but they can so easily lead to ungodliness as people try to outdo one another. Paul knew this and that is why he told Timothy, his son in the Lord, not to waste time with vain babblings, which lead to ungodliness.

Let's talk about things that pertain to the kingdom of God: constructive, encouraging, and life-building conversations. Be a person who is known as a warrior of Jesus Christ so that when people see you coming they will change the conversation and stop their filth, swearing and blaspheming.

Shun profane and idle babblings.

Strong in the grace of Jesus

"You therefore, my son, be strong in the grace that is in Christ Jesus."
— 2 Timothy 2:1

Without the grace of God, this world would be totally without hope. To be strong in grace means to find our strength in the favour and blessing of our Lord Jesus Christ.

I used to be a power lifter, spending hours in the gym building my strength, but that is not the kind of strength God is speaking about. It is not our strength but His, which is given to us because of His undeserved, unmerited favour. God says we must be strong in that and not trust in our own ability.

It's all about Him. If you have been given the gift of healing, preaching, prophesying, or whatever, it has nothing to do with you. It is because of God's goodness (grace) and He gets the glory. They teach you in the corporate world to get to the top at all costs but in the kingdom of God it works the opposite way. As you give, so you receive. As you prefer your brother, so God promotes you. We do not have to prove anything to anyone because any good that is in me comes from God and my strength lies in that knowledge.

Are you strong today in the Lord Jesus Christ? Or are you still persisting in doing your own thing? My dear friend, if you are, then repent and plug into the most powerful source of energy the world has ever known – the Lord Jesus.

Witnessing

"Let the redeemed of the LORD say so, whom He has redeemed from the hand of the enemy," – Psalm 107:2

When the Brazilian soccer team won the World Cup, a few of the players lifted their jerseys and underneath they had on T-shirts with the slogan, "I love Jesus. I belong to Jesus." I think about two billion people watched the World Cup Final and these young men were not ashamed of the gospel. Jesus must have been so proud of them that day!

It thrills my heart and brings tears to my eyes when I see sportsmen and sportswomen unashamedly stand up for Jesus and give glory to Him when they receive their gold medal at the Olympics, or win the World Cup in rugby or soccer.

We must take every opportunity to point men and women to the Lord Jesus Christ, their only hope in this world and the next. Never be ashamed to share your testimony with those around you. What God has done for you, He can do for others.

Let the redeemed of the Lord SAY SO, whom He has redeemed from the hand of the enemy.

God is not mocked

"For the gifts and the calling of God are irrevocable." – Romans 11:29

Some years ago a young, dynamic evangelist came home and told his wife that he no longer loved her. He intended to divorce her and marry his secretary because, he said, she understood his ministry. Blessing appeared to follow his ministry thereafter and he was in great demand as signs, wonders and healings took place. People were not interested in his lifestyle, nor did they realise that every time he stepped into the pulpit he brought a spirit of adultery with him. But God is not mocked. One night he and his secretary (who was now his second wife) had a head-on collision and were killed instantly. That was the end of that young man's ministry.

The word "irrevocable" in the Collins Dictionary means "not to be revoked, changed or undone; unalterable." The gifts and calling of God are irrevocable. It is a serious responsibility for any man or woman of God to watch over the divine calling or gifting God has put on their life.

If you know people who are operating in the gifts of the Spirit, and you know them well enough to recognize that they are not living the life, pray for them urgently that they might repent and start again. How dreadful it will be for them to hear the words of Jesus recorded in Matthew 7:22, 23. "Many will say to Me in that day, 'Lord, Lord, have we not prophesied in Your name, cast out demons in Your name, and done many wonders in Your name?' And then I will declare to them, I never knew you; depart from Me, you who practice lawlessness!" (Matthew 7:22,23).

Do not be overly impressed with signs, wonders and miracles. Be interested more in the man or woman's lifestyle and the Word that they preach. All that glitters is not gold.

Actions speak louder than words

" ...and though I have all faith, so that I could remove mountains, but have not love, I am nothing." – I Corinthians 13:2

I once heard a sad story of a man who went to a large church gathering to hear a very gifted speaker preach a powerful message. At the end of the service, he tried to tell the preacher how the message had touched his heart, but he was brushed aside. Although the preacher had a powerful message, love was not evident in his actions. That influenced this man so much that he never went back to that church again. We need to show love, not only tell people we love them. Love is a verb, a doing or action word, and the Lord said Christians would be known by the love they display, not by the miracles, signs and wonders they perform.

I had the privilege of speaking to the troubled farmers in Zimbabwe a few months ago. Many of them thanked me afterwards. What touched their hearts most, they said, was the fact that I had been prepared to go into a troubled area in order to encourage them to trust God. That meant more to them than the preaching. Actions always speak louder than words.

When we have bush fires on the farm in the dry season, many people come along to watch. But it is only a few who arrive with their fire equipment and staff who get stuck in, cut down trees and make firebreaks. They get their hoses out, douse the flames and put the fire out before they stop to talk. They demonstrate their love and support by their actions.

God says that faith to move mountains without love has no value.

Cooperation with the Lord

"I planted, Apollos watered, but God gave the increase." – I Corinthians 3:6

Farming is definitely not a one-man show. There are many contributory factors. Someone has to grow the seed and produce the fertilizer. The tractor drivers have to be supplied, the crop has to be harvested, marketed and sold. It's a combined effort. That is exactly how it is with the gospel of Jesus Christ. There's no such thing as a one-man show.

Our dear intercessor, Peggy O'Neill, prays for me and all of us at Shalom. She is a prayer warrior of note. She goes with me whenever she can and, while I'm preaching, she is praying. Some people think that it is my anointing when they see droves of people coming forward to give their lives to Jesus. What they forget are those who are holding my arms up while I'm preaching, like the elderly man I spoke of earlier who said that he could not go with us, but he was able to stand at the top of the well and hold the rope.

If you can't go down the well, my friend, make sure you are holding the rope for someone else.

The beloved of the Lord

"My beloved spoke, and said to me: 'Rise up, my love, my fair one, and come away...'" – Song of Songs 2:10

Can you hear the Lord beckoning you this morning, calling you and saying, "Come away, my beloved... come away, my love, my fair one?" How the Lord Jesus Christ loves His own. He wants you to come away from all your needs, problems, worries, and desires and sit down and talk with Him. He is our beloved and our friend, the fairest of ten thousand, the lily of the valley, the bright and morning star – and He wants to speak with you today.

Do you remember when you first fell in love with your husband or wife? How you could do nothing else but think about each other all day long? You made any excuse to telephone or write to one another, longing just to spend time in each other's presence – sometimes not even talking, but just sitting and gazing at your loved one. That's exactly what Jesus wants of you and me today.

How is your relationship with Him? He has not changed and He loves you deeply. The question is, do you love Him? Do you have an intimate relationship with the Master? Or do you treat the Lord Jesus Christ as a crutch? Is He the fairest one in your life?

He says to you today, "Rise up my love, my fair one, and come away. Come away from the cares and the problems of this world, just for half an hour or an hour and talk with me." He wants to hear from you today.

Your winter is past

"For lo, the winter is past, the rain is over and gone." – Song of Songs 2:11

When the Lord Jesus Christ died on the cross of Calvary, He said, "It is finished," and He meant it. He has completed the work of salvation. If Jesus Christ is truly your Lord and Saviour, the winter is past for you. It's a new day. It's a new beginning. Your name is written in the Lamb's Book of Life. You have everything to look forward to and nothing to look back upon. The winter is past in your life.

We need to walk in victory and in the liberty we have in Jesus Christ, our Saviour and Lord. The Lord says, "The winter is past" and that means spring is beginning. With the spring come many new things – new life, new opportunities, new reasons for living. The rain is over and gone. In Africa, when the rain has fallen on the dry ground, there is an incredible fragrance that one cannot describe. When the sun comes out and the birds are singing, it feels like a new beginning. That is what the Lord has done in your life and mine.

You may feel that there are areas in your life that are weighing you down. Bring them to the Lord, confess your sins and shortcomings. Ask God to forgive you and to give you the strength not to do it again, and then press on and enjoy this new season in your life. Your winter is past.

God's ways

"For My thoughts are not your thoughts, nor are your ways My ways, says the LORD." – Isaiah 55:8

I read a lovely little story that I want to share with you. It's about two angels who spent the night in the home of a wealthy family. The family were very unfriendly and ushered them into the cold basement. As they made their bed on the hard floor, the older angel saw a hole in the wall and repaired it. When the younger angel questioned him, he responded: "Things aren't always what they seem."

The next night they stopped at the house of a very poor but hospitable farmer. After sharing what little food they had the couple insisted the angels sleep in their bed. The next morning, the farmer and his wife were in tears. Their only cow, whose milk had been their sole source of income, lay dead in the field. The younger angel was infuriated. "How could you have let this happen?" he cried out. "The first family had everything and yet you helped them... This family has nothing but you let their cow die!"

"Things aren't always what they seem," the older angel said. "When we stayed in the basement of the mansion, I noticed there was gold stored in the hole of the wall. Since the owner was so obsessed with greed and unwilling to share his good fortune, I sealed the wall so he wouldn't find it. Last night the angel of death came for the farmer's wife. I told him to take the cow instead. Things aren't always what they seem."

When you have faith in God, you can trust that every outcome will always be to your advantage, even though you might not realise it at the time.

Treasure worth having

"For God so loved the world that He gave His only begotten Son, that whoever believes in Him should not perish but have everlasting life." – John 3:16

The story is told of a wealthy man who loved to collect rare works of art. He had everything in his collection, from Picasso to Raphael. When the Vietnam War broke out, his son died in battle while rescuing another soldier and his father grieved deeply.

One day a young man came to his home with a large package. "I am the soldier for whom your son gave his life," he said. "I'm not much of an artist, but I think you will want to have this picture". It was a portrait of his son and tears filled his eyes at the way his boy's personality had been captured in the painting. "It is a gift," said the young man. That painting became his most prized possession.

A few months later, he died. Many influential people gathered at the auction of his famous collection of paintings. "We will start the bidding with this picture," said the auctioneer, holding up the portrait of the son. "Who will bid for this picture?" There was silence and angry muttering as they waited for the valuable paintings to be auctioned. Finally, a voice came from the back of the room. It was the family gardener. "I will give $10 for the painting. It's all I can afford."

"Give it to him for $10," shouted the crowd. "Let's get on with the auction." The auctioneer pounded the gavel. "Going once, going twice, sold for $10." Then he stood up. "The auction is over," he announced. "The will stipulates that whoever buys the painting of the son inherits the entire estate. The man who takes the son gets everything!"

God gave his Son, Jesus Christ, two thousand years ago to die on a cruel cross. His message today is the same. Whoever takes the Son gets everything.

Strength for the strain

"No temptation has overtaken you except such as is common to man; but God is faithful, who will not allow you to be tempted beyond what you are able..." – 1 Corinthians 10:13a

I was reading my diary the other day and came across an entry I wrote in August 2001 while on a preaching campaign. It was headed "Strength for the Strain" and I want to share it with you today.

"The second expedition of the Seedsower Gospel Truck: I am sitting at a familiar place now, on the banks of the mighty Zambezi River, looking across into Zambia. I am contemplating last year's campaign. It seems like just a couple of months ago that we were last here, and I am thinking about the hardships, the homesickness, the fatigue we went through preaching in eleven campaigns, the setting up of the stage, the sound, the lights, the follow-up material, praying for the sick night after night, before packing up and moving on to the next meeting. The continual, unending stream of people with you all the time, almost day and night, eventually can become quite overpowering. Jesus reminded me very clearly in my quiet time that He would give me 'the strength for the strain,' but only as I need it, and that through the strain, I would learn many new things, mainly about myself. Father has promised that He would not allow me to be tempted above that which I am able. My prayer at the Zambezi River this time is, 'Lord Jesus, please help me to keep the vision, to see the lost, blind and confused folk and to help them. Yes, to bring in the great and mighty harvest'."

I trust this little reading out of my diary will bless you today and that God will remind you, as He has me, that time is of the essence. Trust Him to give you "strength for the strain," sufficient for the day.

One day at a time

"Do you not know that those who run in a race all run, but one receives the prize? ..." – 1 Corinthians 9:24a

We are not running in a hundred-metre dash, we are running the marathon of our lives. The finish line is heaven. It is vital that we do not run too fast, or too slow. We have to pace ourselves so that we will finish strong and receive the prize.

My trips into Central Africa have taught me to pace myself. Our last trip into Africa covered 11,000 kilometres as we travelled across Tanzania and Northern Zambia in the big Seedsower, our twenty-ton Mercedes Benz lorry with a capacity for carrying over thirty thousand Bibles at a time. One of my drivers could not make the trip at the last minute, so I was left to drive this extremely long distance on my own. My young nephew, Fraser, accompanied me, but he had no licence. In order to make the distance, I had to discipline myself. This meant that I had to stop every so often and rest, whether I liked it or not.

Whenever I stopped on the side of the road during that long journey into Central Africa, I took time to meditate on the goodness of Jesus, the call of God on my life, and the glorious future that we have in Him. It's at times like this that we learn the importance of taking one day at a time, and of not looking too far ahead and becoming overwhelmed by the task before us.

That is a good lesson to learn.

Strength from the Lord

" ...Run in such a way that you may obtain it." – I Corinthians 9:24b

In a marathon, many runners start strong and fall out along the way because they overstretch themselves. Are you doing that, my friend, in your life? Are you stopping and taking time to rest? Are you spending time with the Lord Jesus Christ. Are you taking regular breaks with your family? Or are you just pressing on regardless. If you are, you are in danger of failing to finish your race.

The old ivory hunters who penetrated into darkest Africa used to walk for ten days and rest for twenty. Dr David Livingstone was a man on an urgent mission. He wanted to see the horrific trade in human flesh, namely slavery, put to an end once and for all so he walked for twenty days and rested for ten. He knew the importance of pacing himself and waiting upon the Lord.

Even the Lord Jesus Christ Himself regularly took time to go up the mountain and wait upon His Father for strength, direction and guidance. What makes us think we can work until we drop from exhaustion? The bigger the task, the more time we need to spend with Jesus. That is the key to miracles, signs and wonders. It is also the key to renewing our strength (Isaiah 40:31).

DECEMBER

Made holy by His Word

"Sanctify them by Your truth. Your word is truth." – John 17:17

Again this morning, I want to quote from a diary that I kept on some of the expeditions God led me to undertake into Central Africa with the Seedsower.

"These expeditions into Africa always teach me more than I learn in the comfort of my home environment, because I have fewer distractions and am more focused. Just walking in this majestic forest and seeing God's creation brings me back to basics.

Father is busy sanctifying my very soul, my spirit and my body, and He has shown me very clearly that these missionary campaigns into the depths of Africa are as much for me as for the folk who will hear the gospel. I have become more aware that I must display Jesus at all times, not only from the platform but also while driving this big truck and dealing with awkward policemen at road blocks and border crossings, officials who are looking for bribes and the constant presence of poor, rural folk, always begging and asking for something.

Father has shown me that I must release my wife and loved ones into His hands, for He is better able to care for them than I am. These gospel services are beneficial to the lost but they are just as vital for those who bring God's Word, because these are times when God really speaks to my heart. "Lord, sanctify me by your Word, which is the truth."

Spend some time today in a quiet place meditating on His Word and allow the Lord to sanctify you by His truth.

Prayer and fasting

"However, this kind does not go out except by prayer and fasting." – *Matthew 17:21*

The disciples could not heal the epileptic boy and when they talked to Jesus about it, He said that this kind (of devil) did not go out except by prayer and fasting. Have you got any mountains in your life today? Are there problems in your business, on your farm or in your family that you cannot deal with? Have you tried spending time in fasting and prayer?

I'm a talkative person by nature. I find it easy to talk and hard to listen. I also enjoy my food and have a good appetite but I find that when I fast I become quiet and listen more intently to God. Fasting is very healthy and afterwards I always feel cleansed, physically, spiritually and mentally. If you have never fasted – and especially if there is a stronghold in your life that you cannot break – spend time in prayer and fasting.

Jesus said there are some things that require both prayer and fasting. Some folk fast through one meal, others fast through all three. Because I am a farmer and self-employed, I have been able to close myself off, as it were, from the world and go up the mountain, figuratively speaking. Sometimes I don't actually leave the farm, other times I literally do go up the mountain, but I always return totally refreshed, especially after a long fast.

When you fast and pray, those mighty mountains in your life will literally crumble into dust before you. God is more interested in your love for Him – and your relationship with Him – than what you can do for Him. When He sees you go the extra mile, there is nothing in this world that will stop Him blessing you.

Godly sorrow

"Therefore bear fruits worthy of repentance." – Matthew 3:8

Oswald Chambers says," If I cannot repent, I am in darkness." If there is no godly sorrow, there can be no repentance. And if there is no repentance, my friend, there is no salvation.

There is nothing more dangerous than a seared conscience. People who don't care any more and just go on sinning are in a very dangerous place. The only one who can convict us of sin and bring us to a place of repentance is the Holy Spirit, and it is only the forgiven person who can become a holy person.

2 Corinthians 7:10 says that "GODLY sorrow produces repentance leading to salvation, not to be regretted; but the sorrow of the world produces death." There is a big difference between remorse and repentance. Remorse allows you to admit that you have made a blunder, that you're sorry you got caught, and that you are disgusted with yourself. However, repentance causes you to cry out to the Lord for forgiveness and cleansing. The Lord will never, ever, turn away a truly repentant heart. That's why God loved David so much. As great a sinner as he was, he knew how to repent, and God called him a man after His own heart. What an honour!

Once we have been forgiven, let us be careful to bear the fruits of repentance. For example, by stopping filthy language, changing our attitude towards our subordinates and superiors, and displaying the fragrance of the love of Jesus wherever we go. The change in us should be so radical that people will ask: "What has happened to you?," giving us an opportunity to share the gospel freely with them.

The Day of small things

"For who has despised the day of small things?..." – Zechariah 4:10

Every one has to start somewhere. Even the Lord Jesus Christ, the Son of the Living God, spent many years working as a carpenter. Never despise the day of small beginnings or look down on daily toil as unprofitable.

Perhaps you are a student, a housewife, or a farmer working in the fields, and wondering what use you are to the kingdom of God. Be encouraged today and very patient because the Lord your God is busy honing and sharpening you for the task He has ordained for you. It is in our small beginnings, toil and tears, that we learn the lessons of perseverance.

Thank God for your work and do it with all of your heart. Do the best you can, not for your employer only, but as unto the Lord, and see what a wonderful and exciting day you will have. The Lord says that if we are faithful in small things, He will be able to trust us with larger tasks.

My trade as a farmer has opened doors for me that are closed to many theologians. Last year I spent nearly a month in the British Isles, preaching in universities, potato sheds, in a mansion and an agricultural college, ministering among the men of the land as farmers flocked to the meetings.

I thank God for small beginnings. Jesus prepared for His ministry at the carpenter's bench. Allow God to teach you through the trade you find yourself in.

Empowering of the Holy Spirit

" ...But whatever is given you in that hour, speak that; for it is not you who speak, but the Holy Spirit." – Mark 13:11

Whether we have an advanced education or not, is unimportant to the Holy Spirit. His empowering has nothing to do with us. It is all about Him.

I have only a Standard VIII education, but it is exciting to me that the Lord Jesus Christ uses the foolish things of this world to confound the wise. I was invited to address the whole assembly of a very famous private school in the province of KwaZulu–Natal in South Africa. There were possibly a thousand young men present, as well as their lecturers, professors, deans, and principals, and I was truly blessed at the tremendous response to the Word of God. If we are available, God can use anybody.

I was walking down the corridor to address one of the Religious Education classes afterwards, when a young man came running out of a lecture room. "My teacher is an atheist," he said, "But he has given permission for you to address our English class because we are learning about speech giving. Will you come?" I was indeed truly humbled and deeply honoured at the opportunity to share the gospel message with young men who may possibly become leaders of our nation in the future. The Lord says that we do not have to worry about what we are going to say or do. If we put our hand in the hand of God, He will take care of the rest.

Later that day I was able to counsel many of those young men. One by one they wept as they told me their stories. The Holy Spirit had done the work. All I had to do was open my mouth so He could fill it (Psalm 81:10).

Abundant life

" ...I have come that they may have life, and that they may have it more abundantly." – John 10:10b

Jesus says that He came to give you life more abundantly. Are you experiencing that abundant life today? He never came to take your joy away but to increase the quality of your life, your vision, your health and most of all your reason for living. I have never in my life been more excited, challenged and inspired to keep on living for Jesus than I am today.

I don't know where people get the idea that the Christian life is dull, boring and without excitement. The Lord is always inspiring us to trust Him more than ever before and to move on to greater things. He wants us to have "faith like potatoes" – tangible faith that you can see and touch, faith that He can honour. Walking on the water makes life very exciting. Yes, there are times we cry out for help but, when other people are consolidating, thinking of old age pensions and retirement annuities, we are stretching out, doubling up and going across to the other side. At Shalom, we can hardly cope with all the things that are happening on the farm, our orphanage, our school, and our campaigns. People are being healed, delivered and set free and we have ministry invitations to every corner of the globe.

When I was sixteen years old, with a limited education, very few friends and a face full of pimples, I had no self-confidence. Yet I dared to dream that someday I would preach to thousands of people because God has promised me life abundantly. That is exactly what I am doing. God has given me my heart's desire.

God has promised to give you life abundantly. Take that promise and run with it.

Praying specifically

"Until now you have asked nothing in My name. Ask, and you will receive, that your joy may be full." – John 16:24

When Bartimaeus, a blind man, was led to Jesus, the Lord asked him a strange question: "What do you want me to do for you?" He said, "Oh, Rabboni, that I might receive my sight" and the Bible says he was immediately healed. God wants us to be specific when we pray.

God says, "Ask, and you will receive, that your joy may be full." Is your farm in debt? Are you carrying an overdraft that is crippling you? Our crop of corn was suffering very badly recently. I fasted and prayed and asked God for rain. We had forty millimetres (just under two inches) of beautiful soaking, drenching rain and it is still raining this morning. Do the same. And don't forget to thank God when He gives specific answers to your specific prayers.

He is a miracle-working God; nothing is impossible to Him (Luke 1: 37). When you ask, ask humbly, but ask specifically and according to His will. He is a good God and He wants to bless you.

Patience and faith

"So that we ourselves boast of you among the churches of God for your patience and faith in all your persecutions and tribulations that you endure." – 2 Thessalonians 1:4

How does one acquire patience and faith? Only through trials and tribulations. As I have said before, I have never read a biography or an autobiography about a mighty man or woman of God who has not gone through fiery trials, tribulations and persecutions.

I heard about a man from behind the Iron Curtain who was preaching to a restless audience about the suffering of the saints in the eastern bloc countries. Suddenly, he stopped preaching and took his shirt off. The people were stunned when they saw massive scars all over his back where he had been thrashed and beaten. From that moment he had their full attention. Through his tribulation, God had given him a testimony.

I thank God for every fiery trial that I've been through because they have tempered me. When my little nephew fell off the tractor I was driving, that was the most painful fiery trial I have ever had to face. I had to pick up that little broken body and take him back to his father, my brother. I think my faith and patience grew more in that afternoon than from all the conferences, teaching seminars and Christian books that have come my way.

If you are going through tribulation and persecution today, praise God for the lessons He is going to teach you. You will learn patience and faith as He refines and purifies you so that you may become a good soldier for Him.

Spiritual food

" ...Open your mouth wide, and I will fill it." – Psalms 81:10

At a recent conference of evangelists, a dear brother in Christ shared a wonderful concept with us about letting the Lord Jesus fill us with spiritual food so that we, in turn, can go out and spread the Word of God.

How can we feed others if we ourselves suffer from spiritual anorexia? That is a spiritual condition that comes from starving yourself of the Word of God for so long that your spiritual organs cannot digest the Word. Eventually you die spiritually and are unable to feed others. The Lord says we must open our mouth wide, so that He can fill it with good, wholesome food – like faith, wisdom, vision, power, godly standards and so on.

Another danger is to take in junk food. My young son is bordering on becoming a professional rugby player and he has strict instructions from his trainer to avoid junk food. We, as Christians, must be careful what we are taking in. If we are living on junk food, we will have neither the ability nor the strength to walk the Christian walk.

Pray today that the Lord will give you a good spiritual appetite so that you can eat the Word, digest it and share it with your world. Jeremiah 15:16 says, "Your words were found and I ate them..."

Watch your spiritual diet. Make sure you always enjoy a good breakfast of spiritual food every day by reading God's Word and spending time in meditation and prayer.

Listening to God

" ...And Samuel answered, 'Speak, for Your servant hears.'"
— 1 Samuel 3:10

Samuel was one of the greatest prophets that ever lived. He never faltered in his walk with God and was steadfast until the Lord took him home. I believe the main reason was because he listened to what God had to tell him and was obedient. A good idea is not always a "God idea."

A famous Christian singer was overwhelmed when he saw Mother Theresa pulling people out of gutters, washing their decaying bodies and allowing them to die with dignity. He wanted to give up his career and help her but she encouraged him to keep singing and supporting the ministry financially. Many people desire to work in countries like Africa, China or India but, unless God is telling them to go, such a move will end in disaster. We need to hear what God says and act only on that.

Are you listening to God as Samuel did? I believe in the five-fold ministry (apostles, prophets, evangelists, pastors and teachers – Ephesians 4:11), but I want to caution believers to listen to God rather than man. Whatever is spoken into your life must always confirm what God has already told you through His Word. Some people are too lazy to hear from God and they listen to any prophet that comes to town. That is very dangerous. Get a Word first from God and then, if you want to, allow a prophet to confirm it.

We must spend time with God so that we can hear what He has to say. The more you are involved in ministry, or in management, the more time you need to spend with Him. If you haven't got time to listen to God, you are in big trouble because He does not always speak immediately. We have to prepare our hearts to hear.

Families

"No, my sons! For it is not a good report that I hear. You make the Lord's people transgress." – 1 Samuel 2:24

Eli, the High Priest of Israel in Samuel's day, was God's chosen servant but he had two wicked sons. They were disobedient, badly behaved, and lived immoral lifestyles. They were a disgrace to their father and the Lord had to deal with them. The Ark of God was captured and these two men died in the battle. Eli was so shocked when he heard the news that he fell, broke his neck and died.

It is no good being the greatest preacher in the world if you have a wayward wife, and children who are into drugs, alcohol or immorality. There may be a greater need to reap the harvest in your own home than out in the world. Eli lost his anointing from God because he would not check his wayward sons. Make sure today that your family are following the Lord Jesus Christ. If your spouse or children are in a "far country," seek God's face earnestly for them today that they might come home and be saved.

One of the qualities of leadership required by the scriptures is that we have authority in our homes. "This is a faithful saying: If a man desires the position of a bishop, he desires a good work. A bishop then must be blameless, the husband of one wife, temperate, sober-minded, of good behaviour, hospitable, able to teach; not given to wine, not violent, not greedy for money, but gentle, not quarrelsome, not covetous; one who rules his own house well, having his children in submission with all reverence (for if a man does not know how to rule his own house, how will he take care of the church of God?)" (1 Timothy 3:1–5).

I believe today God wants to challenge us concerning our families.

Guarding our blessings

"...beware, lest you forget the LORD who brought you out of the land of Egypt, from the house of bondage." – Deuteronomy 6:12

The most dangerous time for a Christian is when God is blessing you. On our farm we have found that when the going is tough, the drought is on, the debts are high and we don't know which way to turn, we are constantly on our knees, asking God to undertake for us. When He does, the tendency is to slack off and we have to guard against that.

When our houses are "full of all good things, which you did not fill, hewn-out wells which you did not dig, vineyards and olive trees which you did not plant; when you have eaten and are full" (Deuteronomy 6:11), that is the time to be very careful lest you forget that it is the Lord who has given you all these good things, and not your own efforts.

Preachers are especially vulnerable. Unless they remain very humble and close to God, they can begin to think they are "somebody" when, in actual fact, they are "nobody." It is God's Word that saves the sinner, heals the sick, sets the captives free, and brings about miracles, signs and wonders. With man's constant praise, the preacher can fall very quickly. The same thing applies to a businessman. When he starts off, he cries out to God for assistance, but when God blesses him and good things start pouring into his household, it is very easy to forget God.

The Lord says. "Beware! Lest you forget from whence you came." God brought you and me, my dear friend, out of the land of Egypt, the house of bondage. Therefore, at all times, let us be quick to give Him thanks, praise and honour. Let us not allow the blessings that have been bestowed upon us to keep us from waiting on God and hearing from Him.

The faithfulness of God

" ...He is God, the faithful God who keeps covenant and mercy for a thousand generations with those who love Him and keep His commandments;" – Deuteronomy 7:9b

What a beautiful promise! Our Father keeps His covenant with those who love Him and keep His commandments for a thousand generations! That's a long time. All He asks from you and me is that we keep our side of the covenant – to love Him first of all and, secondly, to obey His commandments.

Perhaps you haven't heard from God for a while, or things are not going the way you thought they would and God's promises to you have not yet been fulfilled. I said YET! Believe God's Word that He will keep His covenant for a thousand generations. That is good news!

Just the other day I made out my will. I wrote up an agreement, which I've given to a trustee in the bank. That will stand fast. Have you made an agreement with God? Have you entered into a covenant with God? You can believe His promises because one thing I have learnt, my friend, is that God is not a man that He should lie (Numbers 23:19). We serve a God who will never go back on His Word. That's something that cannot always be said in our business circles today.

God says that His covenant will stand for a thousand generations. You can trust Him. He is faithful to His promises.

The source of our blessings

"And you shall remember the LORD your God, for it is He who gives you power to get wealth..." – Deuteronomy 8:18

How quickly we forget that every good and perfect gift is from God. We grow a beautiful crop of wheat, grapes, barley or maize and when people admire our crops, we are often reluctant to say, "It's a gift from God." Instead we often take the glory ourselves. "We ploughed deeply and did good land preparation. We put the seed in correctly and placed the fertilizer in the right area. We applied the correct amount of herbicide and insecticide and what a beautiful crop we have!" What we forget is that there would be no crop if there was no sun, or wind for pollination, or rain.

In times of great drought, we call the farmers to prayer and the town hall is always comfortably full. But when we call a day of thanksgiving for the rain, hardly anybody arrives. People think their good works, gifting, and abilities brought the blessing, but God reminds us that He is the one who gives power to get wealth.

God always honours His children faithfully, and we must be careful to give thanks to Him for every blessing in our lives. When you receive trophies and awards, be quick to acknowledge that the Lord Jesus Christ gave you the wisdom to achieve. Do you know why, my friend? Because it's the truth! There is no good thing in you or me. Everything we have comes from God.

Acknowledge Him in everything and you will continue to enjoy His blessings in your life.

A good testimony

"Moreover he must have a good testimony among those who are outside..." – *1 Timothy 3:7*

It's one thing to behave as a godly man or woman in the sanctuary, but what happens on Monday morning when we go out into the world? Do you have a good testimony? When you walk down the main street, can people point you out as a man or woman of God? Are your business dealings during the week in line with your testimony on Sundays?

A good testimony stands out when things are tough. That's when people see what you are really made of. When an orange gets squeezed, juice comes out. When a rose petal is crushed, the fragrance is delivered. It is very easy to praise God when everything is going well, but when the going gets tough, and your business is on the line, your farm is taking tremendous strain, or you have problems at home, that is when your testimony speaks the loudest. We have to walk by faith, and not by sight.

Paul says he had learned to rejoice in all situations and that is what we have got to do when we walk amongst the people of the world. We must stand tall, because they are watching us closely. Even though they might not like us, they respect us because they know in their heart of hearts that there is a God and that you and I serve Him. We are probably the only ambassadors they will ever see who will represent God to them.

Make a decision today not to walk by your feelings or emotions. Remember, when you give your life to Jesus Christ, you are no longer your own. It is Christ that you are representing now. Therefore, "walk the talk."

Working hard

"For even when we were with you, we commanded you this: If anyone will not work, neither shall he eat." — 2 Thessalonians 3:10

As Christians, we are often put under tremendous pressure to give, and give, and give again. The day we say that we cannot give any more, we are often branded as hypocrites. "I thought you were supposed to be a Christian," is thrown in our face. But the Lord is very clear that if we do not work, we shall not eat.

The Christian is called to work hard and our standards must be higher than those of the world. General William Booth, the founder of the Salvation Army, fired his best evangelist when he acted against the principles of the Army and received a gold watch and five pounds as a gift. John Wesley did the same when he discovered that some of his preachers were drinking alcohol.

We have to maintain a high standard. If a man is lazy, he needs to be fired! According to the Word of God, he doesn't deserve to eat. If someone employed by you is not doing his job, give him warning and, if necessary, fire him. A fair day's pay for a fair day's work is the Biblical standard.

There is also a difference between hirelings and sons. My sons are farming with me and they know that we don't work by the clock. We put our watches in our pockets and, when the work is finished, we go home. Farming is not a job — it's a lifestyle. These young men are not working for wages; they are working for their inheritance. How much more so in the ministry.

Work hard for the Lord today and, when you eat your food, you will eat it thankfully, with a clear conscience.

The friend of sinners

"This is a faithful saying and worthy of all acceptance, that Christ Jesus came into the world to save sinners, of whom I am chief." – I Timothy 1:15

What a beautiful, encouraging scripture to start the day with. Jesus is known as the friend of sinners. He didn't come to save and heal those who are healthy. He came for the sick, the wretched and those without hope, people like you and me.

Meditate on the truth today that you are not a Christian because you are a good person. Good people don't go to heaven! Believers go to heaven! Those who acknowledge Jesus Christ as Lord and Saviour and confess Him as such will be saved. "For with the heart one believes unto righteousness, and with the mouth confession is made unto salvation." (Romans 10:10).

Never be too quick to judge others. Remember we have been saved by grace (undeserved loving-kindness), through faith, "and that not of yourselves; it is the gift of God" (Ephesians 2:8). God is working in the lives of others in the same way He is working in your life.

Rejoice, above all, that your name is written in the Lamb's Book of Life and be thankful because God has shown you so much loving-kindness and grace.

Seeking God diligently

"I love those who love me, and those who seek me diligently will find me."
— Proverbs 8:17

There's no doubt about it — the early bird catches the worm. Nine times out of ten, in agriculture the early-planted crop yields the best harvest. Seeking God early in the day is a good discipline.

You might find it hard to get up early in the morning but there is nothing more exhilarating than watching the sunrise, listening to the birds sing, and breathing in the fresh air of a new day as you open the Word of God.

Martin Luther was a very busy man. But the busier he got, the earlier he rose in order to spend more time with God. We tend to cut our quiet times down when we are busy but he increased his. That is why God was able to use him so mightily. We need to be good managers of our time. Some Christians believe that it is unnecessary to have a quiet time because they are talking with God all day. Jesus Christ did not believe that. He spent whole nights in prayer, waiting on His Father for instruction and strength and preparing for the next phase of His ministry.

We get up early to go to the gym, or to go jogging, canoeing, or riding, but when the time comes to pray we are reluctant. The Lord says that those who seek Him diligently (early) will find Him. Now that I'm preaching the gospel full-time and my sons are running the farm, my lifestyle has changed. Often I get to bed in the early hours of the morning because of campaigns and travelling. Yet, I still find that if I give the Lord my undivided attention first thing in the morning, it makes an enormous difference in my life.

Consider the scripture today, if you love Him, get up early in the morning and spend time with Him.

Prayer, the Christian's heartbeat

"LORD, You have been our dwelling place in all generations." – Psalms 90:1

Moses wrote Psalm 90. He had an incredible responsibility as he led the children of Israel through the wilderness but he never forgot to pray and spend time with God. "Establish the work of our hand," he prayed (verse 17), because he knew that he could do nothing without the presence of God in his life. Because he was a man of prayer, God used him mightily. Moses had a personal relationship with the Lord. He didn't just bring a shopping list to God but spoke to Him often, and God answered him. The Bible says that the Lord spoke to Moses face to face. What an honour!

I once visited the prime minister of Swaziland and, when I came into his grand office, that dear man sat there with a notepad and a pen diligently writing down every scripture I shared with him. He needed direction from God in order to govern his nation effectively and he was serious. The more God blesses you in your business or work situation, the more time you need to spend on your knees in prayer, seeking direction and guidance from Him. How much time are you giving to prayer at this moment in your life? Is your business and your career being soaked in prayer?

Nothing is too big, or too small for God. Bring all your concerns to the Lord in prayer. Speak to Him first before you make any decisions. Pray His protection over your loved ones. Let's get into a habit, like Moses, of speaking to God constantly and listening for direction. You will be amazed at the results.

Using time effectively

"LORD, make me to know my end, and what is the measure of my days, that I may know how frail I am." – Psalms 39:4

This is a prayer of David. He asked God to show him just how long he had on this earth. I think that's a good request because, when we realise just how frail, small and insignificant we are, we will start to trust God in a greater measure.

Some folk believe the whole world is going to stop because they have arrived. It's quite a blow to their ego when they finally realise that, whether they are there or not, the world continues to turn and the sun comes up in the morning and goes down every evening. That is a very humbling fact and we need to always remember that God is not dependent upon us. It is only when we realise how frail we are, that God can use us. Pride caused satan to fall from heaven and he loves to encourage that vice in people. God despises pride and arrogance more than anything else.

Moses prayed, "Teach us to number our days that we may gain a heart of wisdom." He acknowledged that we are only here for a short time and was asking God to help him use that time effectively, and not to waste it.

Make that your prayer today. The Lord said, "Do you not say, 'There are still four months and then comes the harvest?' Behold, I say to you, lift up your eyes and look at the fields, for they are already white for harvest!" (John 4:35). My dear friend, the Bible says it is a wise man who busies himself with the task of winning souls while he has time.

Use your time profitably. If you have any relationships that need to be restored, do it today. Don't leave things for tomorrow, because your days are numbered. Keep short accounts with God and with man.

Limiting God

"Now to Him who is able to do exceedingly abundantly above all that we ask or think, according to the power that works in us." – Ephesians 3:20

The Lord does not want us to limit Him. "Is there anything that is too hard for me?" he asks in Genesis 18:14. He can do exceedingly, abundantly, above all that you can even ask or think through the power of the Holy Spirit in your life. How big is your vision? If it doesn't scare you, it's not big enough.

DL Moody was a shoe salesman, but God used to him speak to over one hundred million people. He saw the fire of God come down. When he went to Britain, whole trainloads of people followed him from meeting to meeting, because God worked mightily in and through his life. He was a man who yielded himself to the power of the Holy Spirit.

God is looking for men and women like that at this time to change the nation of South Africa, and indeed the world. He's looking for people with that reckless kind of faith, who will trust God at all costs and be prepared literally to walk on water, people who will be willing to lay down their lives and reputations. When you've got no reputation, you've got nothing to lose and then you will do whatever the Holy Spirit tells you.

The Lord specialises in taking the nobodies (like me and maybe like you), who have been disregarded by this world, anointing us with His Holy Spirit and changing us into potential giants for His service. Will you take up the challenge?

Grieving the Holy Spirit

"And do not grieve the Holy Spirit of God..." – Ephesians 4:30

So often we fail to acknowledge the Holy Spirit, taking Him for granted or ignoring Him, neglecting to show Him respect and reverence. He is the third person of the Holy Trinity. He is holy and it is possible to grieve Him. When we blaspheme and speak filth, when bitterness, wrath, quarrelling, evil speaking and all kinds of malice come out of our mouths, we grieve the Holy Spirit.

We grieve the Holy Spirit by stifling Him, and not recognising His power. Keith Greene, a pop star and talented pianist, had a radical conversion. At the age of 29, when his mission had been accomplished, the Lord took him home in a plane crash. He was playing the piano at a leading Bible college in the USA, when he suddenly stopped. "There are homosexuals among you," he said. "You need to repent and ask God to forgive you." With that he knelt down and began to weep. A thousand students sat in stunned silence, and then some started crying out to God for forgiveness. These were Divinity students, ministers in training. The Principal abruptly closed the meeting. "There's no need to come forward," he said, "You can deal with it in your own way, between you and God." Never do that. Allow the Holy Spirit to move in your midst and to bring conviction of sin. Let us not grieve Him by stopping His work in the lives of men and women.

Another way of grieving the Holy Spirit is by unbelief. Be alert to the move of God. If the Holy Spirit is not given liberty and freedom to move in the nation of South Africa, there will never be revival. Let us pray that God will soften our hearts so that Jesus can move in our midst by the power of the Holy Spirit.

Dealing with anger

"Be angry, and do not sin: do not let the sun go down on your wrath." –
Ephesians 4:26

God says, "Do not let the sun go down on your wrath." Be angry if you must but do not sin by staying angry. In other words, have it out, sort it out, put it behind you and press on. Especially if you are married! Or do you have the proverbial "blue room" that I've heard some folk talk about? "He's been relegated to the 'blue room,'" they say. "He has to sleep there for a week until they patch up their problems." That is not a laughing matter, but an abomination in the sight of God because it goes contrary to His Word.

The same thing applies to those you are working with. You may not hold a grudge against another person if you are a Christian. "But, Angus," you may say, "You don't know what that person did to me." Take another look at Jesus Christ on the cross of Calvary. Hear Him pray, "Father, forgive them, for they do not know what they are doing," as He was nailed to the tree.

Nowhere in the Bible does it say that it is easy to be a Christian. It is not easy but it is the only way. The Lord demands that we forgive before the sun goes down. Whether it is your fault or not is not the issue. There is no such thing as a one-sided argument. There are always two sides to every story. Ask that person to forgive you for your part in the quarrel, misunderstanding or fight and do not allow the sun to go down on your wrath. If they refuse to forgive you, there is nothing you can do about that, except to pray for them and make sure there is nothing in your life that is hindering reconciliation. Do it today.

Immanuel, God with us

"Behold, the virgin shall be with child, and bear a Son, and they shall call His name Immanuel, which is translated, 'God with us.'" – Matthew 1:23

The greatest miracle that has ever taken place happened when our Lord Jesus Christ, Son of the living God, left His throne in glory and chose to be born in a cave in Bethlehem.

I believe in miracles. I believe that Jesus Christ is the Son of the living God. I believe that He was born of the virgin Mary. I believe He was conceived through the Holy Spirit. I believe that He lived on this earth for thirty-three years, was falsely accused, crucified and buried. I believe He took the sins of the world upon His shoulders. I also believe He rose from the dead on the third day and is seated at the right hand of God, the Father Almighty.

My dear friend, if ever there was a perfect mentor, someone to look up to and model your life on, then it is Jesus Christ, the Son of God. He is my champion and hero. He is everything to me. He gives me strength to get up in the morning and face the day. He is my hope, and my very reason for existence. If He can change my life, He can change anyone's. All He asks is that we believe in Him. Come to Him with all your problems, faults and shortcomings and He will take care of every one of them.

Have a wonderful Christmas season, rejoicing in the truth that we serve a miracle-working God who has never changed. He is the same yesterday, today and forever. Let us tell the world about the greatest birthday that has ever taken place, the day when God came to live with us. Truly, He is Immanuel – God with us.

The miracle of rebirth

"For God did not send His Son into the world to condemn the world, but that the world through Him might be saved." – John 3:17

One of the most powerful miracles experienced by mankind is the miracle of rebirth. John Newton writes about it in his magnificent hymn "Amazing Grace." "I once was lost, but now am found. I was blind, but now I see. Amazing grace, how sweet the sound in a believer's ear. It soothes his sorrows, heals his wounds and drives away his fear."

On this day, the 25 December, we remember the birth of our Lord Jesus Christ in Israel just over 2,000 years ago. That wonderful and most powerful miracle opened the way for the miracle of rebirth. I have experienced it in my own life and seen countless thousands do the same. When you experience the miracle of the rebirth – when you are "born again" – your whole life changes because, just as Jesus came into the world, He comes into our hearts. He came that first Christmas, not to condemn us, but to save us from eternal damnation.

As you enjoy your Christmas today with your children, parents and loved ones, take time to contemplate what Christmas is really about. It was the day Christ Jesus came into the world to bring us salvation, the most wonderful gift anyone could ever have – and it is completely free!

Let the fragrance of Christmas flow through you, pointing others to the one who brings joy, hope, liberty, freedom and forgiveness to all who will call on His Name. Share freely the truth that you are "born again" and that you are a new person because of what Jesus Christ did for you 2,000 plus years ago.

Have a wonderful and blessed Christmas.

Intercessors

" ...since He always lives to make intercession for them." – Hebrews 7:25b

Jesus is in heaven at this very moment. He is an intercessor by occupation and He is standing in the gap for you and me right now. You might be a farmer, a pilot, a ship's captain, a student, an engineer or a street sweeper. Jesus is an intercessor.

Charles Finney, a mighty man of God, lived in America many years ago. When he came into town and held revival meetings, the whole town changed. It is said that over eighty per cent of his converts remained true to the Lord. Those are incredible statistics. He preached holiness, repentance, fire and brimstone – and he had amazing results.

Few people realise that an elderly man by the name of Father Nash always came into town a few days before Finney arrived. He would check into the hotel, close the door, get down on his knees and start praying. When Finney arrived, Father Nash moved on to the next town on the itinerary.

Today, I want to pay tribute to and give thanks for intercessors, men and women who stand in the gap and wait on God. When believers pray, God works. Maybe, as you read this, God is calling you to become an intercessor, someone who will consistently intercede on behalf of others.

If things are not going well in your life, perhaps you need to call upon intercessors to stand in the gap for you. Do you have anybody praying for you today? If not, ask God to show you those who can stand in the gap for you while you do His bidding.

Faith with feet

"Thus also faith by itself, if it does not have works, is dead." – James 2:17

There is an area in the Great Lakes of Central Africa where a tribe of Africans live in the marshlands. A group of well-meaning Christians visited the area and promised the Chief machinery and equipment. Everyone was excited and many gave their lives to Jesus. Then the Christians returned home and were never heard from again. About three years later another group of Christians arrived and went to pay their respects to the Chief. The tribe nearly stoned them to death. "You are all the same," they shouted. "You make empty promises and we do not believe you any more." Sadly, it took a long time to regain their trust and confidence.

Preaching the Word of God must be backed up with active service. Practical ministry is very important, especially in Africa. If you are a farmer and can teach people how to plant a crop of maize, potatoes, ground nuts or vegetables, they will willingly listen to you talk about Jesus. If you can repair a vehicle in Central Africa, where there are few spares, the people will regard you as a miracle worker and the door will be wide open for you to share the gospel.

As preachers of the Word, we must not be afraid to roll up our sleeves and get our hands dirty. I believe that our Lord Jesus Christ had a firm handshake and strong hands, after thirty years spent working at a carpenter's bench. We must keep in touch with society so that we become salty and relevant.

We have to lead from the front. A little plaque on my wall says: "People may doubt what you say, but they will always believe what you do."

Priorities

"Finally, brethren, whatever things are true, whatever things are noble, whatever things are just, whatever things are pure, whatever things are lovely, whatever things are of good report, if there is any virtue and if there is anything praiseworthy; meditate on these things." – Philippians 4:8

The Lord desires that we get our priorities in order and learn what to put first in our lives and give our attention to.

I was preparing to leave for a preaching campaign in the British Isles, when my youngest daughter came to visit me. She is a second year medical student in a hospital, some eighty-odd kilometres away from our farm and she wanted to see me before I left. It touched my heart deeply and I promised that I would take her horse riding in the morning.

I stopped writing this journal, saddled two horses and took her on a long ride. We had wonderful fellowship together. When she went back to her studies, it was in the knowledge that it had been time well spent. She had spent time with her dad.

My friend, are you going to put aside that busy schedule of yours for one of your children? Why not make a decision today to spend time having a cup of tea with someone – perhaps an elderly person – instead of pressing on with something that can wait for a couple of hours.

Keep your priorities in order. Put God first, your family second, and everything else third.

Protection

"But the Lord is faithful, who will establish you and guard you from the evil one." – 2 Thessalonians 3:3

When Smith Wigglesworth came to South Africa in the early 1940s, he stayed in a remote farmhouse. In the middle of the night he heard the most dreadful noise in his room. He reached for his candle and saw a most grotesque monster. It was a demon, attempting to terrorise him. "Oh," he said, "It's only you." With that he blew out the candle and went back to sleep.

The devil is a defeated foe. Do not fear him or give him any place in your life. He is destined for hell and is going to burn forever. Our faith depends on the faithful one, the Lord Jesus Christ, and the Bible promises that He will guard and protect us from the evil one and establish us. I dislike talking about the devil, witchcraft, wizards and witches. We need to keep our focus on the Lord Jesus Christ. I John 4:4 says, "Greater is He that is in you than he that is in the world." We have nothing to fear. People who are demonised and involved in witchcraft cannot contend or fight against the power of the Holy Spirit. They will run for their lives.

I have known of people who have made churches out of covens, plundering hell and populating heaven, as Reinhardt Bonnke loves to say. The Word of God is so simple, powerful and true that nothing can stand against it. God is faithful and He will establish us in the faith, if we spend time with Him, put Him first in our lives, acknowledge Him as King of Kings and Lord of Lords, and give the devil no time at all.

Traditions

"Therefore, brethren, stand fast and hold the traditions which you were taught, whether by word or our epistle." – 2 Thessalonians 2:15

There are good traditions to which we need to hold fast and we must be careful that we do not throw the baby out with the bathwater. Tradition has its place, like insisting on good manners at home.

I believe that the Word of God should be read at every worship service because it is Jesus in print. If you do not regularly hear the voice of the Living Word ministered through the Written Word, then be very cautious. I also believe that we should participate in Holy Communion regularly, as the Lord commanded His disciples, and that we should not ignore the Lord's Prayer. It is the prayer the Lord Jesus Christ taught us to pray and it covers our every need.

I love the old hymns because many of them are firmly grounded on the scriptures. I also love the new songs, because they have beautiful melodies and were composed by people who love God. There is a place for both in our worship and we lose much when we ignore either.

Let us keep good traditions. Pray with your staff before you start work today. Pay your tithe to the storehouse from which you receive your (soul) food and give offerings and alms generously. That is not just a good tradition, by the way – it is a command from God. Give yourself to prayer and the ministry of God's Word. Love your spouse. Worship regularly with other Christians.

If we keep traditions like these, our lives will be far less complicated and more fulfilled than we could ever imagine. Christians have been doing these things for two thousand years. Why should we change now? Let us embrace everything God has given to the church.

Seasons in our lives

"To everything there is a season, a time for every purpose under heaven:"
– Ecclesiastes 3:1

As we come to the end of another year, it is good to reflect on what God has done for us. This is the time to count our blessings and thank Him for His goodness. It is also a good time to learn from our mistakes. Nothing is wasted if we learn something from it.

The Lord tells us that there is a season and a purpose for everything under heaven, no matter how severe or painful. The scripture goes on to say that there is "a time to be born, and a time to die; a time to plant, and a time to pluck what is planted ... a time to break down, and a time to build up; a time to weep, and a time to laugh; a time to mourn, and a time to dance" (Ecclesiastes 3:2–4).

Romans 8:28 sums it up for us. "And we know that all things work together for good to those who love God, to those who are called according to His purpose."

Many times we do not understand why things are happening to us and we become confused. At times like that, trust in the Lord and count your blessings. Thank God that He has brought you thus far. By His grace you are going to face a new year tomorrow.

No matter how deep a valley you have been in this past year, or how much pain you have suffered, be assured of this – tomorrow you are going to be one day closer to seeing Jesus face to face, and that is good news! What a privilege to be a child of God!

God bless you richly as you face a new year, with your hand in the hand of our Saviour and Lord.

More Books by the Authors

Angus Buchan

Faith like Potatoes by Angus Buchan with Jan Greenough and Val Waldeck
Published by Monarch Books

The Seed Sower Jesus ... a Farmer and miracles
Co-authored by Angus Buchan and Val Waldeck

Available from:
SHALOM MINISTRIES
PO BOX 373,
Greytown, KwaZulu–Natal,
South Africa 3250
email: shalom@futuregtn.co.za
Web. www.shalomtrust.co.za Tel: +27 33 417 1695

Val Waldeck

I Can't Keep My Eyes Off the Clouds – compelling evidence
    for the soon return of Christ.
What do they believe?
Hell, the Unspoken Truth
Nostradamus,
    Prophet or Clairvoyant?
Various e–books – www.onlinesaints.com

Available from:
PILGRIM PUBLICATIONS SA
PO Box 44066, Bluff, Durban, SA 4036 email: vwaldeck@iafrica.com
Web: www.selah.co.za